Catherine van Valkenburg Waite

The Mormon Prophet and his Harem

Or: An Authentic History of Brigham Young, his Numerous Wives and Children

Catherine van Valkenburg Waite

The Mormon Prophet and his Harem
Or: An Authentic History of Brigham Young, his Numerous Wives and Children

ISBN/EAN: 9783743337220

Manufactured in Europe, USA, Canada, Australia, Japa

Cover: Foto ©ninafisch / pixelio.de

Manufactured and distributed by brebook publishing software (www.brebook.com)

Catherine van Valkenburg Waite

The Mormon Prophet and his Harem

THE MORMON PROPHET

AND

HIS HAREM;

OR,

AN AUTHENTIC HISTORY OF BRIGHAM YOUGN,

HIS

NUMEROUS WIVES AND CHILDREN.

BY

MRS. C. V. WAITE.

> ——— "And with a piece of scripture,
> Tell them,— that God bids us do good for evil.
> And thus I clothe my naked villainy
> With old odd ends, stol'n forth of Holy Writ,
> And *seem* a saint, when most I play the devil."

FIFTH EDITION, REVISED AND ENLARGED.

CHICAGO:
J. S. GOODMAN AND COMPANY,
CINCINNATI:
C. F. VENT AND COMPANY,
1868.

Entered according to Act of Congress, in the year 1866, by

CATHARINE V. WAITE,

In the Clerk's Office of the District Court of the United States for the Second Judicial District of the Territory of Idaho.

RIVERSIDE, CAMBRIDGE:
STEREOTYPED AND PRINTED BY
H. O. HOUGHTON AND COMPANY.

PREFACE.

No apology is offered for presenting to the public the only authentic account of Brigham Young, of his polygamous family, and of that complicated and incongruous system of social and political machinery, called Mormonism.

The only form of religion in this country which refuses to conform either to the spirit of progress and improvement and enlightened humanity which characterizes the age in which we live, or to our laws and the genius of our free institutions, — drawing constantly from foreign countries hosts of votaries, impelled hither *not* by a love of republicanism, but rather by a desire to exchange a political for a religious monarchy, — is Mormonism, which presents an antagonism to our Government, and can scarcely fail to result in national trouble.

The elements of a second rebellion are in active progress in Utah, and, as in the case of the slavery rebellion, the great danger lies in failing to place a proper estimate upon the power of those elements for mischief, and to take the proper precautions in time. Religious fanaticism is more active, and, when hostile, more dangerous, than political ambition; hence the arrogant and intolerant spirit, and the bitter hostility of the Mormons, are more worthy the serious attention of our statesmen than would be the opposition of so many mere political traitors.

Again; their power for mischief is much increased by the position they occupy upon the great thoroughfare between the eastern and western portions of our country.

It is with the view of calling the attention of the Government and of the people of the country to the dangerous character of this monarchy growing up in the midst of the Republic, that the political history of Utah has been written.

The chief interest of the work, however, with a large class of readers, will doubtless consist in the information it contains, relative to the family and social relations of the celebrated Mormon leader. These, and all other facts contained in this volume, may be relied upon as true, and many of them are now published for the first time.

The subject of polygamy is treated thoroughly, and as dispassionately as the writer's utter abhorrence of the system will permit. A residence of two years in the midst of this state of society, could not fail to afford me a tolerably good view of its inside workings, and this view I have presented to my readers.

Some of the facts narrated in this volume have been furnished by persons in Salt Lake, who are thoroughly conversant with them; in some cases, by persons who have long been in the service of Young, and know whereof they relate. While I am not at liberty to mention their names, I take this opportunity to return them my thanks for such valuable information.

This book is believed to be a desideratum demanded by the social and political well-being of the country, and as such it is presented to the consideration of the people of this country, and especially to my own sex, who are deeply interested in preventing the framework of our social system from being broken up and superseded by the customs and maxims of the worst ages of barbarism.

To the suffering women of Utah, I especially dedicate this result of my labors in their behalf; and I am not without hope that many of them may, upon a perusal of its pages, be induced to retrace their steps, and rescue themselves from the snares of the religious impostors now seeking their destruction.

CONTENTS.

CHAPTER I.
EARLY HISTORY OF BRIGHAM YOUNG.

PAGE

The Birth and Parentage of Brigham Young. — His Brothers and Sisters. — He embraces Mormonism, and becomes a Leader. — Is appointed President of the Twelve, and finally placed at the Head of the Church, to succeed Joseph Smith. — Establishes the Mormons in Salt-Lake Valley.................................... 11

CHAPTER II.
POLITICAL.

Brigham as Governor of Utah and Superintendent of Indian Affairs. — Formation of the State of Deseret. — Proceedings of the Utah Legislature. — Brigham's Proclamations. — Difficulties with the Federal Officers. — Proceedings of the First Judges...................... 21

CHAPTER III.
POLITICAL HISTORY CONTINUED.

Colonel Steptoe and Brigham Young. — Brigham reappointed Governor. — John F. Kinney. — Western Utah, or Nevada. — Letter of Hon. James M. Crane. — Judge Stiles and the Records. — W. W. Drummond 36

CHAPTER IV.
POLITICAL HISTORY CONTINUED. — THE MORMON WAR.

Report of the Secretary of War. — Proclamation of Governor Brigham Young, declaring Martial Law. — Correspondence. — Sermons of Young and Kimball. — Proclamation of Governor Cumming. —

His Echo Canyon Adventures. — Col. Kane. — The Mormons leave Salt Lake. — Commissioners appointed by the President. — Peace restored... 50

CHAPTER V.
POLITICAL HISTORY CONTINUED.

The Mountain Meadow Massacre, and other Crimes of the Mormons. — Attempts to bring the Perpetrators to Justice. — Doings of Judge Cradlebaugh. — Governor Cumming and the Military Officers. — Judge Sinclair's Court. — Governor Dawson and his Misfortunes. — New Governor and Associate Justices appointed................ 70

CHAPTER VI.
POLITICAL HISTORY CONTINUED.

Arrival of the New Federal Officers, in July, 1862. — Colonel Connor arrives with his Command. — The Message of Governor Harding. — The Mormons Indignant. — The Legislature refuse to print the Message. — Action of the United States Senate thereon. — Forgery in the Mormon Legislature. — Bill of Judge Waite to amend the Organic Act. — Indignation Meeting. — Governor Harding and Judges Waite and Drake requested to leave the Territory. — Their Replies. — Brigham. — The Federal Officers............................ 88

CHAPTER VII.
BRIGHAM AS PRESIDENT OF THE CHURCH.

Organization of the Mormon Church. — Functions of the various Officers. — The Two Priesthoods. — Mode of treating Dissenters or "Apostates." — Divisions in the Church. - - The Gladdenites. — History of the Morrisites. — The Josephites. — Return to the True Mormon Church.. 128

CHAPTER VIII.
BRIGHAM AS TRUSTEE IN TRUST FOR THE CHURCH.

Nature of the Trusteeship. — The Tithing System. — Brigham's Private Speculations. — The Emigration Fund. — The Hand-Cart Company 148

CHAPTER IX.
BRIGHAM AS PROPHET, SEER, AND REVELATOR.

Brigham's Position as Head of the Church. — Mormon Theology. —

Brigham's Theology, or Utah Mormonism. — Adam as God. — Brigham Young as God. — Human Sacrifice. — Introduction of Polygamy. — Polygamy no part of the Original Mormon Religion. — The Revelation, or Celestial Marriage. — The Ceremony of Sealing. — Consequences and Incidents of the Doctrine. — Incest. — Summary of the Mormon Religion.................................. 169

CHAPTER X.

BRIGHAM AS LORD OF THE HAREM.

Brigham's Block. — The Lion House. — The Tithing-House. — The Bee-Hive House, Office, etc. — Description of the Harem, — Plan, Rooms, etc., of each Floor, and who occupies the same. — Life at the Harem. — Brigham at Home................................. 195

CHAPTER XI.

THE WIVES OF BRIGHAM YOUNG.

Mary Ann Angell Young, the first wife. — Her Family. — Lucy Decker Seely, the first wife in Plurality. — More of "My Women": Clara Decker, Harriet Cook, Lucy Bigelow, Twiss, Martha Bowker, Harriet Barney, Eliza Burgess, Ellen Rockwood, Susan Snively, Jemima Angell, Margaret Alley, Margaret Pierce, Mrs. Hampton, Mary Bigelow, Emeline Free, or the Light of the Harem. — Proxy Women: Miss Eliza Roxy Snow, Zina D. Huntington, Amelia Partridge, Mrs. Cobb, Mrs. Smith, Clara Chase, the Maniac. — Amelia, the last love. — The Prophet in love the Thirtieth Time........... 211

CHAPTER XII.

POLYGAMY.

Condition of Woman among various Heathen Nations. — Influence of Christianity. — Mormonism and Woman. — Brigham offers to set the Women Free. — Arguments in Favor of Polygamy. — The Argument against it. — Abraham and Sarah. — Appeal to Mormon Women. — Their Unhappy Condition. — Evil Effects of the System. — Illustrations.. 235

CHAPTER XIII.

THE ENDOWMENT,

A Mormon Drama.. 264

CONTENTS.

CHAPTER XIV.

BRIGHAM AS GRAND ARCHEE OF THE ORDER OF THE GODS.

Organization of the Order of the Archees. — The Grand Archees. — The Archees. — The Danites. — Organization of Brigham's Celestial Kingdom. — Doctrine of Adoption. — Case of Dr. Sprague. — Description of Leading Danites: Bill Hickman, Porter Rockwell, Robert T. Burton. — Affidavits.................................... 281

CHAPTER XV.

RECENT EVENTS. — CONCLUSION.

Personal Appearance and Character of Brigham Young. — His Aims and Purposes. — Solution of the Mormon Question. — New Complications. — Military Reviews of Mormons. — Governor Durkee. — Counteracting Influences. — The Mines and Miners. — Rev. Norman McLeod. — The " Salt Lake Vedette." — Administration of General Connor. — Murder of Brassfield. — Order of Young for the Expulsion of the Gentiles. — Order for the Murder of Eighty Men. — Difficulties concerning the Public Lands. — Murder of Dr. Robinson. — The Gentiles flee in Terror. — The Government fails to protect its Officers and Citizens. — The Hero of Three Wars of the Republic hunted through the Territory. — Rev. Mr. McLeod warned not to return to Utah. — The Reign of Terror commenced. — The Gentiles call for Help.. 293

THE MORMON PROPHET.

CHAPTER I.

EARLY HISTORY OF BRIGHAM YOUNG.

The Birth and Parentage of Brigham Young.—His Brothers and Sisters.—He embraces Mormonism, and becomes a Leader.—Is appointed President of the Twelve, and finally placed at the Head of the Church to succeed Joseph Smith.—Establishes the Mormons in Salt Lake Valley.

BRIGHAM YOUNG was born at Whitingham, Windham County, Vermont, June 1, 1801. A short sketch of the family of this noted adventurer may not be uninteresting. The following extract is from his autobiography:—

"My grandfather, John Young, was a physician and surgeon in the French and Indian war.

"My father, John Young, was born March 7, 1763, in Hopkinton, Middlesex County, Massachusetts. He was very circumspect, exemplary and religious, and was, from an early period of his life, a member of the Methodist Church. At the age of sixteen he enlisted in the American Revolutionary War, and served under General Washington; he was in three campaigns in his own native State, and in New Jersey. In the year 1785 he married Nabby Howe, daughter of Phineas and Susannah, whose maiden name was Goddard.

"In January, 1801, he moved from Hopkinton to Whitingham, Windham County, Vermont, where he remained for three years, opening new farms.

"He moved from Vermont to Sherburn, Chenango County, New York, in 1804, where he followed farming, enduring many hardships and privations, incidental to new settlements.

"My father's family consisted of five sons and six daughters, viz.:—

"Nancy, born in Hopkinton, Middlesex County, Massachusetts, August 6, 1786.

"Fanny, born in the same place, November 8, 1787.

"Rhoda, born in Platauva District, New York, September 10, 1789.

"John, born in Hopkinton, Middlesex County, Massachusetts, May 22, 1791.

"Nabby, born in same place, April 23, 1793.

"Susannah, born in same place, June 7, 1795.

"Joseph, born in the same place, April 7, 1797.

"Phineas Howe, born in same place, February 16, 1799.

"Brigham, born in Whitingham, Windham County, Vermont, June 1, 1801.

"Louisa, born in Sherburn, Chenango County, New York, September 25, 1804.

"Lorenzo Dow, born in same place, October 19, 1807."

It is worthy of remark, that all of Brigham's family became Mormons. His father, John Young, was constituted first patriarch of the church, and died at Quincy, Illinois, October 12, 1839. His brothers are all at Salt Lake, and are the devoted followers and satellites of the Prophet.

Through the plurality system, the Youngs have formed connections so numerous, that almost half the people at Salt Lake are in some way related to the ruling dynasty. This is striking evidence of Brigham's ingenuity in consolidating and perpetuating his power.

His early life was that of a farmer's son, but he afterwards acquired the trade of a painter and glazier, which he followed until his conversion to Mormonism. In 1832, being then thirty-one years of age, he heard and embraced this new religion. He was convinced by Samuel H. Smith, brother to the prophet Joseph, and was baptized by Eleazer Miller, now living at Salt Lake.

Brigham "gathered" with the saints, at Kirtland, Ohio, and soon became intimate with Joseph Smith. He was ordained an elder, and began preaching. His shrewdness, and almost intuitive knowledge of character, soon attracted the attention of his brethren, and gave him influence and position in this weak and despised church. They recognized in him a man born to rule and lead the masses. They were attracted by his strong, electrical will; and from that time his power in the church has been undisputed.

In 1835, on the 14th of February, at Kirtland, Brigham Young was ordained one of the newly-organized quorum of the Twelve Apostles. Armed with his new power, and fired with a zeal worthy of a better cause, he went forth, and preached and proselyted with marked success.

Thomas B. Marsh having apostatized, Brigham was chosen to succeed him, as President of the Twelve Apostles, in 1836.

Then came the dark days of Mormonism. Many of the prominent men of the church apostatized. The saints were driven from Kirtland. Smith fled to save his life; Brigham accompanied him, and after many hair-breadth escapes, many trials and hardships, they again planted a new colony, and settled in Far West, Missouri.

But the saints were destined again to endure persecution for their faith. In a few years they were driven from Missouri, seeking a home this time in Illinois. During all this time Brigham stood firm, counselling and directing his brethren, and, like the rock amid the storms, gathering fresh power of resistance as the waves of persecution increased in fury.

In 1839 he was appointed, with others, to "open up the gospel" to the inhabitants of the British Isles. They landed at Liverpool on the 6th of April, 1840, and immediately commenced preaching. Brigham superintended affairs, issued an edition of the "Book of Mormon," and commenced the publication of the "Millennial Star," a periodical still living. In 1841 he sailed for New York, having shipped seven hundred and sixty-nine of the faithful, and leaving many churches, with organizations completed.

Brigham was cordially received by Smith, and the saints generally, who appreciated and acknowledged his services, and it was evident that his influence and fame were rapidly increasing.

In 1844 the whole aspect of affairs was changed. Smith was shot, Nauvoo threatened by a mob, and the Twelve Apostles scattered. Sidney Rigdon assumed the Presidency, he being Smith's first counsellor. Divisions were numerous, and the church was in imminent danger of falling into hopeless ruin.

Brigham, with true Napoleonic foresight, saw his opportunity, and was not slow to improve it. He came hurriedly to Nauvoo, denounced Rigdon as an impostor and his revelations as emanations from the Devil, cut off both him and his adherents from the true church, cursed Rigdon, and "handed him over to the buffetings of Satan for a thousand years," and was himself elected President by an overwhelming majority.

This exhibition of energy silenced all opposition. Those who did not love, feared him; and all suffered themselves to be led, because they dared not resist, a man so determined to rule.

Thus much accomplished, and visions of future power and aggrandizement, perchance of temporal sovereignty, floated through the brain of this modern Mohammed. He dreamed of the kingly robe and the jewelled crown in some far-off valley of the Rocky Mountains, where gentiles or their laws could not annoy the saints, or hinder the normal development of Mormonism. How and in what manner these dreams came so near fulfilment, will be seen as the reader peruses these pages.

But he did not lose sight of the present in these glowing visions of the future. He completed the Temple, the Mansion-House was in a forward state, Nauvoo was increasing rapidly, and with it his power and popularity.

Brigham, however, with his usual foresight, saw the storm arising. The saints were again to be driven. So he hurried the people through their endowments, bound them to him by oaths which made them shudder to recall, and still, by an art equal to that of Loyola, so inwound himself in their affections that they loved and reverenced him the more. He aroused their deepest hatred toward the "gentiles;" wrought upon their pride, ambition, and revenge, until they were ready to do and dare anything for their religion and their leader. When his power was thus fully established, he revealed to them "the will of the Lord concerning them." They must leave their beautiful Nauvoo, their sacred temple, their altars and their homes, and follow him as the Moses of the new dispensation, and he would find for them a Canaan, a land flowing with milk and honey, where the gentiles should never come. This was a trial of their faith. Should they yield to the temptation, and, hankering after the flesh-pots of Egypt, lose their birthright? They wept, they hesitated, but the strong will and iron nerve of Brigham conquered, and they obeyed.

In February, 1846, they crossed the Mississippi on the ice, and leaving home, property, and kindred, they took up their line of march for the land of the setting sun. As the long trains rolled by, Brigham comforted, counselled, and blessed the weeping emigrants. He told them of the land where they should worship "under their own vine and fig-tree, with none to molest or make them afraid." Alas for their fainting hearts! Little did they suspect that the cruel ambition of their God-man would lead them to a land as barren as the Desert of Sahara, and as devoid of vegetation as the Rock of Gibraltar.

They established themselves in winter-quarters at Kanesville, now Council Bluffs, Iowa. Here new difficulties arose. The church was poor, and means were needed to supply the current necessities, as well as to defray the expense of the journey to their new Zion. Various schemes were resorted to for the purpose of "raising the wind." A band of Danites was sent out to steal cattle and horses, and convey them beyond the jurisdiction of the State authorities. Others were detailed to make and circulate counterfeit money. While these little speculations were progressing, Brigham was trying his hand at diplomacy. He is reported to have sent James C. Little to Washington, to request the **privilege** of raising a battalion of Mormons for the Mexican **war.**

This movement was prompted by several considerations. First, it was thought necessary for the safety of the church that they should make a show of patriotism; secondly, these soldiers would draw pay from the government, which Brigham could appropriate; and thirdly, they were to be discharged in Mexico, where, at that time, he designed to found his theocratic monarchy. It has been asserted by some persons that Brigham received $20,000 from the government, as a bonus, for raising the battalion; but I find no evidence to substantiate this assertion. The following affidavit will show in what manner he was benefited by this transaction:—

"Territory of Utah, }
Great Salt Lake City. }

"Alexander McCord says that he was mustered into the **U. S. service in** the Mormon Battalion, August 16th, 1846. That **an advance of** $42.50 **was issued by** the government per man, ostensibly **for the** purpose of clothing the command, making a total to the battalion of $22,500. That **this** amount was received by Parley P. Pratt, and forwarded by him to Brigham Young, who proffered to apply the same for the benefit of the families of the battalion, who were in a state of destitution. That he, Brigham, informed them he would send to St. Louis, purchase goods, and deal **them** out for the benefit **of** said families at wholesale prices. Also **made** a covenant with them, calling upon God and angels to witness the same. That he would transport their families to them **in** Mexico, now California, even if he had to leave his own family behind; also would provide houses for them. **That** in his public address to the battalion, in relation **to** this **subject, he** strongly urged the advantages that would accrue to his church by their compliance with this requisition, making **it** entirely **a** matter of self-interest, with the sole view of accomplishing certain private ends; and not in anywise appealing to their loyalty, or setting forth the necessity of rendering assistance to the parent government.

"That he did not fulfil the promises he had made. Some few articles were served out to their families at enormous rates, — his (McCord's) wife having to take sole-leather, for which she had no use. That when their wives appealed to him, expecting in good faith to receive according to promise, he laughed, mimicked, and made fun of them on the public stand; showing how they cried and whined. On the arrival of the money at Council Bluffs, some of the women, being entirely destitute, desired their husbands' share, and some cried for the want of it. Young ridiculed them, and told them if they insisted upon having the money, they must not look to him for support or protection; thus compelling them to accept of his terms.

"Two agents, John D. Lee and Major Egan, followed the battalion to Santa Fe, and there received a draft on Leavenworth, for the first month and a half's pay, with the understanding from the soldiers it was to be paid to their families. The authorities of the church drew the amount, and then took out the tithing for themselves, one tenth.

"One of the inducements held out by the government, was to discharge them, with their arms in Mexico, which was done. When he (McCord) arrived in Utah, October, 1847, he found his family not here, and was prevented by the church authorities from going after them; and was not permitted to leave until January following. When he reached his family at Winter Quarters, Missouri, he found no preparations made for their being forwarded to Utah, and there were none made afterwards.

(Signed,) ALEXANDER McCORD.

"*Territory of Utah*, ss.

"Alexander McCord, being duly sworn, says that the facts set forth in the foregoing statement by him subscribed, of his own knowledge, are true, and those set forth upon information and belief he verily believes to be true.

(Signed,) ALEXANDER McCORD."

"Subscribed and sworn to before me, this 4th day of May, 1864.
"THOMAS J. DRAKE,
"*Associate Justice U. S. Sup. Court, Utah.*"

By this operation, Brigham must have realized the neat little sum of $10,000. This enabled him to fit out an expedition to explore the country west of the Rocky Mountains. Accordingly, in the spring of 1847, with one hundred and forty-three of his tried adherents, he made the journey to Salt Lake, where they arrived July 24, 1847. A colony was at once established, and a part of the number left to commence farming operations. Brigham, with the remainder, returned to "Winter Quarters." Here he found the people on the point of starvation, while fevers and the cholera were rapidly thinning their ranks. Brigham at once commenced alleviating their suffering, and in the excess of their gratitude, these poor deluded creatures did not see that he was the cause of all their misery.

Young was now ready to enact another scene in this Mormon drama. He was ruling the church in the capacity of President of the Twelve Apostles. He desired greater power; he wished to occupy the place of the Prophet of the Lord. This was the more difficult, as the people venerated the memory of Joseph Smith, sanctified as it was by the remembrance of his cruel and untimely death. Brigham knew well the extent of this feeling, and that it would be impossible to supplant Joseph in their affections, and extremely difficult to occupy his position. But his plans demanded that he should be in form what he was in fact,— the absolute head of the church. He resolved to execute a brilliant *coup d'état*, and risk the consequences.

On the morning of the 24th of December, 1847, he ascended the pulpit to preach; and with that power of mimicry and imitation for which he is so remarkable, aided, doubtless, by works of art to enable him to represent the features and *personnel* of Smith, he so completely assumed the tone and manner, and presented the appearance of Joseph, that the congregation believed that their dead prophet stood before them. The effect was electrical. Women screamed and fainted; strong men wept; the delusion was complete. "*The mantle of Joseph had fallen upon Brigham;*" he was henceforth their Prophet, Seer, and Revelator, the rightful successor to the Presidency. One old brother told me that he really believed that Joseph was present in the flesh, so strong was the personal resemblance at the time. As soon as the tumult subsided, the people elected Brigham " President of the Church of Jesus Christ of Latter Day Saints in all the world." He appointed Heber C. Kimball and Willard Richards as his counsellors. These three constituted the " First Presidency." This action was subsequently confirmed, at a conference held April 6, 1848, at the same place. Brigham was now the nominal as well as the real leader of this strange community.

A greater trial demanded his forethought. The whole church was to be removed over a thousand miles, through an almost unknown country, full of dangers and difficulties.

The following account of the manner in which this difficult undertaking was executed, is from the pen of John Hyde, Jr.:—

" Some ability is required to efficiently remove bodies of armed troops over such new and pioneering obstacles: well supplied, equipped, and mounted, it takes a commander's skill; but here were poor, unprovided, feeble men, women, and children, shaking with ague, pale with suffering, hollow and gaunt with recent hunger. Without strife, without discord, almost without a murmur, this heterogeneous mass moved off. Many groaned with anguish, but none with complaint. Brigham's energy inspired them all; his genius controlled them all. Marking their road with their gravestones, they arrived at Salt Lake Valley, destitute and feeble, in 1848. The desert to which they had come was as cheerless as their past history. From cruel foes they had fled to as unfeeling a wilderness. Renewed difficulties demanded a renewed effort from Brigham. Everything depended on him. Starvation and nakedness stared in the gloomy faces of the desponding people. Murmurs and complaints were uttered. He quelled everything, scolded, plead, threatened, prophesied, and subdued them. With a restless but resistless energy he set them to work, and worked himself as their example. He directed their labors, controlled their domestic affairs, preached at them, to them, for them. He told foolish anecdotes to make them laugh, encouraged their dancing to make them merry, got up theatrical performances to distract their minds, and made them work hard, certain of rendering them contented by-and-by. Feared with a stronger fear, venerated with a more rational veneration, but not loved with the same clinging tenderness that the people still felt for Joseph Smith, Brigham swayed them at his will. They learned to dread his iron hand, and were daunted by his iron heart." *

While he was thus consolidating his power, laying plans for the foundation of a monarchy more despotic than that of Austria, important changes were going on in the political condition of the country. Mexico was conquered, and much of its territory, including Utah, was annexed to the United States, and the Mormons thus again brought within the jurisdiction of the Federal Government.

From this era in Mormon affairs Brigham appears in so many different characters that his history can only be fully written by considering him in his various *rôles*, — as " Governor of Utah and Superintendent of Indian Affairs ; " " President of the Church, Prophet, Seer, and Revelator ; " " Trustee in Trust for the Church ; " " President of the Emigration Company ; " " Lord of the Harem ; " " Eloheim, or Head God ; " and " Grand Archee of the Order of the Gods."

* *Mormonism; its Leaders and Designs*, by John Hyde, Jr. New York: W. P. Fetridge & Co. 1857. Page 144.

CHAPTER II.

POLITICAL.

Brigham as Governor of Utah and Superintendent of Indian Affairs. — Formation of the State of Deseret. — Proceedings of the Utah Legislature. — Brigham's Proclamations. — Difficulties with the Federal Officers. — Proceedings of the first Judges.

By the treaty of Guadalupe Hidalgo, concluded between the United States and Mexico in 1848, the country now embraced in the Territory of Utah was transferred from the jurisdiction of the latter to that of the former, and on the 9th of September, 1850, Congress passed an Act to organize the Territory of Utah.

The Mormons arrived in the Salt Lake Valley on the 24th of July, 1847, while the Territory yet belonged to Mexico. When the peace between the United States and Mexico was concluded, the Mormons were left without a government. They took advantage of this opportunity to set up an independent government.

Early in 1849 they met in convention to frame a constitution for "the State of Deseret." The following is an abstract of the minutes of that convention: —

On the 15th of March, 1849, the convention appointed the following persons a committee to draft a constitution for the State of Deseret, to wit: Albert Carrington, Joseph L. Heywood, William W. Phelps, David Fullmer, John S. Fullmer, Charles C. Rich, John Taylor, Parley P. Pratt, John M. Bernheisel, and Erastus Snow.

March 18, 1849, Albert Carrington, chairman of the committee, reported the following constitution, which was read, and unanimously adopted by the convention: [The preamble only is here given.]

"Constitution of the State of Deseret.

"Whereas a large number of the citizens of the United States, before and since the treaty of peace with the Republic of Mexico, emigrated to and settled in that portion of the territory of the United States lying west of the Rocky Mountains, and in the great interior basin of Upper California; and whereas, by reason of said treaty, all civil organization originating from the Republic of Mexico became abrogated; and whereas the Congress of the United States has failed to provide a form of civil government for the territory so acquired, or any portion thereof; and whereas civil government and law are necessary for the security, peace, and prosperity of society; and whereas it is a fundamental principle in all republican governments that all political power is inherent in the people, and governments instituted for their protection, security, and benefit, should emanate from the same:

"Therefore your committee beg leave to recommend the adoption of the following *Constitution*, until the Congress of the United States shall otherwise provide for the government of the Territory hereinafter named and described, by admitting us into the Union.

"We, the people, grateful to the Supreme Being for the blessings hitherto enjoyed, and feeling our dependence on Him for a continuance of those blessings, *do ordain and establish a free and Independent Government*, by the name of *the State of Deseret;* including all the territory of the United States within the following boundaries, to wit: [Here follow the boundaries of the proposed new State.]

It will be noticed by the phraseology of the foregoing preamble that this government was to be "free and independent," and was intended to remain such until the new State, thus constituted, *should be admitted into the Union*. In other words, they intended, through the machinery of this independent State, to harass and annoy the government, and the gentiles, until the "saints" could force themselves into the Union upon their own terms. This theory is fully sustained by the subsequent history of this inchoate State. The very first steps taken were independent of, and in hostility to, the officers appointed by the Government of the United States, as will more fully appear in the following pages.

The formation of this government for the State of Deseret was the first effort to throw off the yoke of the Federal Government, — an effort which has been persistently persevered in to the present time.

There never has been a time since Brigham Young crossed the Rocky Mountains, when he has honestly entertained the idea of being a good and loyal citizen of the United States.

The following were the first officers of this infant monarchy: —

Governor, BRIGHAM YOUNG.
Lieutenant-Governor, HEBER C. KIMBALL.
Chief Justice, DANIEL H. WELLS.

The Assembly met, and after listening to the Governor's Message, proceeded to frame a code of laws. This *pseudo* State government remained in force until the 22d of September, 1851, when the Territorial Legislature convened.

In the mean time Brigham, having been appointed Governor of the newly organized Territory, and Superintendent of Indian Affairs, and seeing a fair prospect of lining his pockets from the treasury of the United States, concluded to forego for a time his ambitious projects, and consented that the new "State" should be merged into a United States Territory.

The federal officers were appointed during the session of 1850-51, but owing to the difficulty of transportation, did not arrive until July, 1851. Young, who had been appointed Governor, had, on the 3d of February, 1851, taken the oath of office before Wells, *Chief Justice of Deseret.*

The first session of the Territorial Legislature was convened, in pursuance of the proclamation of the Governor, on the 22d day of September, 1851, and continued by adjournment from time to time, until the 18th day of February, 1852. This was succeeded by a special session, called by proclamation of the Governor, commencing the following day, and continuing until the 6th day of March, 1852. What there was in the political condition of this community, subjected as they were, in almost all the relations of life, to a complete and comprehensive system of religious government, to require a continuous session of the Territorial Legislature for nearly six months, has never yet been explained.

The following is extracted from the published proceedings of the first Legislative Assembly:—

"REPRESENTATIVES' HALL, Tuesday, Sept. 23, 1852.

"10 o'clock, A. M. Both houses of the Legislative Assembly met in joint session, according to previous arrangement. The President of the Council in the chair.

"The committee appointed to that duty appeared, escorting his Excellency Brigham Young, Governor of Utah Territory, who was seated immediately in front of the Speaker's chair.

"The joint committee appointed to wait upon the Judges of the Supreme Court, and the Secretary of the Territory, appeared, escorting the Hon. Z. Snow [Mormon], one of said Judges. They reported that they had visited the Hon. Perry E. Brochus, and Mr. Secretary Harris. But the answer returned by them was so vague and indefinite that they did not know whether they would respond to the invitation or not. The committee also reported that they did not see the Hon. Judge Brandenburg. The United States District Attorney, Seth M. Blair, Esq., [Mormon,] was also seated within the bar."

The hostility to the federal officers had already been so openly and offensively manifested, that the respect which these gentlemen owed to themselves and the government and people whom they represented, would not permit them to be present at the first meeting of the Legislative Assembly. It will be noticed that one of them was not seen at all, and the reply of the other two was not even reported!

"The House was called to order by the President of the Council, who then informed his Excellency the Governor, that the two Houses were now ready to receive any communication he might be pleased to make."

The Governor then presented his Message, as follows: —

"*Fellow-citizens of the Council and House of Representatives of Utah Territory:* —

"Having called you from your various avocations to convene in general assembly at an earlier day, and upon shorter notice than may appear desirable, I will proceed without delay to lay before you the chief reason for so doing, as well as such other suggestions as to me shall appear necessary and proper, and as shall occur to my mind." . . .

"Through the munificence of the General Government, we have extended unto us increased facilities for spending our time for the public weal; for, however much the honest pride of gratuitous public service may flatter its humble recipient, yet whilst it impoverishes all but his honorable name and his country's cause, his anxieties will scarcely be lulled, his daily supplies but rarely replenished."

He again addressed them, January 5, 1852: —

" . . . The enjoyment of a *free and independent people* can be accomplished only through this principle: produce what you consume. Draw from the native elements the necessaries of life; permit no vitiated taste to lead you into expensive luxuries, which can only be obtained by involving yourselves in debt. Let home industry produce every article of home consumption." . .

This Legislature, besides passing a code of laws for the government of the Territory, sent some twenty memorials to Congress, most of them calling for appropriations of public money, and divided up the canyons, ferries, pasture-lands, woodlands, water privileges, and, in fact, all the most valuable portion of the public domain, among prominent "saints," giving always to Brigham the "lion's" share. To this he was entitled by his recognized appellation of "the Lion of the Lord."

To this day he holds, by virtue of an Act of the Legislature, the most valuable canyon, near Salt Lake, called City Creek, or Brigham's Canyon, — having taken actual possession of the same, by fencing in the mouth of the canyon completely, and thus preventing all ingress or egress, except upon the payment of toll. General Connor, upon his arrival in Utah, in the fall of 1862, was justly indignant to find himself fenced out from one of the national thoroughfares, but thought it prudent not to add to the causes of irritation by interfering.

During this session Brigham issued eight proclamations. The following is the most celebrated of these *State Papers:*—

"**TERRITORY OF UTAH.**

"*A Proclamation for a Day of Praise and Thanksgiving.*

"It having pleased the Father of all good to make known his mind and will to the children of men in these last days, and through the administration of his angels to restore the holy priesthood unto the sons of Adam, by which the gospel of his Son has been proclaimed, and the ordinances of life and salvation are administered; and through which medium the Holy Ghost has been communicated to believing, willing, and honest minds; causing faith, wisdom, and intelligence to spring up in the hearts of men, and influencing them to flow together, from the four quarters of the earth, to a land of peace and health, rich in mineral and vegetable resources, reserved of old in the councils of eternity for the purposes to which it is now appropriated; a land choice above all other lands; far removed from the strife, contentions, divisions, moral and physical commotions, that are disturbing the peace of the nations and kingdoms of the earth,—

"I, Brigham Young, Governor of the Territory aforesaid, in response to the time-honored custom of our fathers at Plymouth Rock, by the governors of the several States and Territories, and with a heart filled with humiliation and gratitude to the Fountain of all good, for his multiplied munificence to his children, have felt desirous to, and do, *proclaim* Thursday, the 1st day of January, eighteen hundred and fifty-two, a *Day of Praise and Thanksgiving,* for the citizens of this our peaceful Territory, in honor of the God of Abraham, who has preserved his children amid all the vicissitudes they have been called to pass; for his tender mercies in preserving the nation undivided in which we live; for causing the gospel of his kingdom to spread and take root upon the earth, beyond the power of men and demons to destroy; and that he has promised a day of universal joy and rejoicing to all the inhabitants who shall remain when the earth shall have been purified by fire, and rest in peace.

"And I recommend to all good citizens of Utah, that they abstain from everything which is calculated to mar or grieve the spirit of their Heavenly Father on that day; that they rise early in the morning of the first day of the new year, *and wash their bodies with pure water;* that all men attend to their flocks and herds with carefulness, and see that no creature in their charge is hungry, thirsty, or cold; while the women are preparing the best of food for their households, and their children ready to receive it in cleanliness and cheerfulness; then let the head of each family with his family, bow down upon his knees before the God of Israel, and acknowledge all his sins, and the sins of his household; call upon the Father, in the name of Jesus, for every blessing that he desires for himself, his kindred, the Israel of God, the universe of man; praying with full purpose of heart and united faith that the union of the United States may be preserved inviolate, against all the devices of wicked men, until truth shall reign triumphant, and the glory of Jehovah shall fill the earth. Then, in the name of Jesus, ask the Father to bless your food; and when you have filled the plates of your household, partake with them with rejoicing and thanksgiving; and if you feel to make merry in your hearts, sing a song of thanksgiving; and lift up your hearts continually, in peace and acknowledgment of the unbounded mercies you are momentarily receiving.

"I also request of all good and peaceful citizens, that they abstain from all evil thinking, speaking, and acting, on that day; that no one be offended by his neighbor; that all jars and discords cease; that neighborhood broils may be unknown; that tattlers and strife may not be remembered; that evil surmising may be forgotten; that all may learn the truth, and have no need of priests to teach them; that all may be well, and have no need of doctors; that all may cease their quarrels, and starve the lawyers; that all may do as they would be done unto, so that perfect love, which casteth out all fear, may reign triumphant, and there shall be nothing to disturb the quiet of an infant in all the Territory of Utah; that there be no contention in the land; and that the same peace may extend its influence to the utmost bounds of the everlasting hills, and from thence to the habitation of every man and beast, to the ends of the earth; till the leopard shall lie down with the kid, the lion shall eat straw like the ox, and the babe shall lay his hand upon the cockatrice's den, and find peace to its soul.

"I further request, that when the day has been **spent in doing** good, in dealing your bread, your butter, your **beef and your** pork, your turkeys, your molasses, and the choicest of **all the** products of the valleys of the mountains, at your command, **to the** poor; **that you** end the day in the same order, and on the same principle **that you** commenced **it**; that you eat your supper with singleness of heart, as **unto** the Lord, after praise and thanksgiving, and songs of rejoicing; remembering that you cannot be filled with the Holy Spirit, and be preparing for celestial glory, while **the** meanest menial under your charge **or control** is in want of the smallest thing which **God** has given you power to supply; remembering that it **is** dependent on you for **its** comforts, as you are dependent on your **God for** your constant support.

"Retire to your beds early, that you may be refreshed, **and** rise early again, and so continue, until times and seasons are changed; or finally, I say unto you, let the same process be continued from day to day, until you arrive unto one of the days **of Kolob,** [where a day is 1000 of our years,] the planet nearest to the habitation of the Eternal Father; **and** if you do not find peace and **rest to your** souls by that time, in the practice of these things, and **no one else** shall present himself to offer you better counsel, *I will be there*, and knowing more, will tell **you** what you ought to **do next.**

"Done at the Executive Office, Great Salt Lake City. In witness whereof, I have hereunto set my hand and caused the seal of the Territory to be affixed, this 19th day of December, A. D. 1851, and **of** the Independence of the United States **the** seventy-sixth.

[SEAL.]

"By the Governor, BRIGHAM **YOUNG.**
"W. RICHARDS, Sec. *pro tem., appointed* **by the** *Governor.*"

Amidst the verbosity of **this** singular document will be seen expressions of attachment to the Federal Union. The sincerity of these professions must be judged of in the light of his contemporaneous acts. The officers appointed by the

General Government were then in the States, or at Washington, representing truly the condition of things in Utah, and the conduct of Brigham and his associates, which effectually obliged them to leave the Territory, by rendering their presence in Utah not only useless but dangerous. It is for our readers to say how much weight is to be given to that portion of the fulmination of the Prophet put forth under such circumstances.

At this first session of the Legislature, Brigham proceeded to give, in his Message, his views in relation to African slavery, fully indorsing it, and prescribing regulations for its establishment in the Territory. His views upon this subject may be gathered from the following extract:—

"Thus while servitude may and should exist, and that too upon those who are naturally designed to occupy the position of servant of servants, yet we should not fall into the other extreme, and make them as beasts of the field, regarding not the humanity that is in the colored race; nor elevating them, as some seem disposed, to an equality with those whom nature and nature's God has indicated to be their masters, their superiors."

In accordance with the foregoing suggestions, the Legislature passed a law regulating slavery in the Territory, and it has existed in full force and effect to the present time. There are now a considerable number of African slaves in the Territory, and a large number of Indians, "held to service."

During the same session, the Legislature memorialized the President, setting forth that the federal officers had abandoned the Territory; reciting the formation of the provisional government of Deseret, and complaining that "all the authorities of the Territory, including the governor and both houses of the Assembly, and marshal, had been set at naught as exercising their functions illegally and unconstitutionally."

The causes which led to this petition were as follows:—

When the Territory was organized, in the winter of 1850-51, the following named officers were appointed:— Brigham Young, Governor; Lemuel C. Brandenburg, Chief Justice;

Perry E. Brochus and Zerubbabel Snow, Associate Justices Seth M. Blair, Attorney General, and B. D. Harris, Secretary. These officers did not arrive in Utah until July, 1851. Previous to their arrival, **Brigham Young** had issued a proclamation ordering an election for delegate to Congress and members of the Legislature, and providing for taking the census.

The Secretary considered that Young had exceeded his authority, and on this ground refused to pay over the moneys in his hands for the expenses of the Legislature.

The Supreme Court being then in session, Harris applied to the court for an injunction to stay the proceedings of the Legislature, which the court granted. This order, however, was nugatory, as the court had no power to enforce its judgments. This, of course, enraged the Mormons; and the Governor instructed Blair, the District Attorney, who was a Mormon, to sue out a writ of injunction upon the Secretary, to prevent him from taking the money out of the Territory. The court decided against the injunction, thus again sustaining the Secretary.

Again, Congress had appropriated $20,000 for the erection of suitable buildings at the capital of the Territory. Brigham and his tools, the members of the Legislature, attempted to appropriate this money, and in exchange, palm off upon the government, for $20,000, a building which never cost over $8,000.

These circumstances engendered much feeling between the Mormons and the gentile officers; and this was in nowise lessened by an incident which occurred about this time.

Hon. Perry E. Brochus, one of the Supreme Judges, in some remarks made in a Mormon assembly, commented rather severely upon the peculiar institution. He commenced by addressing the women upon the subject of spiritual wife-ism; pointing out to them its wickedness and the unhappy results that must follow to them and to their children, if the practice should be persisted in. He said it was against the laws of man and God. This was undoubtedly the first time, at Salt Lake, that a gentile had ever spoken in public against Mormon institutions.

The women were excited; the most of them were in tears, before he had spoken many minutes. The men were astonished and enraged, and one word of encouragement from their leader would have brought on a collision. Brigham, with his usual shrewdness, saw this, and was equal to the occasion. When the Judge sat down, he rose, and by one of those strong, nervous appeals, for which he is so famous among his brethren, restored the equilibrium of the audience. Those who, but a moment before, were bathed in tears, now responded to his broad sarcasm and keen wit, in screams of laughter; and having fully restored the spirits of the audience, he turned to the Judge, and administered the following rebuke: "I will kick you," he said, "or any other gentile Judge from this stand, if you or they again attempt to interfere with the affairs of our Zion."

The Judge saw that he was beaten, and finding his life threatened and in danger, soon after left the Territory.

After his departure, Brigham preached the following sermon: —

"I am at the defiance of the rulers of the greatest nations on the earth, with the United States all put together, to produce a more loyal people than the Latter Day Saints. Have they, as a people, broken any law? No, they have not. Have the United States? Yes. They have trampled the Constitution under their feet with impunity, and ridden recklessly over all law, to persecute and drive this people. Admit, for argument's sake, that the Mormon elders have more wives than one, yet our enemies never have proved it. If I had forty wives in the United States, they did not know it, and could not substantiate it; neither did I ask any lawyer, judge, or magistrate for them. I live above law, and so do this people. Do the laws of the United States require us to crouch and bow down to the miserable wretches who violate them? No!

"I defy the world to prove that we have infringed upon that

law. You may circumscribe the whole earth, and pass through every Christian nation, so called, and what do you find? If you tell them a 'Mormon' has two wives, they are shocked, and call it dreadful blasphemy. If you whisper such a thing in the ears of a gentile, who takes a fresh woman every night, he is thunderstruck with the enormity of the crime. . . . .

"Now, let me tell you the great, killing story. 'Governor Young has sixteen wives and fourteen babies.' Now, they did not see that sight, but the circumstance was as follows: I took some of my neighbors into the large carriage, and rode down to Father Chase's to eat watermelons. When driving out of the gate, in the evening, Brother Babbitt walks up, and I invited him into the carriage, and he rode up into the city with me, and I suppose he told the United States officers. That, I believe, is the way the story of the sixteen wives and fourteen children first came into circulation.

"But this does not begin to be the extent of my possessions, for I am enlarging on the right hand and on the left; and shall soon be able, Abraham-like, to muster the strength of my house, and *take my rights*, asking no favors of judges or secretaries."

At another time he used the following language: —

"When the officers returned from this Territory to the States, did we send them away? We did not. I will tell you what I did, and what I will do again. I did chastise the poor, mean ruffian, — the poor, miserable creature who came here by the name of Brochus, — when he arose before this people, to preach to them, and tell them of meanness which he supposed they were guilty of, and traduce their characters.

"It is true, as it is said in the report of these officers, if I had crooked my little finger he would have been used up. But I did not bend it. If I had, the sisters alone felt indignant enough to have chopped him in pieces. I did not do it, however, but suffered him to fill up the measure of his shame and iniquity, until his cup is running over.

"I have no fears whatever of Franklin Pierce excusing me from office, and saying that another man shall be the Governor of this Territory. At the beginning of our settlements, when we sent Almon W. Babbitt to Washington with our constitution for a State government, and to ask leave to adopt it, he requested that

I should not sign my name to it as Governor; 'for,' said he, 'if you do, it will thwart all our plans.' I said, 'My name will go as it is in that document, and stay there, from this time henceforth and forever. Now,' I continued, 'if you do not believe it, you may go to Washington, and give those papers to Dr. Bernheisel, and operate against him, and against our getting a State government, and you cannot hinder it.'

"I will be Governor still, after you have done everything you possibly can to prevent it. We have got a Territorial Government, and I am and will be Governor, and no power can hinder it, until the Lord Almighty says, 'Brigham, you need not be Governor any longer;' and then I am willing to yield to another Governor."

This "sermon" was preached at Great Salt Lake City, June 19, 1853, and is published in the "Journal of Discourses," vol. i. p. 188.

Brigham had appointed his second counsellor, Willard Richards, to fill the vacancy occasioned by the departure of Secretary Harris. So the saints had fairly succeeded in ridding themselves of the obnoxious officials, — the remaining Judge, and the District Attorney, being Mormons in good standing.

The Hon. Z. Snow then proceeded to hold his court, unmolested by gentile law or judges. He tried and convicted several Spaniards of buying Indian children for slaves, took the children from the Spaniards, and turned them over to the "brethren."

The Indians now began to be hostile, and the brethren were obliged to cease pursuing the gentiles, and prepare to defend themselves against the "Lamanites." During the years 1852–53–54, more or less disturbances prevailed.

In October, 1852, Judge Shaver arrived, as successor to Judge Brochus; and Lazarus H. Reed, of New York, was appointed Chief Justice, to succeed Judge Brandenburg. Judge Reed arrived in the Territory in June, 1853. Of these, Brigham said,—

"One of our judges, Judge Shaver, has been here during the

winter, and, as far as he is known, he is a straightforward, judicious, upright man, and a good adjudicator in the law. He and Judge Reed, who has lately arrived, I believe will do the best they can, and all is right."

Judge Snow continued to hold his office until succeeded by Judge Stiles, in the fall of 1854.

Judge Shaver lived among the saints until his death, and was "buried with the faithful."

It is currently reported, and believed by many, that Judge Shaver died from the effects of poison, administered by the hands of a Mormon. He was a Southerner by birth, agreed very well with the Mormons, gave suppers, and drank with them, and was considered a "hail-fellow well met." There was, however, some difficulty between the Judge and the Prophet, the nature of which was not distinctly known. The difficulty increased, and one morning the Judge was found dead in his bed. The heads of the church took great pains to have the affair investigated, and came to the conclusion that the Judge had died of some "disease of the head." He was followed to the grave by a large concourse of people, and preceded by a band of music.

Less regard would be paid to these invidious reports, were it not for the fact that Brigham Young's connection with the violent death of divers other persons is too notorious to be denied. To say nothing of the Mountain Meadow massacre, in which he is distinctly implicated by evidence of an overwhelming character, there are other cases in which his agency in causing in some way the death of the party, is scarcely denied by himself.

For instance, the death of Almon W. Babbitt, at the hands of "Indians," on the Plains. In the summer of 1862, Brigham was referring to this affair, in a tea-table conversation, at which Judge Waite and the writer of this were present. On that occasion, after making some remarks to impress upon the minds of those present the necessity of maintaining friendly relations between the federal officers and the authorities of the church, he used language substantially as follows: —

"There is no need of any difficulty, and there need be none, if the officers do their duty, and mind their own affairs. If they do not, if they undertake to interfere in affairs that do not concern them, I will not be far off. *There was Almon W. Babbitt. He undertook to quarrel with me, but soon afterwards was killed by Indians.* He lived like a fool, and died like a fool."

People determined to believe only that Brigham Young is a good citizen, and that he and his people are mostly in the right in their difficulties with the federal officers, will doubtless be able to put an innocent construction upon the foregoing language. But to the minds of those who heard it, and who were most interested in its meaning, it never had but one signification, and went far to disclose the dark and damning character of the man.

But to return to our narrative. Judge Reed seems to have been more fortunate in his intercourse with these people. The Mormons wished to eradicate from his mind all unfavorable impressions created by the sudden departure of his predecessors. They therefore treated him with marked consideration. They hoped, through his influence, to reinstate themselves with the authorities at Washington, and they partially succeeded. The Judge formed quite a favorable opinion of the Mormons, though not indorsing the administration of Brigham Young. He remained in the valley about a year, and then went to the States, intending to return, but died suddenly, while at his home, in Bath, Steuben County, New York.

CHAPTER III.

POLITICAL HISTORY CONTINUED.

Col. Steptoe and Brigham **Young.** — Brigham reappointed Governor. — John F. Kinney. — Western Utah, or **Nevada.** — Letter of Hon. James M. Crane. — Judge Stiles and the Records. — **W. W.** Drummond.

In 1854 **Col. Steptoe**, with about 300 **men, came to Salt Lake.** His **command was** intended for California and Oregon, but spent the winter **of** 1854–55 at Salt Lake City.

About this time John F. Kinney, of Iowa, was appointed Chief Justice, to succeed Reed, and George P. Stiles, Associate Justice; Joseph Hollman, also **of Iowa,** Attorney-General, **and** Almon W. Babbitt, Secretary. In the spring of **1855, W. W.** Drummond, of Illinois, was appointed **Associate** Justice.

During the winter of **1854–55,** news reached Salt Lake **that** President Pierce **had** commissioned **Col.** Steptoe as Governor of Utah. This alarmed the saints exceedingly. The Lion of the Lord was roused. Something must be done.

Col. Steptoe had the appointment under consideration for several weeks, and finally *refused to accept it*, and joined with Chief Justice Kinney and others in recommending the continuance in office **of Governor Young.**

The question naturally **arises, Why did Col. Steptoe** refuse to accept the appointment, **and** recommend Brigham Young? Mormons would tell you, in confidence, that Brigham "put **a** hook in his nose," and he was compelled to do **as he** did. The Prophet of the Lord had said he would be Governor, **and no power** but the Lord Almighty could hinder it.

Daring and unscrupulous as a brigand, having the means at his command, and the ingenuity to use them, why should he not outwit the government and deceive the people of the United States? He was determined not to relinquish, without an effort to retain them, the power and emoluments of his position. The following narrative of the manner in which he accomplished his purposes, has been furnished by a Mormon who was residing in Salt Lake City at the time, and the employment of similar appliances on more than one occasion afterward, gives the coloring of truth to the story.

There were in Salt Lake City, at that time, two beautiful and fascinating women, one of whom was by marriage nearly related to the Prophet; the other was an actress in the church theatre. Their husbands were both " on a mission." These ladies were a great deal in the society of Col. Steptoe and his officers. Much attention was paid to the military officers, and it would be but natural that these men should be both pleased and flattered by the attention of sisters occupying so high a place in the hierarchy. According to report, however, the character of these women was not such as their exalted position in the church would seem to require.

One evening Brigham called " the girls " to him, and explained that he had a plan in which he needed their assistance. They at once consented to do anything he might desire. The plan was soon agreed upon. He placed his Danites at a convenient distance around the Colonel's office, and calmly awaited developments. In a short time one of the " police " came to the Prophet, and signified that it was time for him to appear on the field. He went immediately down to the Colonel's office, which was on Main Street, and knocked for admittance. For some time no one responded, but the knocking continuing violently, Col. Steptoe asked who was there. " Brigham Young," said the angry Prophet; " and I want to come in, and I will come in." At this Steptoe opened the door, and Brigham entered the front office. He seemed excited, and without being seated, asked if Mary and Mrs. —— were there; adding,—"I want the girls." Steptoe denied their presence; but could a prophet be deceived? "I know better," said he; "I know they are here;" at the same time walking into the back office. There, on the sofa, sat two young gentlemen dressed in the highest style, but wearing their hats. Brigham advanced, lifted the hats of the fancy gentlemen, and the ladies he was seeking sat before him. Of course, the righteous indignation of the Prophet knew no bounds. He threatened Steptoe with exposure and prosecution, and told him his life would not be safe if the friends of the ladies came to hear of the affair. He censured the girls, and told them to go home, and finally calmed down, and left the office.

Steptoe was greatly alarmed, and, as a compromise, offered to recommend Brigham for the appointment which had just been tendered to himself. With ill-concealed satisfaction on the part of Brigham and his friends, the proposition was accepted, and "the matter arranged."

Soon after, a petition was sent to the President, dated December 30, 1854, and asking for the reappointment of Young as Governor. This was signed by Col. Steptoe and most of his officers, and by all the federal officers then in Utah.

This array of gentile names was not to be disregarded, and Brigham Young was reappointed Governor of Utah.

In 1854 John F. Kinney was appointed, by Franklin Pierce, Chief Justice of Utah, and came to the valley with his family and a large stock of goods the same year. He was known in Iowa as a "Jack Mormon," and subsequent events have proven that he was such. He sold goods and kept a boarding-house; and at once entered into favor with the Mormon administration. He was pecuniarily interested in keeping the good-will of his trading customers; and this fact, together with his undoubted sympathy with the church, will satisfactorily account for the course pursued by him in the complicated condition of the Territory.

It is not our purpose to detract from the merits of any one We desire to do justice to all. But the impartial truth of history requires us to say that the uniform course of Judge Kinney has been to aid and abet Brigham Young in his ambitious schemes, with but little regard to the advancement of the interests of the whole country, or the requirements of indiscriminate justice.

As to his merits as a jurist, the writer of these pages cannot undertake to decide. But it would seem, to one uninitiated, that a Judge cannot be very profound who will try, convict, and sentence men not within the jurisdiction of his court, and even men not in the land of the living. This was done by Judge Kinney, in the case of the Morrisites, — dissenters or apostates from the Mormon Church.

In the spring of 1863 a large number of these men were tried, convicted, and fined $100 each. Many of them were out of the Territory at the time, and one was dead. This statement is fully substantiated by affidavits which were taken at the time. Over ninety were tried and convicted, about twenty of whom were out of the Territory, and one had died before the trial commenced.

When the cases were called on for trial, it was stated that some of the accused were absent. The Judge remarked, it made no difference; he was gratified that so many had made their appearance, and directed the trial to proceed. All were found guilty, and sentenced to pay a fine of $100 each, except a few of the leaders, who were sentenced to the penitentiary, — one of them for fifteen years.

These men were accused of resisting the Mormon officers who came to arrest them. Robert T. Burton, the sheriff of Salt Lake County, who was the principal one thus "resisted," had shot Morris, their Prophet, in cold blood, after he and his party had surrendered; and yet, while the Morrisites were so severely punished, Burton went scot free. The grand jury of Salt Lake County would not even find a bill of indictment against him. Burton stands high in the community, and was afterwards appointed Collector of Internal Revenue.

But this is not all. Not only were all of the accused tried and convicted, but the bonds of those absent were declared *by the clerk* to be forfeited, and execution was issued against those resident in Utah, to collect the penalty of the bonds. At the same time, *the records showed no judgments against the delinquents.* One of these Morrisites, named Abraham Taylor, found his property, worth $2500, suddenly levied upon, under one of these executions. There being no gentile lawyer at Salt Lake, he applied to Judge Waite, who investigated the matter, and found there was no judgment of record. He then advised Mr. Taylor to apply to Judge Kinney for an injunction against the officer. This was done; but the application was refused by Judge K. *on the ground that if there was no judgment he could render one, as the court had not permanently adjourned, but only to meet on his own motion.* This response to the application of a suitor is a sufficient indication of the ability of Judge Kinney, and of his desire to administer impartial justice.

The result of the whole matter was, that the homestead of Mr. Taylor was sold under the execution, *to the clerk of Judge Kinney's court, for* $200; the family of Taylor impoverished, and literally turned into the street. After remaining out of doors, in front of the house, for a day or two, they took refuge at the camp of Gen. Connor.

In his personal appearance Judge Kinney is pompous and conceited. He is of the medium size, rather stout, with dark complexion. Brusque and ready in conversation, and never declining to drink when invited, he is well adapted to the country in which he resides, and is immensely popular in the community in which he was placed "to administer the law," and which he now represents in Congress. He is an open apologist and advocate of polygamy.

Mrs. Kinney is a sister of Judge Hall, of Iowa, and an accomplished lady. She was utterly disgusted with Mormon society, and returned, with her daughters, to the States.

Judge Kinney remained in Utah until 1856. In 1860 he

was reappointed. Thus he was absent from the Territory during all the exciting scenes of 1857–8 and 9, and returned after something like harmony had been restored in the affairs of the Territory. He managed, however, by having his leave of absence extended from time to time, to retain the office and its emoluments until 1858. Since 1860 he has been back and forth, spending about half his time in either portion of the country, but retaining his position as Chief Justice, until elected to Congress in 1863.

Judge Stiles, who was appointed to succeed Snow, was assigned to the third, or Carson District. He immediately proceeded to his district, and held a term of court.

The present Territory of Nevada was included mostly in the third judicial district, and much difficulty occurred between Mormons and the miners in that section.

A full account of the proceedings which go to make up the history of this part of Utah, will be found in a letter from the Hon. James M. Crane to Hon. William Smith, published in 1859.

This letter is so complete and truthful in its statements, and presents such a correct view of the character and tendencies of Mormonism, that we insert it, nearly entire:—

"WASHINGTON, January 17, 1859.

"DEAR SIR,—

"As you may need some facts not reported at length in the memorial and other documents, relating to the proposed Territory of Nevada, I herewith submit them.

"The Mormons and Anti-Mormons began the settlement of Western Utah in the latter part of 1854. The former, however, succeeded, in 1855, in obtaining a numerical majority; and the Legislature of Utah, on being informed of this fact, organized the whole western part of the Territory, under the name of Carson County, and Governor Young appointed Orson Hyde, the President of the Quorum of Twelve Apostles, its Probate Judge. Soon after the Judge arrived, adventurers from California, as well as from the Atlantic States, settled in Carson and other valleys on the eastern side of the Sierra Nevada, for the purpose of mining, farming, and raising stock. As they increased very fast, the Mormons became alarmed, and determined to expel them.

"They therefore ordered them to leave the country. Of course the Christians, or Anti-Mormons refused to do so. The Mormons then assembled their forces, and attempted to expel them, *vi et armis*. The Anti-Mormons also organized, and fortified themselves, with a view of defending their lives and property against their assailants.

"For two weeks their armies camped nearly in sight of each other, without coming to a direct battle.

"By this time, news had reached the miners in California of this state of affairs, and a large number had determined to cross the mountains, and afford protection to the Anti-Mormons. On hearing this, the Mormons became satisfied that, unless they retraced their steps, they would be driven themselves from the country, instead of the Anti-Mormons. They therefore proposed a truce, and agreed that all should enjoy a common heritage in that part of the Territory.

"The Mormons now became satisfied that the Christians not only could, but would occupy these fertile valleys, on the ground that they were the common property of the United States. When the Legislature of Utah heard of this affair, that body, in violation of every constitutional right, repealed the county organization, recalled the Probate Judge, and removed all the county and court records to Salt Lake City, where they have ever since remained. Amongst these records were several indictments against certain persons for high crimes and misdemeanors. By this flagrant violation of all sacred, individual, collective, and constitutional rights, the people of Western Utah were not only denied all legal protection to life and property, but they were disfranchised. They have ever been unrepresented in the Legislature and in Congress. The history of our country presents no such a record of open defiance of law, and such cruelties to men under the form of laws.

"For years the Anti-Mormons have been applying, both to the Territorial Legislature and to Congress, for protection, without success.

"Their situation has ever been, and still is, peculiarly unsafe and annoying. Recently a Probate Judge was surreptitiously appointed for Carson Valley, with a view of reorganizing the county of Carson, and thus extend over the people there the Mormon statutes of the Territory.

"The Judge, soon after he received his commission, undertook to force on an election of county officers. Enough of the Anti-Mormons, however, turned out, to defeat his purpose, by the election of an opposite ticket, who, on being elected, refused to qualify, because they were required to obey the Mormon statutes. The Judge has been notified that if he undertakes to enforce the Mormon statutes he will be resisted, — peaceably if they can, forcibly if they must.

"They will not introduce, nor permit others to introduce among them, the vices of that wicked, perverse, and adulterous generation, who have so long wielded the sceptre of authority in the Great Basin. They will not allow, with impunity, their wives and daughters to be kidnapped, dishonored, and defiled; nor submit to laws made by such a people, nor allow themselves to be ruled by men who practise and uphold vices and crimes so revolting to the moral sense of the world; and if the Mormons persist in their present course, blood will flow.

"The only loyal people of Utah are oppressed, annoyed, and scandalized, by a government intended by Congress to secure them in their rights, and to protect them in their property; and while the present Territorial organization exists, the Mormons, who have control of the Legislature, will never 'let up on the gentiles.'

"The only remedy for this unnatural war, now raging between the Mormons and the Anti-Mormons in Utah, is to be found in the immediate separation of these people under two distinct governmental organizations. One thing is inevitable, — the Mormons and Anti-Mormons will never, and can never live together in peace, under one government. The conflicts which took place between them in Ohio, Missouri, Illinois, and Iowa, and which are now going on in Utah, ought to convince any intelligent man of the justice and truth of this declaration. Indeed, the Mormons themselves acknowledge it; and so long as they adhere to their belief, — a belief founded upon their own scriptures, — that an absolute theocracy is the only government under which they can and should live, they never will be loyal to our government and countrymen, and hence their hostility to our institutions and people, and their inflexible devotion to their own.

"In every State where the Mormons have lived, it has cost the loyal people of the State thousands of dollars, as well as the loss of many lives, to compel them to obey the laws. In every instance they have resisted our laws, and in every State necessity demanded their expulsion.

"In Utah, while they were charged with the administration of the government and execution of the laws, they proved themselves not only traitors to our people, but treacherous to the government, and openly rebelled against them and defied their authority, and it cost the Federal Government millions to conquer them. They have still control of the Territory, and they are inflexibly bent upon subduing the Anti-Mormons of Western Utah; and if the latter are not separated from them, and protected by law, it will require the expenditure of millions more to restore order in Utah. Congress can count the cost in this matter, while we will have the melancholy duty of burying our dead. The people of Nevada will never be conquered,— never be ruled by the Mormons. Come what will, they will resist to the bitter end. They prefer death to dishonor, and the government may choose which of these shall be meted out to them.

"In addition to the above considerations, which should, I believe, present conclusive and imposing evidence, sufficiently satisfactory to induce Congress to organize the Territory of Nevada, I may likewise mention others.

"While the people of Western Utah have, in the Mormons, open and avowed enemies, they have likewise the savage tribes to defend themselves against. Some of these tribes are professed Mormons, while others are under their influence. Many conflicts have taken place between the Christians and some of these tribes, as well as between the emigrants, while crossing the Plains to the North Pacific, and the aforesaid savages; and there is no hope of establishing amicable relations with these Indian tribes, until they are brought under other and better relations with the Anti-Mormons of Utah. Peace does not reign in Utah, and never will, under the present order of things. . . . .

"When our common country shall call forth her sons to defend her rights, the people of Nevada will come forth. They will be ready and willing to meet the enemy, on the beach and on the frontier, with a sword in one hand and a torch in the other. They will dispute every inch of ground, burn every blade of grass, and the last intrenchment of liberty will become their graves, rather than permit a foreign enemy to contaminate the soil of our country. Can this be said of the Mormons? I think not. If we can protect our countrymen abroad, why should we not, on our own soil?

"Very respectfully, yours,
"JAMES M. CRANE,
"*Delegate elect from Nevada.*

"To Hon. Wm. Smith."

"Having read the above statement of Judge Crane, delegate from the proposed Territory of Nevada, I will state from my own observation, having resided in the Territory of Utah for over three years, for a portion of which time I was in Carson Valley, that I heartily concur with him, and fully indorse his statement in relation to the condition of things in Western Utah, and seriously believe that the wants and necessities of the people of that portion of the Territory demand its immediate organization.

"GEORGE P. STILES,
"*Late Associate Justice for Utah.*"

Nevada was erected into a Territory, and has made rapid and gigantic strides in all the essentials of a high civilization. Her mines are celebrated throughout the world, and she annually adds millions of dollars to the circulation of the country.

Already are her valleys teeming with the life of the husbandman, and her soil yielding up its rich harvests of golden grain, for the sustenance of her brave and patriotic sons. She has sent several hundred men into the field, and with unshaken loyalty stands ready to send more, if the cause of her country calls, — thus literally fulfilling the promise of Judge Crane made in the foregoing letter. Mark the contrast between loyal and Christian Nevada, and disloyal and Mohammedan Utah! One rushing on to a glorious and happy destiny, and the other falling rapidly back into the habits and customs of heathen nations. The genius of Liberty sits enthroned among the mountains of free Nevada, while despotism of the most hideous character clanks her chains in Utah. May the day of deliverance for the oppressed thousands of Utah soon dawn. Then will she take her place among her sisters in the family of States, and the hand of oppression be no more felt in all her fair borders.

When Brigham Young found that the gentile element was gaining ground rapidly in Carson County, his Legislature attached it to Great Salt Lake County, for judicial and other purposes. A large number of Mormons were sent on to colonize, and if possible to retain, the fertile Valley of Nevada. These missionaries were recalled in 1857, as well as many others, who were settling in different parts of California.

Slowly and sullenly they relinquished their hold upon this rich and prosperous portion of the Republic. It rapidly advanced in population, and not only prospered as a Territory, as already mentioned, but has lately been admitted as one of the States of the Union. The admission of Nevada, carved out of Utah, while the mother Territory still remains out in the cold, ought to be a sufficient hint that Congress and the people of the United States are not yet prepared for the establishment in their midst of a polygamic monarchy.

Judge Stiles returned to Salt Lake City, and there held several courts.

In the fall of 1856 a conflict arose, in regard to the jurisdiction of the United States Marshal. Heretofore this officer had acted with the Mormons, and all had passed off smoothly. But a real gentile was now appointed, and this was the signal for Mormon opposition. The Mormons claimed that the Territorial Marshal, instead of the United States Marshal, should act in the United States courts when doing territorial business. The United States Marshal contended that he should officiate in all business transacted in the United States courts, whether sitting as federal or territorial courts. Judge Stiles issued certain writs, directed to the officer, which he found it impossible to serve. The people, instigated by the Mormon leaders, refused to obey the precepts of the court, and set at naught its authority, proclaiming that the time had come when their laws, and none others, should be enforced in Utah.

The question of jurisdiction was brought before the court, and James Ferguson, Hosea Stout, and J. C. Little, Mormon lawyers, loudly demanded that the Judge should decide in their favor. Ferguson, backed by an armed mob, told Judge Stiles, in open court, that if he dared to decide contrary to their wishes, he "would take him from the bench d—d quick"; that the boys were there to do it, and he, with others, by threats and intimidations, finally compelled the Judge to adjourn his court.

Judge Stiles then appealed to Brigham Young, as Governor of the Territory, to sustain him, and protect him in the discharge of his duties. In reply, he was coolly told that "the courts had already cost him [Brigham] too much trouble; that the boys had got their spunk up, and he would not interfere." He advised him, "if he could not sustain and enforce their [the United States] laws and institutions, the sooner he adjourned his court the better."

These proceedings had a tendency to bring the Judge into disrepute with the Mormons. Thomas Williams, a lawyer, had his office with Judge Stiles, on Main Street. Williams, though a Mormon, was an independent man, and had openly opposed Brigham on some question of politics. He had also denounced some prominent murders, and was becoming obnoxious, and even dangerous, to Brigham and his compeers. The Prophet once said to Williams's father and mother: "If Tom don't behave himself better, and stop causing me trouble, I must attend to him." Soon after, Williams apostatized, and started for California, intending to remain, and send back for his family. He met the fate of Babbitt. He was waylaid and killed by "Indians" on the Plains. It is well understood at Salt Lake that these were white Indians, and that Williams was put to death by order of the church authorities.

The records of the United States District Courts were in Judge Stiles's office. He, and Wiliiams also, had a good many law books, which were private property. Brigham asserted that the records were suffered to "lie around loose," and suggested to the boys that they had better be cared for. This was sufficient, and "the boys" proceeded to "'tend to it." James Ferguson, Hiram B. Clawson, and several others, repaired to the office of the Judge when he was absent, and stationing one of the number to watch, they gathered up the records of the courts, first of all, and conveyed them to a fire-and-burglar-proof-safe, belonging to Young, and under the control of Clawson, who was his confidential clerk and son-in-law.

Having deposited them safely, they returned, and taking some of the Judge's papers, tore them in pieces, and scattered them over the floor, and in the direction of an outhouse. About the same time a large number of the law books found their way into the houses of certain Mormon lawyers, where they have ever since remained. They then took some of the books from the office, and placed them in the outhouse, set fire to the building, and burned it to the ground.

When Judge Stiles returned he found the office robbed, and the books and papers, as he supposed, burned.

Thus all business was suspended, and the records of the United States Courts and government property burned and stolen from the custody of the legal authorities.

Judge Stiles left Utah in the spring of 1857, and when in Washington, made affidavit to the foregoing facts. It may be well here to state that Judge S. was entirely conscientious in making his affidavit, and the prevailing impression in the community was that the records had been destroyed.

In the summer of 1855 W. W. Drummond, of Illinois, arrived in Utah, as Associate Justice of the Supreme Court. The Mormons allege that he deserted his wife, and brought with him a mistress. This caused much righteous indignation among the saints! The Judge also professed to be a warm friend and advocate of Senator Douglas, whom the Mormons hate.

When Drummond was about to hold court, he intimated that he would set aside all judgments rendered by probate Judges, and annul all their proceedings, except such as pertained to the usual and legitimate business of the probate courts. Here was a direct issue, and a conflict was inevitable.

The court being about to be held in Fillmore, a Jew was hired for $25 to quarrel with Drummond. As a part of the programme, also, he was to strike the Judge. The Jew played his part, except the blow, which, for want of opportunity or courage, was omitted. Instead of this he sent to the Judge an insulting message, by the hands of a colored " boy " belonging to Drummond. The boy was sent back with a raw hide, and instructions to " lay on " the same to the back of the Israelite, which Cuffy obeyed with much spirit. Complaint was made by the Jew to a local magistrate. A warrant was issued, and Drummond and his negro were both arrested.

The result of this *émeute* was a sort of compromise, in which it was understood that the Judge should not interfere with the probate courts, and he was set at liberty.

After adjourning his court at Fillmore, Drummond located in Utah County in the winter of 1856. The following summer he went to Carson to hold court for Judge Stiles. Thence he proceeded to California and to the States, and as the Mormons allege "contributed largely to the getting up of Buchanan's crusade."

CHAPTER IV.

POLITICAL HISTORY CONTINUED. — THE MORMON WAR.

Report of the Secretary of War. — **Proclamation** of Gov. Brigham Young declaring Martial Law. — Correspondence. — Sermons of Young and Kimball. — Proclamation of Gov. Cumming. — His Echo Canyon Adventures. — Col. Kane. — **The Mormons leave** Salt Lake. — **Commissioners appointed by** the President. — Peace restored.

By these and similar outrages the Mormons had succeeded in ridding themselves of all the federal authorities, and were really in open rebellion against the Federal Government.

As Congress was not in session, the matter was taken in hand by Floyd, Secretary of War, and President Buchanan.

After due consultation it was deemed advisable to appoint new men to all the civil offices of the Territory, and to accompany them with a military force sufficient for their protection and the enforcement of the laws. Accordingly, President Buchanan, during the summer of 1857, made the following appointments for Utah: — Governor, A. Cumming; Chief Justice, D. R. Eckels; Associate Justices, John Cradlebaugh and Charles E. Sinclair; Secretary, John Hartnett.

An army of about 3000 men was armed and equipped, and ordered to march for Utah, early in the fall of 1857.

Brevet Brigadier-General W. S. Harney was originally named as commander of this force, but it was subsequently deemed inadvisable to detach that officer from the special duties of his department in Kansas, and the troops sent to Utah were placed under the orders of Col. A. S. Johnson.

The Secretary of War, in his report, dated December 5 1857, says:—

"The Territory of Utah is peopled almost exclusively by the religious sect known as Mormons. . . . They have substituted for the laws of the land a theocracy, having for its head an individual whom they profess to believe a prophet of God.

"This Prophet demands obedience, and receives it implicitly from his people, in virtue of what he assures them to be authority derived from revelations received by him from Heaven. Whenever he finds it convenient to exercise any special command, these opportune revelations of a higher law come to his aid. From his decrees there is no appeal; against his will there is no resistance. . . .

"From the first hour they fixed themselves in that remote and almost inaccessible region of our territory, from which they are now sending defiance to the sovereign power, their whole plan has been to prepare for a successful secession from the authority of the United States, and a permanent establishment of their own. . . .

"'This Mormon brotherhood has scarcely preserved the semblance of obedience to the authority of the United States for some years past; not at all indeed, except as it might confer some direct benefit upon themselves, or contribute to circulate public money in their community. . . . I need not here recite the many instances in their conduct and history on which these general allegations are founded, especially the conduct they have adopted within the last twelve months towards the civil authorities of the United States.

"It has, nevertheless, always been the policy and desire of the Federal Government to avoid collision with this Mormon community. It has borne with the insubordination they have exhibited, under circumstances when respect for its own authority has frequently counselled harsh measures of discipline. And this forbearance might still be prolonged, and the evils rife among them be allowed to work out their own cure, if this community occupied any other theatre, isolated and remote from the seats of civilization, than the one they now possess.

"But, unfortunately for these views, their settlements lie in the great pathway which leads from the Atlantic States to the new and flourishing communities growing up upon the Pacific seaboard.

They stand a lion in the path; not only themselves defying the civil and military authorities of the government, but encouraging, if not exciting, the nomad savages who roam over the vast, unoccupied regions of the continent, to the pillage and massacre of peaceful and helpless emigrant families traversing the solitudes of the wilderness. The rapid settlement of our Pacific possessions; the rights, in those regions, of emigrants, unable to afford the heavy expenses of transit by water and the Isthmus; the facility and safety of military, political, and social intercommunication between our eastern and western populations and States, — all depend upon the prompt, absolute, and thorough removal of a hostile power besetting this path, midway of its route, at a point where succor and provisions should always be found, rather than obstruction, privation, and outrage. . . .

"From all the circumstances surrounding this subject at the time, it was thought expedient, during the past summer, to send a body of troops to Utah, with the civil officers recently appointed to that Territory. . . . Great care has been taken, in preparing for the march to Utah, that nothing should seem to excite apprehension of any action on the part of the army in the least conflicting with the fixed principle of our institutions, by which the military is strictly subordinate to the civil authority. The instructions of the commanding officer were deliberately considered, and carefully drawn, and he was charged not to allow any conflict to take place between the troops and the people of the Territory, except only in case he should be called upon by the Governor for soldiers to act as a *posse comitatus* in enforcing obedience to the laws.

"In conformity with this sentiment, and to assure these people of the real intention of the movement, an active, discreet officer was sent in advance of the army to Utah, for the purpose of purchasing provisions for it, and of assuring the people of the Territory of the peaceful intentions of the Government. This officer found, upon entering the Territory, that these deluded people had already, in advance of his arrival, or of any information, except as to the march of the column, determined to resist their approach, and prevent, if possible, and by force, the entrance of the army into the Valley of Salt Lake. Supplies of every sort were refused him.

"The day after his departure from the city, on his way back,

Brigham issued his Proclamation, substantially declaring war against the United States, and at the same time putting the Territory under martial law."

The following is a copy of this celebrated document: —

"PROCLAMATION

"OF GOVERNOR BRIGHAM YOUNG.

" *Citizens of Utah*, — We are invaded by a hostile force, who are evidently assailing us to accomplish our overthrow and destruction. For the last twenty-five years we have trusted officials of the Government, from constables and justices, to judges, governors, and presidents, only to be scorned, held in derision, insulted, and betrayed. Our houses have been plundered and then burned, our fields laid waste, our principal men butchered, while under the pledged faith of the Government for their safety; and our families driven from their homes, to find that shelter in the barren wilderness, and that protection among hostile savages, which were denied them in the boasted abodes of Christianity and civilization.

" The Constitution of our common country guarantees unto us all that we do now, or have ever claimed. If the constitutional rights which pertain unto us as American citizens were extended to Utah, according to the spirit and meaning thereof, and fairly and impartially administered, it is all that we could ask, — all that we have ever asked.

" Our opponents have availed themselves of prejudice existing against us, because of our religious faith, to send out a formidable host to accomplish our destruction. We have had no privilege or opportunity of defending ourselves from the false, foul, and unjust aspersions against us, before the nation.

" The Government has not condescended to cause an investigating committee, or other persons, to be sent to inquire and ascertain the truth, as is customary in such cases. We know those aspersions to be false, but that avails us nothing. We are condemned unheard, and forced to an issue with an armed, mercenary mob, which has been sent against us at the instigation of anonymous letter-writers, ashamed to father the base, slanderous falsehoods which they have given to the public; of corrupt officials, who have brought false accusations against us, to screen themselves in their own infamy; and of hireling priests and howling editors, who prostitute the truth for filthy lucre's sake.

"The issue which has thus been forced upon us compels us to resort to the first great law of self-preservation, and stand in our own self-defence,— a right guaranteed to us by the genius of the institutions of our country, and upon which the Government is based. Our duty to ourselves — to our families — requires us not to tamely submit to be driven and slain, without an attempt to preserve ourselves. Our duty to our country — our holy religion — our God — to freedom and liberty, requires that we should not quietly stand still, and see those fetters forging around us, which are calculated to enslave and bring us in subjection to an unlawful military despotism, such as can only emanate, in a country of constitutional law, from usurpation, tyranny, and oppression.

"Therefore, I, Brigham Young, Governor and Superintendent of Indian Affairs for the Territory of Utah, in the name of the people of the United States in the Territory of Utah, forbid, —

"*First.* All armed forces, of whatever description, from coming into this Territory, under any pretence whatever.

"*Second.* That all the forces in said Territory hold themselves in readiness to march at a moment's notice, to repel any and all such invasion.

"*Third.* Martial law is hereby declared to exist in this Territory, from and after the publication of this proclamation; and no person shall be allowed to pass or repass, into, or through, or from this Territory, without a permit from the proper officer.

"Given under my hand and seal, at Great Salt Lake City, Territory of Utah, this fifteenth day of September, A. D. eighteen hundred and fifty-seven, and of the Independence of the United States of America the eighty-second.

"BRIGHAM YOUNG."

This proclamation was forwarded to the commander of the United States forces, then on the Plains. It was accompanied by the following letter: —

"FORT BRIDGER, September 3, 1857.

"SIR, — I have the honor to forward you the accompanying letter from his Excellency Governor Young, together with two copies of his proclamation, and a copy of the Laws of Utah, 185, chap. 7, containing the Organic Act of the Territory.

"It may be proper to add, that I am here to aid in carrying out the instructions of Governor Young. General Robinson will deliver these papers to you, and receive such communication as you may wish to make.

"Trusting that your answer and action will be dictated by a proper respect for the rights and liberties of American citizens, I remain,

"Very respectfully,
"DANIEL H. WELLS,
"*Lieut.-General commanding Nauvoo Legion.*"

"GOVERNOR'S OFFICE, UTAH TERRITORY,
GREAT SALT LAKE CITY, September 29, 1857.

"Sir, — By reference to the Act of Congress, passed September 9, 1850, organizing the Territory of Utah, published in a copy of the Laws of Utah, herewith, p. 146, chap. 7, you will find the following: —

"'SEC. 2. *And be it further enacted,* That the executive power in and over said Territory of Utah shall be vested in a governor, who shall hold his office for four years, *and until his successor shall be appointed and qualified,* unless sooner removed by the President of the United States. The governor shall reside within said Territory, shall be commander-in-chief of the militia thereof,' &c., &c.

"I am still the Governor and Superintendent of Indian Affairs for this Territory, no successor having been appointed and qualified, as provided by law, nor have I been removed by the President of the United States.

"By virtue of the authority thus vested in me, I have issued and forwarded you a copy of my proclamation, forbidding the entrance of armed forces into this Territory. This you have disregarded. I now further direct that you retire forthwith from the Territory by the same route you entered. Should you deem this impracticable, and prefer to remain until spring in the vicinity of your present encampment, Black Fork, or Green River, you can do so in peace, and unmolested, on condition that you deposit your arms and ammunition with Lewis Robinson, Quartermaster-General of the Territory, and leave in the spring, as soon as the condition of the roads will permit you to march. And should you fall short of provisions, they can be furnished you by making the proper applications therefor.

"Gen. D. H. Wells will forward this, and receive any communications you may have to make.

"Very respectfully,
"BRIGHAM YOUNG,
"*Governor and Superintendent of
Indian Affairs, Utah Territory*

"To the Officer commanding the Forces
now invading Utah Territory."

The legitimate result of this violent and treasonable proclamation, as might be supposed, was to incite the people to revenge and bloodshed. Every man who could bear arms was at once taken from his usual avocation and trained in the art of war. Clothing was at this time very scarce, as no trains of goods had arrived from the States. The "sisters" were called upon to make up every article which they could possibly spare into uniforms for the troops. Accordingly the "brethren" appeared arrayed in pieces of bed-quilts, carpets, and old clo' made over, and presented to the eye as motley and miserable a crew as those of "the right valiant Sir John Falstaff." If we look at the leaders of these classical armies, however, the parallel fails. The chivalric Jack had at least the courage to march at the head of his soldiers; while Brigham, who acknowledges himself to be a natural coward, preferred to remain snugly ensconced among his numerous wives and children. The Lion of the Lord, though seemingly aroused, only shook himself and roared loudly several times. He then quietly lay down, and remained thenceforth *couchant* during the war. With all the assurance and assumption of Joseph Smith, he lacked his personal courage and manly daring.

But the rank and file of these "warriors of the Lord" lacked neither courage nor enthusiasm. Their Zion was threatened, — their institutions in danger, — and with the fire of revenge burning in their hearts, at the remembrance of former injuries, they rushed forth, to conquer or to die.

Many joined their brethren in Echo Canyon, without even

shoes to their feet, wading through snows several feet deep. Such devotion and heroism were worthy of a better cause.

The feeling and determination of the people cannot be better expressed than by extracts from the sermons of their leaders at this critical period.

Sunday morning, September 16, 1857, Brigham Young, in his public discourse, said : —

"This people are free; they are not in bondage to any government on God's footstool. We have transgressed no law, and we have no occasion to do so, neither do we intend; but as for any nation's coming to destroy this people, God Almighty being my helper, they cannot come here. [The congregation responded a loud 'Amen.'] . . .

"We have borne enough of their oppression and hellish abuse, and we will not bear any more of it, for there is no just law requiring further forbearance on our part. And I am not going to have troops here to protect the priests and hellish rabble in efforts to drive us from the land we possess; for the Lord does not want us to be driven, and has said, 'If you will assert your rights, and keep my commandments, you shall never again be brought into bondage by your enemies.' . . .

"They say that their army is legal; and I say that such a statement is as false as hell, and that they are as rotten as an old pumpkin that has been frozen seven times, and then melted in a harvest sun. Come on with your thousands of illegally ordered troops, and I will promise you, in the name of Israel's God, that you shall melt away as the snow before a July sun. . . .

"You might as well tell me that you can make hell into a powder-house, as to tell me that you could let an army in here, and have peace; and I intend to tell them, and show them this, if they do not stay away. . . . And I say our enemies shall not slip the bow on old 'Bright's neck' again. God bless you. Amen."

In the afternoon of the same day, the "lion" again roars, as follows : —

"There cannot be a more damnable, dastardly order issued, than was issued by the Administration to this people, while they were in an Indian country in 1846. Before we left Nauvoo, not less than two United States Senators came to receive a pledge from us that we would leave the United States; and then, while we were doing our best to leave their borders, the poor, low, degraded curses sent a requisition for five hundred men to go and fight their battles! That was President Polk; and he is now weltering in hell, with old Zachary Taylor, where the present Administration will soon **be,** if they do not repent.

"Liars have reported that this people have committed treason, and upon their lies the President has ordered out troops to aid in officering this Territory; **and if** those officers are like many who have previously been sent here, — and we have reason to believe that they are, or they would not come where they know they are not wanted, — they are poor, miserable blacklegs, broken down political hacks, robbers **and** whoremongers; men that are not fit for civilized society **; so** they **must** dragoon them upon us for officers. I feel that I won't bear such cursed treatment, **and that is** enough to say, — for we are just as free as the mountain air. . .

"I have told you that if this people will live their religion, all will be well; and I have told you that if there is any man or woman who is not willing to destroy anything or everything of their property that would be of use to an enemy if left, I wanted them to go out of the Territory. And I again say so to-day ; **for** when the time comes to burn and lay waste our improvements, **if** any man undertakes to shield his, he will be sheared down ; **for** 'judgment will be laid to the line, and righteousness to **the** plummet.'

"Now, the faint-hearted can go in peace; but should that time come, they must not interfere. Before I will suffer what I have in times gone by, there shall not be one building, nor one foot of lumber, nor a stick, nor a tree, nor a particle of grass or hay that will burn, left in reach of our enemies. I am sworn, if driven to extremity, to utterly lay waste, in the name of Israel's God."

On the same subject, Heber C. Kimball, first counsellor **to** Brigham, used the following language : —

"Is there a collision between us and the United States? No; **we** have not collashed; that is the word that sounds nearest to what I mean. But now the thread is cut between them and us, and we will never gybe again, — no, never, worlds without end. [Voices, 'Amen.'] . . .

"Do as you are told, and Brigham Young will never leave the

governorship of this Territory, from this time henceforth and forever. No, never. And there shall no wicked Judge with his w—— ever sit in our courts again; for all who are against Israel are an abomination to me and to our God.

"The spirit that is upon me this morning is the Spirit of the Lord, that is, the Holy Ghost,— though some of you may think that the Holy Ghost is never cheerful. Well, let me tell you, the Holy Ghost is a man; he is one of the sons of our Father and our God, and he is that man that stood next to Jesus Christ,— just as I stand by brother Brigham. . . . You think our Father and our God is not a lively, sociable, and cheerful man; he is one of the most lively men that ever lived. . . . Brother Brigham is my leader, he is my Prophet and my Seer, my Revelator; and whatever he says, that is for me to do, and it is not for me to question him one word, nor to question God a minute."*

Many sermons were delivered, composed, throughout, of such material as the foregoing extracts. The genius of Mormonism is here fully displayed,— implicit obedience to their leaders, and especially to the teachings of Brigham Young. The people were commanded to be ready to leave their homes at an hour's notice, and flee to the mountains,— and this too, as the snows of winter were falling around them. They were commanded to have the torch ready to set fire to their dwellings, and the axe to cut down all their fruit-trees; and they were ready to obey! The question naturally presents itself, Can blind faith and fanaticism thus lead and control a whole community? That some should be thus blindly infatuated, is not strange; but that a whole community should thus lose their reason, and be willing to beggar themselves and families, in obedience to the call of their leader, is almost beyond belief.

It is safe to say, had the Mormons been left free to choose, at least one half would have remained at home, and even welcomed the troops into the city.

But the fiat of despotism had gone forth. "When the time comes to burn and lay waste our improvements, if any

* *Deseret News*, November 18, 1857.

man undertakes to shield his, he will be sheared down; for 'judgment will be laid to the line, and righteousness to the plummet.'" This means, in plain English, that any man who refused to obey Young should be put to death; and the people well understood it. As it was certain death to resist his will, they vied with each other in seeming to render a willing obedience to a tyrant whom many hated, and all feared.

They fortified Echo Canyon, a narrow pass, about eighteen miles in length, eastward from the city. Piles of huge stones were heaped up along the borders of the precipices, ready to be dashed against the troops, as they should essay to pass the gorge. Intrenchments were thrown up, and such other warlike preparations made as their facilities afforded.

The United States troops had entered the Territory of Utah, and were encamped in Green River County, near Fort Bridger, a distance of 118 miles from Salt Lake City. From this place Governor Cumming issued the following proclamation:—

"GREEN RIVER COUNTY, near Fort Bridger,
UTAH TERRITORY, 21st November, 1857.

"*To the People of Utah Territory:*—

"On the 11th day of July, 1857, the President appointed me to preside over the executive department of the government of this Territory. I arrived at this point on the 17th of this month, and shall probably be detained some time, in consequence of the loss of animals during the recent snow-storm. I will proceed at this point to make the preliminary arrangements for the temporary organization of the territorial government. Many treasonable acts of violence have recently been committed by lawless individuals, supposed to have been commanded by the late executive. Such persons are in a state of rebellion.

"Proceedings will be instituted against them in a court organized by Chief Justice Eckels, held in this county, which court will supersede the necessity of appointing military commissions for the trial of such offenders.

"It is my duty to enforce unconditional obedience to the Constitution, and the organic law of this Territory, and to all the other laws of Congress applicable to you.

"To enable me to effect this object, I will, in the event of resistance, rely first upon a *posse comitatus* of the well-disposed portion of the inhabitants of this Territory, and will only resort to a military *posse* in case of necessity. I trust this necessity will not occur. I have come among you with no prejudices or enmities; and by the exercise of a just and firm administration I hope to command your confidence.

"Freedom of conscience, and the use of your own peculiar mode of serving God, are sacred rights, the exercise of which is guaranteed by the Constitution, and with which it is not the province of the Government or the disposition of its representatives in this Territory to interfere. In virtue of my authority as commander-in-chief of the military of this Territory, I hereby command all armed bodies of individuals, by whomsoever organized, to disband, and return to their respective homes.

"The penalty of disobedience to this command will subject the offenders to the punishment due to traitors.

"A. CUMMING,
"*Governor of Utah Territory.*"

During this time the Mormon troops were busy stealing stock, burning supply-trains, and in every way weakening and embarrassing the United States forces. Being familiar with the country, they had greatly the advantage; and could break suddenly upon a herding party, from some side canyon, capture their stock, and before the alarm could be given, be safely ensconced in their own quarters. Much valuable stock was acquired in this way.

"Forts Bridger and Supply were vacated and burned down. Orders were issued by Daniel H. Wells (Lieut.-General Nauvoo Legion,) to stampede the animals of the United States troops on their march, to set fire to their trains, to burn the grass and the whole country before them and on their flanks, to keep them from sleeping by night surprises, and to block the roads by felling trees, and destroying the fords of rivers.

"On the 4th of October, 1857, the Mormons, under Capt. Lot Smith, captured and burned, on Green River, three of our supply trains, consisting of seventy-five wagons, loaded with provisions and tents for the army, and carried away several hundred animals."

POLITICAL HISTORY CONTINUED.

Late in the fall of 1857 "the Army of Utah" arrived at Bridger, and made an encampment, which was called Camp Scott.

As the winter was severe, and the snow very deep, little progress was made by the army in quelling the Mormon rebellion, while much suffering was endured by the soldiers. Some time during the winter of 1857–58 Col. Kane set out for Utah, to ascertain, if possible, the exact state of affairs in that Territory. He was not sent as the agent of the Government, as is generally supposed, but his mission was approved by President Buchanan, and the War Department. He went *incognito*, and by the southern route, and arrived in Utah in the month of January. He was accompanied by a servant only, and while on the desert to the south of Salt Lake City, was taken sick, and came near losing his life. Amasa Lyman and others were out exploring, with a view of ascertaining whether the Mormons could be attacked from the south. They found Col. Kane and his man on the desert. Lyman took him into his carriage, "laid hands on him, and administered unto him." Kane still remained unknown to him, but told him that he had business of importance to transact at Salt Lake,—important both to the Mormons and to the nation. He was immediately taken to Salt Lake, where, for the first time, he made known his business and his name.

Brigham was agreeably surprised to find an old friend and *quasi* Mormon in his guest, and of course treated him with the greatest consideration. It was well understood at Salt Lake that Col. Kane was baptized by the Elders some years before, while on a tour of exploration to the Rocky Mountains.* How much of Mormonism he imbibed is not known, but certain it is, that the saints rely on his aid and influence, under all circumstances.

---

* John Hyde, Jr., in his work on Mormonism, page 146, says: "Fillmore, by the advice and intercession of Col. Kane, *who had embraced Mormonism in Iowa*, appointed Brigham as the Governor of Utah."

The negotiations were of the most friendly character, and Kane proceeded soon after, in his character as pacificator, to the "Head-quarters of the Army of Utah," at Fort Bridger. He was escorted by Porter Rockwell and Daniel Kimball past the limits of the Mormon camp. He held interviews with the officers of the army and with Governor Cumming, and succeeded in inducing the Governor to accompany him to Salt Lake.

Of this journey Governor Cumming says:—

"I left camp on the 5th, *en route* for this city, accompanied by Col. Kane, as guide, and two servants. . . . I was escorted from Bear River Valley to the western end of Echo Canyon,— the journey through the canyon being performed, for the most part, in the night; it was about eleven o'clock when I arrived at Weber Station.

"I have been everywhere recognized as the Governor of Utah, and, so far from having encountered insults and indignities, I am gratified in being able to state that, in passing through the settlements, I have been universally greeted with such respectful attentions as are due to the representative of the executive authority of the United States. . . .

"When it was arranged with the Mormon officer in command of my escort that I should pass through Echo Canyon in the night, I inferred that it was with the object of concealing the barricades and other defences. I was therefore agreeably surprised by an illumination in honor to me. The bonfires kindled by the soldiers, from the base to the summit of the hills, completely illuminated the valley, and disclosed the snow-covered mountains which surrounded us."

The following is the Mormon account of the *entrée* of Governor Cumming into the Valley of Salt Lake, and may go to explain to him why the journey was made through Echo Canyon in the night.

Upon entering the Mormon lines they were rejoined by Rockwell and Kimball, who commanded the Governor's escort to Salt Lake City. Echo Canyon is a narrow pass, about eighteen miles in length, and commands the entrance to Salt Lake Valley from the east. The Mormons had fortified this canyon at several points. They also had four camps, or places of rendezvous, at convenient distances. Upon arriving at Cache Cave, the first "post," the party of the Governor came to a halt. His Excellency was escorted into camp with due honor, and an ox was slain to celebrate the occasion. After partaking of a sumptuous repast, the troops were ordered out for the Governor to review. About 150 men were "drawn up," and after the review, the Governor "made a speech." He complimented "the boys" on their order, discipline, and skill.

Col. Kimball then proceeded to read various orders to the troops. Various imaginary companies were ordered to relieve various other imaginary companies. Several new posts were ordered to be established, and others abandoned. Meanwhile, the Governor, *not to be deceived*, was noting down the different companies as they were called. This done, they again took the road. It was now about sundown; and as they passed the stations, the troops were arranged on each side of the road, to salute the Governor, and be reviewed by him. Everything passed off smoothly until they reached the third station, when it suddenly occurred to Col. Kimball that the pickets at that post had not been apprised of their coming. He remarked, on nearing the camp, that "he saw no pickets, and he guessed the boys were in ambush." He therefore mounted a horse, and telling the driver to be sure and "halt" as soon as he heard the word, rode off. In a moment more, the guard shouted, "Halt! who goes there?"—and before a reply could be given, the crack of a rifle was heard. The Governor, trembling with fright, cried out, "I am your friend, the Governor of Utah; don't fire, boys; for God's sake, don't fire!" "I know nothing about Governors, nor anybody else," replied the picket; "I must do my duty. This way, Sergeant of the Guard." By this time quite a company rode up, and, as the Governor supposed, he was about to be taken prisoner. Col. Kimball now appeared, explained the whole matter, and relieved his Excellency from his embarrassing position. But the Governor was entirely innocent of the joke, and believes, to this day, that he had a hair-breadth escape.

They then passed on to the mouth of Echo Canyon, where the troops were again reviewed; and as the party bivouacked for the night, hundreds of camp-fires gleamed along the rugged sides of the canyon, furnishing incontestable evidence of the great number of the Mormon soldiers. There were at this time about 150 men, all told, in the canyon, and *these the Governor had reviewed at every station.*

The next morning the Governor proceeded on his journey, prepared to assert that the Mormons had from two to three thousand men under arms in and near Echo Canyon. When the company arrived at Sessions, ten miles from Salt Lake City, they were met by a large concourse of citizen soldiery, preceded by a band of music, accompanied by the roaring of cannon. The Echo Canyon boys were also there, to see the fun. The Governor was quite bewildered by all this parade, and made up his mind that the Mormons were very numerous, and both ready and willing to " wipe out " the handful of Government soldiers, whenever they could get permission from their leader.

Upon arriving at the " Holy City," the best lodgings and the best brandy were provided for his Excellency. Brigham called in due time, and paid his compliments; invited Governor Cumming to his office, and tendered to him " the hospitalities of the city." Governor Cumming was delighted, and in a few days called at the office of Governor Young. This wily personage put on one of his blandest smiles, resigned his office of Governor, turned over the papers and documents of the office to his legal successor, and, to crown all, produced the *records of the courts*, in the highest state of preservation.

Governor Cumming was perfectly amazed. Was it possible his eyes did not deceive him? Were these the veritable records about which so much had been said? They were; and the Mormons had been belied, and the Government deceived. He immediately wrote to the President and to Col. Johnson, and explained how matters stood.

The gifted and accomplished Col. Kane was the bearer of these documents to his venerable friend James Buchanan, who read with delight these "signs of repentance" on the part of his dear children, and immediately commenced writing their pardon.

It has been supposed by many that Col. Kane was, at that time, acting as the agent of the United States Government. But the following extract from a letter to him, written by President Buchanan, dated December 31, 1857, will at once determine the position which the Colonel occupied: —

"My dear Sir, — You furnish the strongest evidence of your desire to serve the Mormons, by abandoning the comforts of friends, family, and home, and voluntarily encountering the perils and dangers of a journey to Utah, at the present inclement season of the year, at your own expense, and without official position. . . . Nothing but pure philanthropy, and a strong desire to serve the Mormon people, could have dictated a course so much at war with your private interests."

While the President was penning his proclamation of pardon, the Mormons were leaving their property and homes, and taking up their line of march for the South. Governor Cumming was unable to control the movements of Col. Johnson, who was acting under instructions from the Secretary of War. Hence Cumming could not save to Brigham, however much he might feel disposed to do so, the humiliation of seeing the streets of the city filled with the federal soldiers, against whom he had been hurling his anathemas. Finding this catastrophe could not possibly be averted, he promulgated an order, purporting to emanate from the Almighty, commanding the people to leave their homes and start for the South. This order was prompted partly by the fact that the "President of the Church" was committed to this course by his repeated declarations, and partly by the wish on his part to test his power over " this people." It was readily and implicitly obeyed by his deluded followers. They knew not where they were going. Many believed they were destined for Sonora. They only knew the Prophet of the Lord had spoken, and they must obey.

On the 6th of April, 1858, their long trains moved southward, taking with them their household gods, and provisions for the journey. Brigham, Heber, and the principal men, also removed their families from their comfortable homes, again to encounter the toils and privations incident to life on the Plains. They went to Provo, 50 miles from the city, and there halted. The snow was still on the ground, and the pilgrims suffered much from the inclemency of the weather.

On the 12th of April, Mr. Buchanan appointed L. W. Powell, of Kentucky, and Ben McCulloch, of Texas, Commissioners to Utah, and by them sent on his proclamation of pardon. They reached Salt Lake on the 7th of June, and immediately made known their business to the Mormon authorities. They were instructed to say to the Mormons, in the language of the proclamation, " If you obey the laws, keep the peace, and respect the just rights of others, you will be perfectly secure, and may live in your present faith, or change it for another at your pleasure. Every intelligent man among you knows very well that the Government has never, directly or indirectly, sought to molest you in your worship, to control you in your ecclesiastical affairs, or even to influence you in your religious opinions."

The following extracts from the report of the Commissioners will serve to show the result of their mission :—

" We stated that we wished a free conference with them, and were ready to hear what they had to say. Ex-Governor Brigham Young, Lieut.-Governor Wells, and others, spoke. They expressed their gratification that the President had sent commissioners to Utah. They stated that they were attached to the Constitution and the Government of the United States; they spoke harshly of many of the officials who had held office in the Territory; they spoke of the wrongs and injuries hitherto done them; they said they desired to live in peace, under the Constitution of the United States. They denied that they had ever driven any officials from Utah, or prevented any civil officer from entering the Territory. They admitted that they burned the army trains, and drove off the cattle from the army last fall, and for that act they accepted the President's pardon. All the charges that had been made against them, except the one last named, they denied. . . . We are pleased to state that the conference resulted in their agreeing to receive, quietly and peaceably, all the civil officers of the Government, and not to resist them in the execution of the duties of their offices; and to yield obedience to the authorities and laws of the United States.

"That they would offer no resistance to the army; that the officers of the army would not be resisted in the execution of their orders within the Territory. In short, they agreed that the officers, civil and military, of the United States, should enter the Territory without resistance, and exercise, peaceably and unmolested, all the functions of their various offices."

The Mormons, on their part, stipulated that the army should not be encamped within forty miles of the city; that they should protect private property; that they should march directly through the city, without halting; and should not encamp until they crossed the Jordan. These conditions were substantially complied with. "On the 26th of June General Johnson marched the army under his command through Salt Lake City, and encamped on the banks of the river Jordan, just without the city limits. The place selected for a permanent camp was in Cedar Valley, about forty miles south of Great Salt Lake City, and known as Camp Floyd, now Fort Crittenden."

On the 5th of July, 1858, the Mormon refugees received orders to return to their homes. With joy and alacrity they prepared to obey the welcome summons.

Governor Cumming had frequently urged them to return, without avail. But when the "mighty man of God" sent forth his mandate, each man sprang to his feet as if by magic, rushed to his teams, and before the morning sun gilded the eastern hills, "the faithful" were again returning to their Mecca.

A company of United States troops were stationed on what was called "the Dug Out," to prevent collision with the Mormons on their return to Salt Lake. The officer commanding related to me the following incident: —

"I witnessed the most extreme destitution among the returning emigrants. I saw a number of women cooking around a campfire, and their clothing was extremely scanty. The supply of a family of fourteen persons could have been compressed into a small-sized trunk. One evening I saw two or three women cooking supper, and observing that they had neither tea nor coffee, I questioned them, and they replied they had had none for two or three years. At this time, according to report, it took a four-mule team to draw the Prophet's gold and silver, besides some that went in other conveyances."

The saints again entered into possession of their deserted homes, and began, as well as the lateness of the season would permit, to cultivate their farms and gardens.

Thus ended this crusade against the modern Mohammed and his followers.

CHAPTER V.

POLITICAL HISTORY CONTINUED.

The Mountain Meadow Massacre and other Crimes of the Mormons. — Attempts to bring the Perpetrators to Justice. — Doings of Judge Cradlebaugh. — Governor Cumming and the Military Officers. — Judge Sinclair's Court. — Governor Dawson and his Misfortunes. — New Governor and Associate Justices appointed.

The darkest chapter of Mormon history is now before us. It becomes my duty to relate one of the most perfidious acts of cruelty and wholesale butchery to be found in the annals of this or any other country. In doing so, free use will be made of the statements of Judge Cradlebaugh and others who were thoroughly conversant with all the facts.

The following is from the able speech of Judge Cradlebaugh, delivered in the House of Representatives on the 7th of February, 1863: —

" As one of the Associate Justices of the Territory of Utah, in the month of April, 1859, I commenced and held a term of the District Court for the Second Judicial District, in the city of Provo, about sixty miles south of Salt Lake City. Upon my requisition, Gen. A. S. Johnson, in command of the military department, furnished a small military force for the purpose of protecting the court. A grand jury was empanelled, and their attention was pointedly and specifically called to a great number of crimes that had been committed in the immediate vicinity, — cases of public notoriety, both as to the offence and the persons who had perpetrated the same; (for none of these things had " been done in a corner"). Their perpetrators had scorned alike concealment or apology, before the arrival of the American forces. The jury thus instructed, though kept in session two weeks, utterly refused to do anything, and were finally discharged, as an evidently useless appendage of a court of justice. But the court was determined to try a last resource, to bring to light and to punishment those guilty of the atrocious crimes which confessedly had been committed in the Territory, and the session continued. Bench warrants, based upon sworn information, were issued against the alleged criminals, and United States Marshal Dotson, a most excellent and reliable officer, aided by a military *posse*, procured on his own request, had succeeded in making a few arrests. A general stampede immediately took place among the Mormons, and what I wish to call your attention to, as particularly noticeable, is the fact that this occurred more especially among the church officials and civil officers. . . .

" Sitting as a committing magistrate, complaint after complaint was made before me of murders and robberies. Among these I may mention, as peculiarly and shockingly prominent, the murder of Forbes, the assassination of the Parrishes and Potter, of Jones and his mother, of the Aiken party, of which there were six in all; and, worst and darkest in the appalling catalogue of blood, the cowardly, cold-blooded butchery and robbery at the Mountain Meadows. At that time there still lay, all ghastly, under the sun of Utah, the unburied skeletons of one hundred and nineteen men, women, and children, the hapless, hopeless victims of the Mormon creed. . . .

" The scene of this horrible massacre at the Mountain Meadows is situate about three hundred and twenty miles west of south from Great Salt Lake City, on the road leading to Los Angelos, in California. I was the first federal Judge in that part of the Territory after the occurrence, — my district extending from a short distance below Salt Lake City to the south end of the Territory. I determined to visit that part of my district, and, if possible, expose the persons engaged in the massacre, which I did in the early part of the year 1859. I accordingly embraced an opportunity of accompanying a small detachment of soldiers, who were being sent to that section by Gen. Johnson, — having requested the Marshal of the Territory to accompany, or to send a deputy. He accordingly sent deputy William H. Rodgers, who went with me.

" The command went as far south as the St. Clara, twenty miles beyond the Mountain Meadows, where we camped, and remained about a week. During our stay there I was visited by the Indian chiefs of that section, who gave me their version of the massacre. They admitted that a portion of their men were engaged in the massacre, but were not there when the attack commenced. One of them told me, in the presence of the others, that after the attack had been made, a white man came to their camp with a piece of paper, which, he said, *Brigham Young had sent,* that directed them to go and help to whip the emigrants. A portion of the band went, but did not assist in the fight. He gave as a reason, that the emigrants had long guns, and were good shots. He said that his brother [this chief's name was Jackson] was shot while running across the Meadow, at a distance of two hundred yards from the corral where the emigrants were. He said the Mormons were all painted. He said the Indians got a part of the clothing; and gave the names of John D. Lee, President Haight, and Bishop Higbee, as the big captains. It might be proper here to remark that the Indians in the southern part of the Territory of Utah are not numerous, and are a very low, cowardly, beastly set, very few of them being armed with guns. They are not formidable. I believe all in the southern part of the Territory would, under no circumstances, carry on a fight against ten white men.

"From our camp on the St. Clara we again went back to the Mountain Meadows, camping near where the massacre had occurred. The Meadow is about five miles in length and one in width, running to quite a narrow point at the southwest end, being higher at the middle than either end. It is the divide between the waters that flow into the Great Basin and those emptying into the Colorado River. A very large spring rises in the south end of the narrow part. It was on the north side of this spring the emigrants were camped. The bank rises from the spring eight or ten feet, then extends off to the north about two hundred yards, on a level. A range of hills is there reached, rising perhaps fifty or sixty feet. Back of this range is quite a valley, which extends down until it has an outlet, three or four hundred yards below the spring, into the main meadow.

"The first attack was made by going down this ravine, then following up the bed of the spring to near it, then at daylight firing upon the men who were about the camp-fires, — in which attack ten or twelve of the emigrants were killed or wounded;

the stock of the emigrants having been previously driven behind the hill, and up the ravine.

"The emigrants soon got in condition to repel the attack, shoved their wagons together, sunk the wheels in the earth, and threw up quite an intrenchment. The fighting after continued as a siege; the assailants occupying the hill, and firing at any of the emigrants that exposed themselves, having a barricade of stones along the crest of the hill as a protection. The siege was continued for five days, the besiegers appearing in the garb of Indians. The Mormons, seeing that they could not capture the train without making some sacrifice of life on their part, and getting weary of the fight, resolved to accomplish by strategy what they were not able to do by force. The fight had been going on for five days, and no aid was received from any quarter, although the family of Jacob Hamlin, the Indian agent, were living in the upper end of the Meadow, and within hearing of the reports of the guns.

"Who can imagine the feelings of these men, women, and children, surrounded, as they supposed themselves to be, by savages? Fathers and mothers only can judge what they must have been. Far off, in the Rocky Mountains, without transportation, — for their cattle, horses and mules had been run off, — not knowing what their fate was to be, — we can but poorly realize the gloom that pervaded the camp.

"A wagon is descried, far up the Meadows. Upon its nearer approach, it is observed to contain armed men. See! now they raise a white flag! All is joy in the corral. A general shout is raised, and in an instant, a little girl, dressed in white, is placed at an opening between two of the wagons, as a response to the signal. The wagon approaches; the occupants are welcomed into the corral, the emigrants little suspecting that they were entertaining the fiends that had been besieging them.

"This wagon contained President Haight and Bishop John D. Lee, among others of the Mormon Church. They professed to be on good terms with the Indians, and represented the Indians as being very mad. They also proposed to intercede, and settle the matter with the Indians. After several hours of parley, they, having apparently visited the Indians, gave the *ultimatum* of the Indians; which was, that the emigrants should march out of their camp, leaving everything behind them, even their guns. It was promised by the Mormon bishops that they would bring a force, and guard the emigrants back to the settlements.

"The terms were agreed to,—the emigrants being desirous of saving the lives of their families. The Mormons retired, and subsequently appeared at the corral with thirty or forty armed men. The emigrants were marched out, the women and children in front, and the men behind, the Mormon guard being in the rear. When they had marched in this way about a mile, at a given signal, the slaughter commenced. The men were most all shot down at the first fire from the guard. Two only escaped, who fled to the desert, and were followed 150 miles before they were overtaken and slaughtered.

"The women and children ran on, two or three hundred yards further, when they were overtaken, and with the aid of the Indians they were slaughtered. Seventeen only of the small children were saved, the eldest being only seven years. Thus, on the 10th day of September, 1857, was consummated one of the most cruel, cowardly, and bloody murders known in our history. Upon the way from the Meadows, a young Indian pointed out to me the place where the Mormons painted and disguised themselves.

"I went from the Meadows to Cedar City; the distance is thirty-five or forty miles. I contemplated holding an examining court there, should Gen. Johnson furnish me protection, and also protect witnesses, and furnish the Marshal a *posse* to aid in making arrests. While there I issued warrants, on affidavits filed before me, for the arrest of the following named persons:—

"Jacob Haight, President of the Cedar City Stake; Bishop John M. Higbee and Bishop John D. Lee; Columbus Freeman, William Slade, John Willis, William Riggs, —— Ingram, Daniel McFarlan, William Stewart, Ira Allen and son, Thomas Cartwright, E. Welean, William Halley, Jabes Nomlen, John Mangum, James Price, John W. Adair, —— Tyler, Joseph Smith, Samuel Pollock, John McFarlan, Nephi Johnson, —— Thornton, Joel White, —— Harrison, Charles Hopkins, Joseph Elang, Samuel Lewis, Sims Matheney, James Mangum, Harrison Pierce, Samuel Adair, F. C. McDulange, Wm. Bateman, Ezra Curtis, and Alexander Loveridge.

"In a few days after arriving at Cedar City, Capt. Campbell arrived, with his command, from the Meadows; on his return, he advised me that he had received orders, for his command entire, to return to Camp Floyd; the General having received orders from Washington that the military should not be used in protecting the courts, or in acting as a *posse* to aid the Marshal in making arrests.

"While at Cedar City I was visited by a number of apostate Mormons, who gave me every assurance that they would furnish an abundance of evidence in regard to the matter so soon as they were assured of military protection. In fact, some of the persons engaged in the act came to see me in the night, and gave a full account of the matter, — intending when protection was at hand, to become witnesses. They claimed that they had been forced into the matter by the bishops. Their statements corroborated what the Indians had previously said to me. Mr. Rodgers, the Deputy Marshal, was also engaged in hunting up the children, survivors of the massacre. They were all found in the custody of the Mormons. Three or four of the eldest recollect and relate all the incidents of the massacre, corroborating the statements of the Indians, and the statements made by the citizens of Cedar City to me.

"These children are now in the south part of Missouri, or north part of Arkansas; their testimony could soon be taken, if desired. No one can depict the glee of these infants, when they realized that they were in the custody of what they called 'the Americans,'—for such is the designation of those not Mormons. They say they never were in the custody of the Indians. I recollect of one of them, 'John Calvin Sorrow,' after he found he was safe, and before he was brought away from Salt Lake City, although not yet nine years of age, sitting in a contemplative mood, no doubt thinking of the extermination of his family, saying: 'Oh, I wish I was a man; I know what I would do; I would shoot John D. Lee; I saw him shoot my mother.' I shall never forget how he looked.

"Time will not permit me to elaborate the matter. I shall barely sum up, and refer every member of this House, who may have the least doubt about the guilt of the Mormons in this massacre, and the other crimes to which I have alluded, to the evidence published in the appendix hereto."

To the foregoing thrilling recital, I will only add:— The train consisted of 40 wagons, 800 head of cattle, and about 60 horses and mules. As near as can be ascertained, there were about 150 men and women, besides many children. They passed through Salt Lake City, and were there joined by some few Mormons, who were disaffected, and sought to travel under their protection.

A revelation from Brigham Young, as Great Grand Archee, or God, was despatched to President J. C. Haight, Bishop Higbee, and J. D. Lee, commanding them to raise all the forces they could muster and trust, follow those cursed gentiles (so read the revelation), attack them, disguised as Indians, and with the arrows of the Almighty make a clean sweep of them, and leave none to tell the tale; and if they needed any assistance, they were commanded to hire the Indians as their allies, promising them a share of the booty. They were to be neither slothful nor negligent in their duty, and to be punctual in sending the teams back to him before winter set in, for this was the mandate of Almighty God.

On the following day a council of all the faithful was held at Cedar City. Many attended from the neighboring settlements; the revelation was read, and the destiny of the unsuspecting emigrants sealed. Plans were suggested, discussed, and adopted, and the men designated to carry out their hellish designs. Instructions were given for them to assemble at a small spring, but a short distance to the left of the road leading into the Meadows, — a number of intervening hills rendering it a fit place for concealment. Here they painted and disguised themselves as Indians, and when ready to commence operations, by a well-known Indian trail proceeded to the Meadows.

For the benefit of those who may still be disposed to doubt the guilt of Young and his Mormons in this transaction, the testimony is here collated, and circumstances given, which go, not merely to implicate, but to fasten conviction upon them, by "confirmations strong as proofs from Holy Writ."

1. The evidence of Mormons themselves, engaged in the

affair, as shown by the statements of Judge Cradlebaugh and Deputy-Marshal Rodgers.

2. The statements of Indians in the neighborhood of the massacre: these statements are shown, not only by Cradlebaugh and Rodgers, but by a number of military officers, and by J. Forney, who was, in 1859, Superintendent of Indian Affairs for the Territory. To all these were such statements freely and frequently made by the Indians.

3. The testimony of the children saved from the massacre.

4. The children and the property of the emigrants found in possession of the Mormons, and that possession traced back to the very day after the massacre.

5. The failure of Brigham Young to embody any account of it in his Report as Superintendent of Indian Affairs. Also his failure to make any allusion to it whatever from the pulpit, until several years after the occurrence.

6. The failure of the "Deseret News," the Church organ, and the only paper then published in the Territory, to notice the massacre, until several months afterward, and then only to deny that Mormons were engaged in it.

7. The flight to the mountains of men high in authority in the Mormon Church and State, when this affair was brought to the ordeal of a judicial investigation.

8. The testimony of R. P. Campbell, Capt. 2d Dragoons, who was sent in the spring of 1859 to Santa Clara, to protect travellers on the road to California, and to inquire into Indian depredations.

In his report to Major E. J. Potter, Assistant Adjutant-General U. S. Army, dated July 6, 1859, he says:—

"These emigrants were here met by the Mormons (assisted by such of the wretched Indians of the neighborhood as they could force or persuade to join), and massacred, with the exception of such infant children as the Mormons thought too young to remember, or tell of the affair.

"The Mormons were led on by John D. Lee, then a high dignitary in the self-styled Church of Jesus Christ of Latter Day Saints, and Isaac Haight, now a dignitary in the same."

Again, after relating briefly the massacre, he says: —

"These facts were derived from children who did remember, and could tell of the matter; from Indians, and from the Mormons themselves."

9. The testimony of Hon. J. Forney, Superintendent of Indian Affairs.

In his letter to the Commissioner of Indian Affairs at Washington, dated Provo City, U. T., March, 1859, he says: —

"Facts in my possession warrant me in estimating that there was distributed, a few days after the massacre, among the leading church dignitaries, $30,000 worth of property."

Again, in another letter to the Commissioner, written from Great Salt Lake City, in August of the same year, he says: —

"From the evidence in my possession, I am justified in the declaration that this massacre was concocted by white men, and consummated by whites and Indians. The names of many of the whites engaged in this terrible affair have already been given to the proper legal authorities. . . . The children were sold out to different persons in Cedar City, Harmony, and Painter Creek. Bills are now in my possession from different individuals, asking payment from the Government. I cannot condescend to become the medium of even transmitting such claims to the Department."

The following is from the Annual Report of Superintendent Forney, made in September, 1859: —

"Mormons have been accused of aiding the Indians in the commission of this crime. I commenced my inquiries without prejudice or selfish motive, and with the hope that, in the progress of my inquiries, facts would enable me to exculpate all white men from any participation in this tragedy, and saddle the guilt exclusively on the Indians; but, unfortunately, every step in my inquiries satisfied me that the Indians acted only a secondary part. . . . White men were present, and directed the Indians. John D. Lee, of Harmony, told me in his own house, last April, in presence of two persons, that he was present three successive days during the fight, and was present during the fatal day." . . .

We close the testimony of Forney, by giving entire a letter from him to the Department at Washington, —

"SUPERINTENDENT'S OFFICE, UTAH,
GREAT SALT LAKE CITY, September 22, 1859.

" Sir, — Your letter dated July 2, in which you request me to ascertain the names of white men, if any, implicated in the Mountain Meadow massacre, reached me several weeks since, about 300 miles west of this city.

" I gave, several months ago, to the Attorney-General, and several of the United States Judges, the names of those who I believed were not only implicated, but the hell-deserving scoundrels who concocted and brought to a successful termination the whole affair.

" The following are the names of the persons the most guilty: Isaac T. Haight, Cedar City, president of several settlements south; Bishop Smith, Cedar City; John D. Lee,* Harmony; John M. Higby, Cedar City; Bishop Davis, David Tullis, Santa Clara; Ira Hatch, Santa Clara. These were the cause of the massacre, aided by others. It is to be regretted that nothing has yet been accomplished towards bringing these murderers to justice. I remain,

" Very respectfully, your obedient servant,
"J. FORNEY,
" Sup't of Indian Affairs, Utah Territory.
" Hon. A. B. Greenwood,
" Commiss'r Indian Affairs, Washington, D. C."

So far as Brigham Young himself is concerned, the evidence is not so direct, but is scarcely less conclusive.

In addition to the circumstances mentioned, of his failing to report the massacre, or to make any mention of it in his public discourses, and the testimony of the Indians, already referred to; in addition also to the facts concerning the revelation sent from him, — facts communicated by one intimately acquainted with the secret history of the church; in addi-

---

* John D. Lee is an adopted son of Brigham Young.

tion to these things, if we reflect for a moment upon the framework of the Mormon Church, we will find therein still more cogent evidence.

The organization of the church is such, that no project of importance is ever undertaken without the express or implied consent of Young, who is in temporal, as well as spiritual matters, the head and source of all authority. Now here was a large train which had lately passed through the place where Young resided, and his feelings and views in relation to it would be well known to the leaders of the church. Can it for a moment be admitted, that members of a community so organized would undertake so important a project as the destruction of that train, requiring, as it did, the concerted action of forty or fifty persons, without the express or implied sanction of him who sat at the head of the community, controlling its every action?

And if such a thing can be supposed possible, would not the perpetrators be immediately called to account for assuming so much responsibility? Reason and evidence all point one way; and add this to the many other acts which stamp Brigham Young as a murderer of the deepest dye,— adding to the guilt of homicide that of blasphemy and hypocrisy.

What was the motive which prompted the act? Partly revenge. These emigrants were from Missouri and Arkansas, the scenes of the alleged injuries and persecutions of the Mormons. It was soon after the killing of Parley P. Pratt, in Arkansas, by McLane, whose wife Pratt had abducted. It was at the time, too, when the United States troops were marching to Utah, and a feeling of revenge and retaliation was prevalent, and was, as has been shown, fostered and encouraged by Brigham in his sermons.

But the principal motive was plunder. The train was a very wealthy one. The spoil of the gentile was before them, and it must be appropriated by the Lord's people.

A great portion of the property was taken to Cedar City,

deposited in the tithing office, and there sold out. Forney says, in the Annual Report already quoted from, —

"Whoever may have been the perpetrators of this horrible deed, no doubt exists in my mind that they were influenced chiefly by a determination to acquire wealth by robbery." *

It is not within the scope of this work to enter into a relation of the many other murders and outrages committed by the authority or connivance of the Mormon Church. This is given as the most notable one, — "*ex uno disce omnes.*" Those who wish to examine into these crimes more fully, are referred to the appendix to the printed speech of Judge Cradlebaugh.

The "Mormon War" having closed, the federal officers, as soon as practicable, assumed their functions, and proceeded to transact business. Federal courts were held, and the authority of the United States again, at least nominally, established in Utah.

In October, 1858, Judge Sinclair opened his court in Salt Lake City. Efforts were made to bring several noted criminals to justice, but everything failed. In the grand jury-room no indictments were found, and murderers and thieves were allowed to go "scot free."

At this term of court a motion was made to expel James Ferguson from the bar, for contempt of court. Ferguson offered to retire from the bar, which was not accepted. He then proposed to plead guilty; but the Judge said, as it was alleged that a Judge of the United States had been insulted

---

* Several years after the massacre, Major, now General Carlton, visited that region and erected a monument to the memory of the slain. "It was constructed by raising a large pile of rock, in the centre of which was erected a beam, some twelve or fifteen feet in height. Upon one of the stones he caused to be engraved, 'Here lie the bones of one hundred and twenty men, women, and children, from Arkansas, murdered on the 10th day of September, 1857.' Upon a cross-tree, on the beam, he caused to be painted: 'Vengeance is mine, saith the Lord, and I will repay it.' This monument is said to have been destroyed the first time Brigham visited that part of the Territory."

and intimidated, when in the discharge of his official duty, it was important that the country be put in possession of the facts, and no plea of crimination or stultification should prevent an exposure.

The grand jury did, finally, in this case, make the following presentment:—

"The grand jury find, that James Ferguson, of G. S. L. City, U. T., did use language and threats calculated to intimidate Judge George P. Stiles, U. S. District Judge, while in the discharge of his official duties, and presiding as Judge of this District Court, at the February Term, 1857.

"ELEAZER MILLER, *Foreman.*"

The right of trial by jury is one guaranteed by the Constitution, and with which it would be highly dangerous to interfere, except in cases of extreme necessity, involving the safety of a whole people or community. The Mormons, with their usual shrewdness, take advantage of this, and manage to control the United States Courts through the grand and petit juries. The following extracts will show how it is done.

March 2d, 1856, in his remarks, made in the Tabernacle, Jedediah M. Grant, then one of the "President's" counsellors, said:—

"Last Sunday, the President chastised some of the Apostles and Bishops, who were on the grand jury. Did he fully succeed in clearing away the fog which surrounded them, and in removing blindness from their eyes? No, for they could go to their room and again disagree; though to their credit it must be admitted that a brief explanation made them unanimous in their action."

Again, in the same connection, Grant, speaking of a trial-jury, continues,—

"Several have got into the fog, to suck and eat the filth of a gentile court; *ostensibly* a court in Utah."

Here is the highest evidence of the direct interference of

Brigham Young with the right of trial by jury, and the prostitution of the jury-box to the accomplishment of his schemes. How could he strike a more fatal blow at our free institutions, or at the rights and liberties of American citizens who may happen to live within the sphere of his influence? For this alone he should be hurled from the defiant position he occupies, and brought to the bar of impartial justice.

Though the evidence was perfectly plain and conclusive in the case of Ferguson, he was acquitted. Comment is unnecessary.

The Judge, finding all efforts to bring criminals to justice unavailing, adjourned his court *sine die.*

The Mormon Legislature had never made provision for defraying the expenses of the United States Courts, while doing territorial business, though their attention had frequently been called to the necessity of so doing. Their object was to throw all the business into the probate courts; and in this they eventually succeeded, except in the court presided over by Judge Kinney, — the only one, after the "war," which acted simply as an adjunct and instrument of the church authorities.

"During the sitting of Judge Sinclair's court, the Mormon grand jury promptly found a bill of indictment against one Ralph Pike, a sergeant in Company I, of the 10th Infantry, United States Army, for an assault with intent to kill, committed upon one Howard Spencer, the son of a Mormon bishop, at the military reserve, in Rush Valley. Upon *capias* issued, Pike was arrested, and brought to Great Salt Lake City. The day following, August 11, 1858, about twelve o'clock, M., as Pike was entering the Salt Lake House, on Main Street, Spencer stepped up to him from behind, saying, 'Are you the man that struck me in Rush Valley?' at the same time, drawing his pistol, shot him through the side, inflicting a mortal wound. Spencer ran across the street, mounted his horse, and rode off, accompanied by several noted 'Danites.' Pike lingered in dreadful agony, two days, before he died. The 'Deseret News,' in its next issue, lauded young Spencer for his courage and bravery.

"A man by the name of Drown, brought suit upon a promissory note for $480, against the Danite captain, Bill Hickman The case being submitted to the court, Drown obtained a judgment. A few days afterwards, Drown and a companion named Arnold were stopping at the house of a friend in Salt Lake City, when Hickman, with some seven or eight of his band, rode up to the house, and called for Drown to come out. Drown, suspecting foul play, refused to do so, and locked the doors. The Danites thereupon dismounted from their horses, broke down the doors, and shot down both Drown and Arnold. Drown died of his wounds next morning, and Arnold a few days afterwards. Hickman and his band rode off unmolested.

"Thus, during a single term of the court, held in a Mormon community, the warm life-blood of three human victims is shed upon the very threshold of the court; and although the grand jury is in session, no prosecution is attempted, and not one of the offenders brought to justice."

Judge Cradlebaugh was assigned to the Second Judicial District, and held his first term of court in Provo City, commencing April 8th, 1859. An account of his efforts to bring to justice the Mountain Meadow and other murderers has already been given in his own language.

The following notice of this bold and energetic man is from the "Nevada Territorial Enterprise": —

"Judge Cradlebaugh, of the United States Court of Utah, is making his mark in that Territory, if half that is written of him is true. . . . . Satisfied that many of the leading Mormons had taken part in or instigated the Mountain Meadow massacre, and the murder of Jones, Potter, Forbes, Parrish, and a dozen others, he determined to bring them to punishment. . . . . He spoke and acted with the fearlessness and resolution of a Jackson; but the jury failed to indict, or even report on the charges, while threats of violence were heard in every quarter, and an attack on the troops intimated, if he persisted in his course.

"Finding that nothing could be done with the juries, they were discharged, with a scathing rebuke from the Judge. Sitting as a committing magistrate, he commenced his task alone. He examined witnesses, made arrests in every quarter, and created a consternation in the camps of the saints, greater even than was occasioned by the arrival of the troops within the walls of Zion. At last accounts, terrified elders and bishops were decamping to save their necks; and developments of the most startling character were being made, implicating the highest church dignitaries in the many murders and robberies committed upon the gentiles during the past eight years."

Governor Cumming did not sustain Judge Cradlebaugh, but, under the pretence of impartiality, sought to screen the Mormons from the demands of justice.

Hence various differences between Cumming on one side, and Johnson and Cradlebaugh on the other; and on one occasion the Governor went so far as to publish his protest against the use of the troops in aid of Cradlebaugh's proceedings.

Cumming was a native of Georgia. He had married a daughter of one of the most distinguished physicians of Boston, a lady of many accomplishments, who accompanied him to Utah.

During the dreadful reign of the cholera in 1836 he was Mayor of Augusta, Ga., and is said to have rendered efficient service in saving the lives of the citizens.

For some years he was stationed at Jefferson Barracks, Missouri. At the commencement of the Mexican war he was at Point Isabel, and afterwards on the Southern line, attached to General Scott's staff. Subsequently he was detailed by the Government to visit several tribes of Indians in the far West.

He had performed some service to the country, and was a man of many good qualities; but was very vain, and fond of attention, and was unable to withstand the seductive influences which the Mormons know so well how to bring to bear upon persons of his organization.

Cradlebaugh, finding he was not supported by Buchanan's administration, left Utah, and settled in the Territory of Nevada; whence he has been twice sent as delegate to Congress, and we look to see him, at no distant day, represent the **new State of Nevada** in the Senate of the United States.

In 1860 John F. Kinney was reappointed Chief Justice, succeeding Judge Eckels; and Judges Crosby and Flenniken were appointed Associate Justices, to succeed Sinclair and Cradlebaugh. Judge Cradlebaugh did **not** resign, and not recognizing **the right of the President to** remove the Judges, **he continued** to perform the duties of his office for some time afterward.

On the 3d of October, 1861, John W. Dawson, of Indiana, was appointed by President Lincoln Governor of Utah, to succeed Cumming, who had left the Territory some months previous.

In the appointment of Dawson, Lincoln, to use his own language, was "imposed **on**." The Senate relieved him from the imposition, by refusing to confirm the appointment.

The Mormons, however, anticipated the action of the Senate, and speedily ejected Dawson from the governorship. The history of this *émeute* is briefly as follows:—

Dawson arrived at Salt Lake about the commencement **of the** session of the Legislature. **Having some** notions of **his own concerning** legislative **affairs, and not yielding,** like his **predecessor, to all the** views of Brigham **Young,** he soon **became** involved in difficulties from which he was unable to extricate himself. **He** had not the nerve and ability **to sustain** himself in his position. The Mormons **saw** this, and at once resolved upon, planned, and accomplished a brilliant *coup* d'état, similar to that practised upon Steptoe. Without going into details, the plan may be seen by the result; **which** was the affidavit of a widow woman named Williams, to the effect that Dawson had insulted **her, by making** improper advances, which, of course, **she had scornfully** repelled and rejected.

The indignation of the Mormons was aroused to the highest pitch by this base attempt upon Mormon virtue. Threats were made so freely, that the Governor became very much alarmed, and precipitately fled the Territory. Not satisfied with this, the "boys" waylaid him at one of the stations, and gave him a severe beating.

In contemplating this serio-comic affair, one hardly knows which most to condemn, the lawless spirit which prompted such treatment, or the timidity and weakness which would submit to it.

About the 1st of February, 1862, Judges Flenniken and Crosby left Salt Lake City, and the federal officers there immediately advised the President of the fact by telegraph, and recommended the appointment of their successors. Accordingly on the 3d of February, 1862, Thomas J. Drake, of Michigan, and Charles B. Waite, of Illinois, were appointed Associate Justices, and on the 31st of March following, Stephen S. Harding, of Indiana, was appointed **Governor, to succeed Dawson.**

CHAPTER VI.

POLITICAL HISTORY CONTINUED.

Arrival of the New Federal Officers in July, 1862. — Colonel Connor arrives with his Command. — The Message of Gov. Harding. — The Mormons Indignant. — The Legislature refuse to print the Message. — Action of the United States Senate thereon. — Forgery in the Mormon Legislature. — Bill of Judge Waite to amend the Organic Act. — Indignation Meeting. — Governor Harding and Judges Waite and Drake requested to leave the Territory. — Their Replies. — Brigham. — The Federal Officers.

JUDGES Drake and Waite arrived in Salt Lake City on the 11th of July, 1862. Governor Harding had arrived a few days previous.

For several months everything passed off smoothly, and Brigham was more than once heard to say the officers now in the Territory were "good men." No circumstances occurred to develop any differences, and it was hoped by the federal officers themselves that none would arise.

In the mean time, in October of the same year, Colonel (now General) Connor marched into and through Salt Lake City with his command, and established his camp on the "bench," or high land, about three miles east of the city. His forces at that time consisted of the Third Regiment of Infantry, California Volunteers, and the Second Regiment of Cavalry, under command of Col. George S. Evans.

Some little excitement was caused by the entrance of the troops, and rumors were rife of threats having been made by the Mormons that the volunteers should never "cross the Jordan," a stream a few miles south of the city, and which was directly on their line of march. But the Jordan was crossed, the camp established, and everything went on as usual, until the meeting of the Territorial Legislature in December.

Then the pent-up fires began to break forth. The first pretext used by the Mormons for indulging in words and acts of hostility was the Message of Governor Harding to the Legislature. Therein he called the attention of the people, through their representatives, to the practice of polygamy in their midst, to the anomalous state of society it tended to establish, to its incompatibility with our free institutions, and especially to its violation of an Act of Congress recently passed.

The following are the portions of the Message which gave most offence:—

"*Polygamy.*

"It would be disingenuous if I were not to advert to a question which, although seemingly it has nothing to do in the premises, yet is one of vast importance to you as a people, and which cannot be ignored. I mean that institution which is not only commended but encouraged by you, and which, to say the least of it, is an anomaly throughout Christendom. I mean polygamy, or, if you prefer the term, plurality of wives. In approaching this delicate subject, I desire to do so in no unkind or offensive spirit; yet the institution, founded upon no written statute of your Territory, but upon custom alone, exists. . . .

"I lay it down as a sound proposition, that no community can happily exist with an institution so important as that of marriage wanting in all those qualities that make it homogeneal with institutions and laws of neighboring civilized communities having the same object.

"Anomalies in the moral world cannot long exist in a state of mere abeyance; they must, from the very nature of things, become aggressive, or they will soon disappear, from the force of conflicting ideas.

"This proposition is supported by the history of our race, and is so plain that it may be set down as an axiom. If we grant this to be true, we may sum up the conclusion of the argument as follows: either the laws and opinions of the communities by which you are surrounded must become subordinate to your customs and opinions, or, on the other hand, yours **must yield to theirs. The** conflict is irrepressible.

"But no matter whether this anomaly shall disappear or remain amongst you, it **is** your duty at least to guard it against flagrant abuses. That **plurality of wives is** tolerated and believed **to be right,** may not appear **so** strange; but that a mother and **her** daughters are allowed to fulfil the duties of *wives* to the same husband, **or that a** man could be found in all Christendom who could be induced to take upon himself such **a** relationship, is, perhaps, no less a marvel in morals than in matters of taste.

"The bare **fact that** such practices are tolerated amongst you is sufficient evidence that the human passions, whether excited by religious fanaticism or otherwise, must be restrained and subjected to laws, to which all **must** yield obedience. No community can long exist, **without absolute social** anarchy, unless **so** important an institution as that of marriage is regulated by law. It is the basis of our civilization, and in it the whole question of the descent and distribution of real and personal estate is involved.

"Much to my astonishment, I have not been able to find any law upon the statutes of this Territory regulating marriage. I earnestly recommend to your early consideration the passage of some law that will meet the exigencies of the people.

"*Act of Congress against Polygamy.*

"I respectfully call your attention to an Act of Congress, passed **the 1st** day of July, **1862, entitled 'An Act** to punish and prevent the practice **of** polygamy in **the** Territories of **the** United States, and in other places, and disapproving and annulling certain Acts of the legislative assembly of Utah,' (chap. cxxvii. of the Statutes at Large of the last session of Congress, page 501.) **I** am aware that there is a prevailing opinion here that said Act is unconstitutional, and therefore it is recommended by those in high authority that no regard whatever should be paid to the same; and still more to be regretted, if I am rightly informed, in some instances it has been recommended that it be openly disregarded and defied, merely to defy the same.

"I take this occasion to warn the people of this Territory against such dangerous and disloyal counsels. Whether such Act is unconstitutional or not, is not necessary for me either to affirm or deny. The individual citizen, under no circumstances whatever, has the right to defy any law or statute of the United States with impunity. In doing so he takes upon himself the risk of the penalties of that statute, be they what they may, in case his judgment should be in error.

"The Constitution has amply provided how and where all such questions of doubt are submitted and settled, namely, in the courts constituted for that purpose. To forcibly resist the execution of that Act would be, to say the least, a high misdemeanor; and if a whole community should become involved in such resistance, would call down upon it the consequences of insurrection and rebellion.

"I hope and trust that no such rash counsel will prevail. If, unhappily, I am mistaken in this, I choose to shut my eyes to the consequences.

"*Liberty of Conscience.*

"Amongst the most cherished and sacred rights secured to the citizen of the United States, is the right to worship God according to the dictates of conscience. . . .

"Religion was left a matter between man and his Maker, and not between man and the Government.

"But here arises a most important question, — a question perhaps that has never yet been asked or fully answered in this country, — How far does the right of conscience extend? Is there any limit to this right? — and if so, where shall the line of demarcation be drawn, designating that which is not forbidden from that which is? This is, indeed, a most important question, and, from the tendency of the times, must sooner or later be answered. I cannot, and will not, on this occasion, pretend to answer this question; but will venture the suggestion, that when it is answered, the same rules will be adopted as if the freedom of speech and of the press were involved in the argument.

. . . "There can be no limit beyond which the mind may not dwell, and our thoughts soar in our aspirations after truth. We may think what we will, believe what we will, and speak what we will, on all subjects of speculative theology. . . . But when religious opinions assume new manifestations, and pass from the condition of mere sentiment into overt acts, — no matter whether they be acts of faith or not, — they must not outrage the opinions of the civilized world, but, on the other hand, must conform to those usages established by law, and which are believed to underlie our very civilization."

In the same Message, the Governor, after giving his views upon the national topics of the day, fully sustaining the Administration and the war, proceeded to discuss all the more prominent subjects of local interest in the Territory. He referred to the attempts to procure the admission of **the State of Deseret** into the Union, — giving it as his opinion that those attempts were premature. He referred to provisions of the Organic Act, and claimed the right to nominate to the Council all general territorial officers. These had formerly been elected by the Legislature:

He recommended a thorough revision and codification of the statutes; a change in the mode of voting; referred to the financial condition of the Territory; adverted to the Indian troubles; advised the organization of a common-school system, and closed by assuring them of his willingness and desire to work with them for the common good and welfare of the people of the Territory.

The question of polygamy was boldly met and temperately discussed in this Message, and the people warned against the consequences of disobedience to the Act of Congress. Anything less than this on the part of the Governor would have been simply a neglect of duty.

Yet the Mormons were very indignant, and professed to look upon that portion of the Message as exceedingly hostile and offensive in its character. Their religion had been attacked by the federal authorities!

It may be well here to remark, for the benefit of the tender-footed upon this subject, that polygamy is no part of the Mormon religion, so far as the same has any history, and can be distinguished from the personal edicts of Brigham Young. It is not only not permitted but explicitly condemned in the "Book of Mormon" and the "Book of Doctrines and Covenants," which are the Old and New Testaments of Mormonism. This subject is more fully examined in another chapter of this work.

From the delivery of this Message, the treatment which the Governor received at the hands of the Mormons was entirely changed. From respect it was immediately changed to disrespect and contumely. No contemptuous treatment was too marked, no indignity was too great, to be heaped upon him, for this simple performance of his duty as a sworn officer of the United States Government.

The Message was never printed by the Legislature. The Journals did not even show that the Governor ever appeared before that body for any purpose whatever.

The fact that the Message was not published having been communicated to Washington, a resolution was introduced into the Senate of the United States on the 16th of January, 1863, instructing the Committee on Territories to inquire and report whether the publication of the Message of the Governor of the Territory of Utah to the Territorial Legislature had been suppressed, and if so by what causes, and what was the Message.

In response to this resolution Mr. Wade, chairman of the Committee, on the 13th of February, submitted a Report, accompanied by a resolution, which was adopted, that one thousand copies of the Message be printed, and sent to the Governor for distribution.

This Report of the Committee was less complimentary to the Mormons than the Message itself.

The following extracts will indicate the character of the document: —

"In pursuance of the instruction contained in this resolution, your committee have the honor to report, that they have collected all the facts, and taken all the testimony within their reach, — the substance of which, together with a copy of the Message, is herewith presented.

"These sources of information disclose the fact, that the customs which have prevailed in all our other Territories in the government of public affairs have had but little toleration in the Territory of Utah; but in their stead there appears to be, overriding all other influences, a sort of Jewish theocracy, graduated to the condition of that Territory.

"This theocracy, having a supreme head who governs and guides every affair of importance in the Church, and, practically, in the Territory, is the only real power acknowledged **here,** and to the extension **of whose** interests every person in the Territory must directly or indirectly conduce. . . .

"We have here **the** first exhibition, within the limits of the United States, of a Church ruling **the State.** . . .

"Another opinion — the subject of both public and private teaching — is, that the Government of the United States will not and ought not to stand. They make a difference between the Constitution and the Government of the United States; **to** the Constitution they **claim** to **be** very loyal.

. . . "Because the Governor, **in his** Message, has animadverted upon some of the customs of the Mormons, and has recommended that steps be taken to Americanize the same, he has given offence, and has had his Message suppressed.

"Polygamy of the most unlimited character, sanctioning **the** cohabitation of **a** man with **the** mother and her daughters **indiscriminately, is not** the only un-American thing among them.

. . . "The Message, on examination, is found to contain nothing that should give offence **to any** legislature willing to be governed by the laws of morality.

"It is the opinion **of** your Committee that the Message is an able exposition of the manners and customs of the people in that Territory, and as such, brought down the censure of the leaders of the Mormon Church, and were it not for the animadversions therein contained, it would not have been suppressed."

The printing and distribution of the Message is then **recommended.**

During the session of the Legislature **an event occurred** which caused much indignation **among the** federal officers, and served to render somewhat mutual **the** feelings of hostility which the leading saints already entertained. This was nothing less than a forgery committed in the Legislature upon a bill relating to the terms of one of the District Courts.

The facts were as follows: —

The Territory was divided into three judicial districts. The First, sometimes called the Provo District, comprised a number of counties carved out of the centre of the Territory. This had been assigned to Judge Drake. The Second, called the "Cotton District," was assigned to Judge Waite, and consisted of the three southernmost counties, Beaver, Iron, and Washington. The Third District, Chief Justice Kinney's, comprised the northern part of the Territory, including Salt Lake City.

On the 14th of January, 1863, the Legislature passed a bill, which was signed by the Governor, changing the county seat of Washington County from Washington to St. George, and in the same bill it was provided that the United States Court for the transaction of territorial business, should be held at St. George, on the third Monday of May. This time was the same as that provided by the law previously in force.

This was before the assignment of the Judges had been made.

After Judge Waite had been assigned to the Second District [in which many murders had been committed, and the murderers still at large], the Legislature concluded they did not want court held in that district until fall. They accordingly passed a bill, providing, among other things, for holding the court at St. George on the third Monday of October. But as they had already passed a bill fixing the term of court in May, and as the Judge preferred to hold the term in May, that being near the time when he was intending to hold court for the transaction of United States business in the same district, the Governor declined signing the second bill.

Soon after, having occasion to examine the first bill for another purpose, he went to the Secretary's office and called for the bill, and behold, *the word May had been erased, and the word October inserted instead!* It appeared to have been done by the same hand which had penned the body of the bill. This had been written by one of the clerks of the House of Representatives. The Governor, after signing the bill, had inadvertently returned it to the Legislature, and it had been sent from that body to the Secretary's office, where it should have been sent by the Governor. It had been recorded in that office before the forgery was discovered.

The Governor immediately caused the record to be corrected, changed the bill back from October to May, by erasing the word "October" and interlining the word "May." He then made a statement of the forgery and its detection, over his own signature, on the margin of the bill.

He then sent a special Message to the Legislature, calling their attention to the fact that a forgery had been committed; but, instead of taking steps to ferret out the guilty party, the Legislature made an issue of fact with the Governor, and endeavored to make out that it was all the time October, and that no forgery had been committed. When the matter was up in the House the second time, one member actually produced a paper which he averred was the original draft, and which had October in it. And this in the face of the fact, that five persons had seen the bill in the Governor's office when the word May was in it, and that the bill showed plainly, upon inspection, that it had been changed; the outline of the letter "y," in the word erased, being distinctly visible.

Thus the Legislature, by their collective action, implicated themselves all in the forgery.

On the 16th of January the Legislature adjourned, without printing the Governor's Message, or sending any appropriation bills for his signature.

The day following, "the Legislature of the State of Deseret" met, and commenced doing business under Brigham Young, as Governor. A Message was delivered, and all the forms of legislation gone through with; in reality, this *de facto* government was the only one for which the Mormons maintained even the show of respect.

The judicial system of the Territory was manifestly very defective, and as constituted under the Organic Act of 1850, as the same had been construed by the Federal Judges, was inadequate to the administration of justice.

The greatest difficulty was experienced in the formation of juries, and in the extraordinary jurisdiction assumed by the Probate Judges, all of whom were Mormons.

The jurisdiction of the Probate Court, in the words of the Organic Act, was to be "as prescribed by law." Under this provision several of the United States Judges had held that it was competent in the Legislature to confer upon the Probate Courts any jurisdiction they pleased. The Mormons, never behind in availing themselves of all advantages, had accordingly granted to the Probate Courts concurrent jurisdiction with the District Courts, in all cases civil and criminal.

Again; the juries had been selected by these courts acting with other county authorities, and it was contended that the United States Courts could only try causes before juries thus selected.

To remedy these defects, and to remove all doubt as to these complicated questions, a bill was drawn by Judge Waite, for an Act of Congress amendatory of the Organic Act of 1850. It provided for the selection of United States juries by the Marshal, under the direction of the court, as in other district and territorial courts of the United States.

The question of jurisdiction was to be settled by an express provision that the Probate Court should have no jurisdiction to try any civil action whatsoever. It was to do the usual probate business, and have a limited criminal jurisdiction, subject to appeal to the District Court. The bill also provided for an organization of the militia of the Territory, under the Governor, and contained several other wholesome and salutary provisions.

The bill was carefully drawn, and was submitted to the inspection of his associate, Judge Drake, and of Governor Harding, — Judge Kinney being absent from the Territory. It received the unqualified approval of Drake and Harding, and, with their indorsement upon it, was sent to Washington. In due time it was introduced in Congress by Senator Browning, and referred to the proper committee.

The introduction of this bill was the signal for another outbreak. The news was telegraphed to Salt Lake, and immediately Brigham called a meeting at the Tabernacle.

The meeting was held on the 3d of March, 1863. Notice having been extensively circulated, some two or three thousand persons assembled, excited by exaggerated statements concerning attempts upon the part of the federal officers to "interfere with their rights."

Speeches of the most inflammatory character were made at this meeting, and the resentment and indignation of the ignorant masses of the people were excited to the highest pitch. The following will serve as a specimen of these harangues.

Elder John Taylor said : —

"It has already been stated that these documents speak for themselves. They come from those who are ostensibly our guardians, and the guardians of our rights. They come from men who ought to be actuated by the strictest principles of honor, truth, virtue, integrity, and honesty, and whose high official position ought to elevate them above suspicion, — yet what are the results?

"In relation to the Governor's Message, enough, perhaps, has already been said. . .

"We had a right to look for a friend in our Governor, who would, at least, fairly represent us. Instead, we have had a most insidious foe, who, through misrepresentations, base insinuations, and falsehood, is seeking with all his power, privately as well as officially, not only to injure us before the Government, but as well to sap the very foundations of our civil and religious liberties; he is, in fact, in the furtherance of his unhallowed schemes, seeking to promote anarchy and rebellion, and dabbling in your blood. [Cries of 'hear, hear.'] Such, it would seem, were the Governor's feelings and intentions when he concocted his Message, and such his purposes when he read it before the Legislature. That document was not hastily written, as it shows upon its face that it had been well digested, and every word and sentence carefully weighed.

. . . "That he is the most vindictive enemy we have, is shown by the statement of our representatives at Washington.

"He is the only man, it would seem, who is industriously striving to sap the interests of our people, and to injure their reputation, and yet, as our Governor, he professes to feel a deep interest in our welfare, and to represent our wishes.

"Let us, for a short time, investigate the results of his acts, should his purposes be successful, leaving the allegations of treason from our consideration. [It was contended that the Governor and Judges had committed *Treason against the Territory.*]

"We have thought that we were living under a republican form of government, and had the right of franchise; that we had the privilege of voting for whom we pleased, and of thus saying whom we would have represent us; but it may be that we are laboring under a mistake, and that it is but a political illusion. We have likewise thought that if any one among us was accused of crimes, it was his privilege to be tried by a jury of his peers, among whom he had lived, who would undoubtedly be the best judges of his actions.

"We have further been of the opinion that while acting in a military capacity, when called into service to stand in defence of our country's rights, we had the right of selecting our own officers. We have always had this privilege, in accordance with republican usage; but we can do so no longer should the plotting of Governor Harding and our Honorable Judges be carried into effect. We shall be deprived of franchise, of the right of trial by an impartial jury, and shall be placed, in a military capacity, under the creatures of Governor Harding, or of his successors. In other words, we shall be forever deprived of all the rights of freemen, and placed under a military despotism; such would be the result of the passage of this Act.

"Again, in regard to juries, already referred to, you know what, as regards this matter, the usage has always been. The Governor and Judges want to place the power in the hands of the United States Marshal of selecting such jurors as he pleases, and that, too, without reference as to who they are, or whence they come. This is what is attempted to be done by our honorable Judges and Governor. Your rights as freemen, and your liberties, are aimed at; and you are to be disfranchised, and your liberties trampled under foot, by strangers, and you will have blacklegs and cut-throats sit upon your juries. Mr. Harding wants to select his own military, and have officers of his own selection to lead them, and then if you do not submit, he will have the authority to say, 'I will make you.' [Uproarious applause, and cries all over the house of ' Can't do it.'] We all know he can't do it, but this is what he is aiming at. [Clapping of hands, and great cheering.] When these rights are taken away, what rights have we left? [Cries of ' None.']

"It can scarcely be credited or believed, that any man in his position could so far degrade himself as to introduce such infamous principles, and it is equally a lamentable fact to reflect upon, that men holding the high and responsible position of United States Judges could so far forget themselves as to descend to such depravity, corruption, and injustice. [Applause.] These things are so palpable, that 'he that runneth may read,' and any man with five grains of common sense can readily comprehend them. It is for you to say whether you are willing to sustain such men in the capacity they act in, or not." [Loud clapping of hands, and a universal and emphatic cry of "No!" on the part of the audience.]

Brigham Young's Speech.

At the close of Elder Taylor's speech Brigham arose, and on advancing to the speaker's desk was greeted with vociferous applause, and immediately proceeded to address the assemblage as follows:—

"I have no intention of delivering a lengthy address, but while I am speaking I desire the audience to remain quiet. I know well your feelings, but much prefer that you should suppress any demonstrations of applause to other times and places, when you may have less business and greater leisure.

"You have just heard read the Message of Governor Harding,

delivered to the last Legislative Assembly of this Territory. You will readily perceive that the bread is buttered, but there is poison underneath. When he came to Utah last July, the Governor sought to ingratiate himself into the esteem of our prominent citizens, with whom he had early intercourse, and professed great friendship and attachment for the people of the Territory. He was then full of their praises, and said he was ready to declare that he would stand in the defence of polygamy, or that he should have to deny the Bible; and stated that he had told the President, prior to leaving Washington, that if he were called upon to discuss the question, he would have to take the side of polygamy, or to renounce the authority of the Scriptures.

" In the face of all these professions, what has been his course? While being fair of speech, and specious of promise, and lavish in his expressions of good-will toward us, he has been insidiously at work to prejudice the General Government against us, and in the secrecy of his private room has concocted measures which he urged upon Congress to pass, which, if successful, would deprive us of the dearest rights of freemen, and render us the abject subjects of this man, who has been sent here to govern the Territory. Man, did I say? — thing, I mean, — a nigger-worshipper, — a black-hearted abolitionist is what he is, and what he represents; and that I do naturally despise. He wants to have the telegraph torn down, and the mails stopped and turned by the way of Panama. Do you acknowledge this man Harding for your Governor? [Voices all through the audience responded, 'No, you are our Governor.'] Yes, I am your Governor; and I will let him know that I am Governor; and if he attempts to interfere in my affairs, ' Woe, woe unto him!' [Shaking his uplifted fist in a very excited manner, which was responded to with loud applause, and cries of ' Yes, you are our Governor.']

" Will you allow such a man to remain in the Territory? [Voices, ' No; put him out.'] Yes, I say put him out. Judges Waite and Drake are perfect fools, and the tools of Governor Harding, and they too must leave. If all three do not resign, or if the President does not remove them, the people must attend to it.

" If they could get the power, as they want to do, to have the Marshal choose jurors of cut-throats, blacklegs, soldiers, and desperadoes from California, and we are to be tried by such men, what would become of us?

"In regard to the war now desolating the country, it is but the fulfilment of the prophecies of Joseph Smith, which he told me thirty years ago. Brother Joseph said that the South would rise against the North, and the North against the South, and that they would fight until both parties were destroyed; and for my part I give it God speed; for they have spilt the blood of the Prophet. [To which the audience responded vociferously, 'Amen!']

"I would like to live in peace with the Government of the United States, but have no desire to live with the people who have brought ruin and disgrace upon their own heads. I do not wish to live in, or have anything to do with the United States; I will have a free and independent government for myself, where I may live and enjoy my civil and religious liberties. [Loud cries of 'Amen,' and 'Yes, yes,' on the part of the entire assemblage.]

"When our rights, and the protection of our liberties are taken from us, what is there remaining? [Voices, 'Nothing,' 'Nothing.'] Yes, service to despots, — service to tyrants."

Brigham also said that money had been appropriated for the purpose of turning the mail by the way of Panama; and these men were not above taking money for such a purpose, under pretence of other business.

The injustice and falsity of these statements concerning the bill introduced into Congress, and which was the immediate cause of this outbreak, will be manifest, when it is stated that so far from authorizing soldiers to sit as jurymen, it was expressly prohibited in the bill itself. Again; the right of suffrage was actually extended by the bill, because, while by one section the militia officers were to be appointed by the Governor, the bill in other sections provided that nearly all civil officers of the Territory, who were before elected by the Legislature, should be elected by the people.

The effect of the bill would have been, to enable the people, when they became generally dissatisfied with the spiritual tyranny to which they were submitting, as many of them were already, to throw off the yoke of despotism, by having every question that might arise fairly and impartially adjudicated upon in the courts. This was foreseen by Brigham. He saw that he was about to lose the powerful enginery of the judicial system of the Territory, then under his control. Hence the demonstration.

There are but two ways in which this theocratic despotism can be met and overthrown. One is, by the people of the Territory, aided by some such legislation as that proposed. The other is by the strong arm of military power. The former would be more congenial to our institutions.

Time only can determine which must be resorted to. Doubtless the employment of force will become necessary in either case, — as the course taken by Young and his associates on this occasion shows that a peaceable remedy will be forcibly resisted.

After listening to such speeches, the audience were, of course, ready to adopt or approve of anything; and the following resolutions, prepared for the occasion, were passed without a dissenting voice: —

"*Resolved*, That we consider the attack made upon us by His Excellency Governor Harding, wherein our loyalty is impugned, as base, wicked, unjust, and false; and he knew it to be so when uttered.

"*Resolved*, That we consider the attempt to possess himself of all military authority and dictation, by appointing all the militia officers, is a stretch of military despotism, hitherto unknown in the annals of our Republic.

"*Resolved*, That we consider his attempt to control the selection of juries as so base, unjust, and tyrannical, as to deserve the contempt of all free men.

"*Resolved*, That we consider the action of Judges Waite and Drake, in assisting the Governor to pervert justice, and violate the sacred palladium of the people's rights, as subversive of the principles of justice, degrading to their high calling, and repulsive to the feelings of honest men.

"*Resolved*, That we consider that a serious attack has been made upon the liberties of this people, and that it not only affects us as a Territory, but is a direct assault upon Republican principles in our own nation and throughout the world; and that we cannot either tamely submit to be disfranchised ourselves, nor witness, without protest, the assassin's dagger plunged into the very vitals of our national institutions.

"*Resolved*, That while we will, at all times, honor and magnify all wholesome laws of our country, and desire to be subservient to their dictates, and the equitable administration of justice, we will resist, in a proper manner, every attempt upon the liberties, guaranteed by our fathers, whether made by insidious foes or open traitors.

"*Resolved*, That a committee be appointed by the meeting to wait upon the Governor, and Judges Waite and Drake, to request them to resign their offices and leave the Territory.

"*Resolved*, That John Taylor, Jetu Clinton, and Orson Pratt, Sen., be that committee.

"*Resolved*, That we petition the President of the United States to remove Governor Harding, and Judges Waite and Drake, and to appoint good men in their stead."

The following is the petition to the President, which was signed by several thousand persons:—

"*To His Excellency Abraham Lincoln, President of the United States:*—

"Sir,—We, your petitioners, citizens of the Territory of Utah, respectfully represent that,

"*Whereas*, From the most reliable information in our possession, we are satisfied that His Excellency Stephen S. Harding, Governor, Charles B. Waite and Thomas J. Drake, Associate Justices, are strenuously endeavoring to create mischief and stir up strife between the people of the Territory of Utah and the troops now in Camp Douglas, (situated within the limits of Great Salt Lake City,) and, of far graver import in our nation's difficulties, between the people of the aforesaid Territory and the Government of the United States:

"*Therefore*, We respectfully petition your Excellency to forthwith remove the aforesaid persons from the offices they now hold, and to appoint in their places men who will attend to the duties of their offices, honor their appointments, and regard the rights of all, attending to their own affairs and leaving alone the affairs of others; and in all their conduct demeaning themselves as honorable citizens and officers worthy of commendation by yourself, our Government, and all good men; and for the aforesaid removals and appointments your petitioners will continue most respectfully to pray.

"*Great Salt Lake City, Territory of Utah*, March 3, 1863."

The best reply to the charges contained in the foregoing petition, is the counter-petition sent to the President by the military officers of General Connor's command, of which the following is a copy:—

"HEADQUARTERS, COLUMN FOR UTAH, CAMP DOUGLAS, UTAH TERRITORY, near Salt Lake City, March 8, 1863.

"*To His Excellency Abraham Lincoln, President of the United States:*—

"It is an unusual proceeding for officers of the army to join in representing to the Government their knowledge of facts and opinion of proceedings, having reference to civil authority, or to the actions of the people for expressing their displeasure at the conduct of their officers.

"The condition of affairs in the Territory of Utah, however, and the result of this condition of affairs, which culminated in a mass meeting in Salt Lake City on the 3d inst., in our opinion demands from us a respectful statement to your Excellency of the matter having allusion to ourselves, simply as an act of duty we owe to our Government.

"We do not propose to inquire into recommendations affecting the laws of the Territory, made by the Governor and Associate Judges of the Supreme Court of Utah. The Government must know, as regards the justice or injustice of the proposed amendments to existing laws, made by the officers above named.

"But when the community residing in Salt Lake City solemnly declare in their petition to your Excellency, that Governor Harding, and Judges Waite and Drake are studiously endeavoring to create mischief and stir up strife between the people of the Territory and the troops now at Camp Douglas (situated within the limits of Salt Lake City), they simply assert a base and unqualified falsehood.

"On the contrary, it has been the aim of these gentlemen to

preserve friendly relations between the people of Utah and **the** troops, who have also labored to the same end, now stationed **at** Camp Douglas.

"And further; during a period of nearly five months, we know that Governor Harding, and Judges Drake and Waite 'have attended to the duties of their offices, honored their appointments, regarded the rights of **all, attended** to their own affairs,' and have not disturbed or interfered with the affairs of others, outside **of** their legitimate duty to the Government; 'and in all their conduct,' His Excellency Governor Harding, and Judges Drake and Waite, have, during our **acquaintance with them,** 'demeaned themselves **as** honorable **citizens, and officers worthy of** commendation by your Excellency, our Government, and all good men.'

"And we further represent to your Excellency that these **officers have been true** and faithful **to** the Government, and fearless **in** the discharge **of** their duties **to** all. They have, **on** all proper occasions, spoken plainly to the people of their duty. They have not been subservient to any person or persons, and they stand proudly preëminent as in contrast with other officers who have represented in the past, and who do now represent, the Federal Government in this Territory.

"Our respectful opinion is, that there is no good and true cause for the removal of His Excellency Governor Harding, and **Judges** Drake and Waite, from the offices they now hold.

"With much respect, **we have the** honor **to** remain your Excellency's **obedient servants,** —

"**P. Edward** Connor, Colonel **3d** Infantry, California Volunteers, commanding District of Utah ; Geo. S. Evans, Colonel 2d Cavalry, Cal. Vol.; **P.** A. Gallagher, Major 3d Infantry, C. V.; J. M. Williamson, Surgeon, 2d Cavalry, C. V.; Robert K. Reid, Surgeon 3d Infantry, C. V.; George Wallace, Capt. and Asst. Q. M. U. S. A.; Thomas B. Gately, 1st Lieut. and Reg. **Q. M.;** William L. Ustick, 1st Lieut. and Adjt. 3d Infantry, and A. **A. A. G.**; T. S. Harris, 1st Lieut. and Adjt. 2d **Cavalry, C. V.;** Henry R. Miller, 2d Lieut. **and Reg. C. S.,** 2d Cavalry, **C. V.;** F. A. Peel, 2d Lieut. and Reg. Q. **M.** 2d **Cavalry, C. V.;** Charles Tupper, Captain 3d Infantry, **C. V.**; John B. Urmy, Captain 3d Infantry, C. V.; Samuel N. Hoyt, Captain 3d Infantry, **C. V.**; David Black, Captain 3d Infantry, C. V.; S. P. Smith, Captain 2d Cavalry, **C. V.** Daniel McLane, Captain 2d Cavalry, C. V.; George F. Price, Captain 2d Cavalry, C. V.; David J. Berry, Captain 2d Cavalry, C. V.; Josiah Hosmer, 1st Lieut. 3d Infantry, C. V.; James W. Stillman, 1st Lieut. 3d Infantry, C. V.; Lysander Washburn, 2d Lieut. 3d Infantry, C. V.; Michael McDermott, 1st Lieut. 3d Infantry, C. V.; John Quinn, 1st Lieut. 2d Cavalry, C. V.; Cyrus D. Clark, 1st Lieut. 2d Cavalry, C. V.; Francis Honeyman, 2d Lieut. 3d Infantry, C. V.; S. E. Joslyn, 2d Lieut. 3d Infantry, C. V.; James Finnerty, 2d Lieut. 3d Infantry, C. V.; Edward Ingham, 2d Lieut. 3d Infantry, C. V.; Anthony Ether, 2d Lieut. 2d Cavalry, C. V.; J. Bradley, 2d Lieut. 2d Cavalry, C. V.; Geo. D. Conrad, 2d Lieut. 2d Cavalry, C. V."*

But to return to the meeting, and subsequent proceedings:—

The next morning, the Committee appointed to wait upon the officers and " request " them to resign and leave the Territory, called upon Governor Harding, at his residence, and presented him with a copy of the " Deseret News," containing the reported proceedings of the meeting.

The Governor treated them with much courtesy, and after examining the paper, addressed the Committee, as follows:—

" Gentlemen, I believe I understand this matter perfectly. You may go back and tell your constituents that I will not resign my office, and will not leave this Territory, until it shall please the President to recall me. I came here a messenger of peace and good-will to your people, but I must confess that my opinions have changed in many respects. But I came also, sirs, to discharge my duties honestly and faithfully to the Government, and I intend to do so to the last. It is in your power to do me personal violence, — to shed my blood; but this will not deter me from my purpose. If the President can be made to believe that I have been unfaithful to the trust he confided to me, he will doubtless remove me; and I then shall be glad to return to my home in the States, and will do so, carrying with me no unjust resentments towards you or any one else.

" But I will not be driven away; I will not cowardly abandon

* The above embraces all the commissioned officers then stationed at Camp Douglas.

my post. I may be in danger in staying; but my purpose is fixed. I desire to have no trouble; I am anxious to live and again meet my family, — but if necessary, an administrator can settle my affairs.

"Your allegations in this paper are false, — without the shadow of truth. You call my **Message** insulting, and you dare not print it for fear your people **may read it** for themselves. To say that I have wronged you when **I said** that you are disloyal, is simply preposterous. Your own people — your public teachers and bishops — admit the fact.

"Let me say to you in conclusion, — and as this is said to be a land of prophets, I too will prophesy, — If, while in the discharge of my duties, one drop of my blood be shed by your ministers of vengeance, that it will be avenged, **and not one** stone or adobe in this city will be left upon another. **I have now done,** and you understand me."

During this reply **the Committee sat** quiet, with the exception of Elder Taylor, who several times attempted to make some explanation; but the Governor refused to hear him, **and** went through with his remarks without stopping to listen, **or** reply to any new matter.

Elder Taylor then turned to Judge Drake, and remarked that he might consider the **resolutions** as addressed **also to** him.

The Judge responded **as** follows: —

"The communications you have made are of some importance, and as they are intended to affect me, **I desire** to say something before you go.

"It is no small thing to request a citizen to leave his country. Are you aware of the magnitude or of the baseness of what you have undertaken? I deny that you have any cause for such conduct toward me. I am an American citizen, **and as such have a** right to go to every part of the Republic. I have the right to petition, or ask the Government **to** pass laws, **or** to amend them. You, Taylor and Pratt, are men of experience, and reputed to be men of learning, and ought to know better than to insult a man **by** such means.

"It is mean and contemptible. **On your** part, Taylor, a foreigner, it is impudence unequalled ; and Pratt, a citizen, ought to know better than to trample on the rights of a citizen by engaging in such a dirty enterprise. Your resolutions are false, and those who drafted them knew them to be so ; and I am informed that in the meeting at the Tabernacle, Brigham Young called me a fool, and a tool of the Governor. [Here Taylor admitted that such was the fact.]

" Go back to Brigham Young, your master, — that embodiment of sin and shame and disgust, — and tell him that I neither fear him, nor love him, nor hate him, — that I utterly despise him. Tell him, whose tools and tricksters you are, that I did not come here by his permission, and that I will not go away at his desire, or by his directions. I have given no cause of offence to any one. I have not entered a Mormon's house since I came here; your wives and daughters have not been disturbed by me, and I have not even looked upon your concubines and lewd women.

" I am no skulk from the punishment of crimes. I tell you, if you, or the man whom you so faithfully serve, attempt to interfere with my lawful business, you will meet with trouble of a character you do not expect.

" A horse-thief or a murderer has, when arrested, a right to speak in court; and unless in such capacity, or under such circumstances, don't you ever dare to speak to me again."

The Committee rose to depart, and one of them said, " We have our opinions." " Yes," replied the Judge, " thieves and murderers can have opinions;" and thus closed the interview.

The Committee then proceeded to call on Judge Waite at his residence, where they were received politely and with due consideration. In answer to their request for his resignation and withdrawal from the Territory, he replied as follows: —

" To comply with your wishes, gentlemen, under such circumstances, would be to admit, impliedly at least, one of two things, — either that I was sensible of having done something wrong, or that I was afraid to remain at my post and perform my duty.

" I am not conscious either of guilt or fear. I must therefore respectfully decline to accede to your request."

These replies were published in California, and in the Eastern papers, and gave general satisfaction. The people rejoiced that at last the Government had representatives in Utah who could neither be wheedled nor bullied out of their rights, nor frightened from the performance of their duty.

In Utah the excitement for a time ran high, and doubtless nothing but the presence of the military saved the federal officers from personal violence.

The state of popular feeling there is well shown by the following extracts from the correspondence of the "Chicago Tribune":—

"Excitement ran high, and groups of men were to be seen on the corners of the various streets, busily engaged in canvassing the subject, their earnest gestures and eager attitudes portraying the depth and intensity of the frenzied feeling which actuated them.

"One of the Judges sought to be ostracised (Judge Waite) was accosted, while passing quietly along the sidewalk, by a group of excited men, and threats of an alarming character made use of to intimidate him.

. . . "The few 'gentiles' resident here were also to be observed in earnest discussion of the question, and with compressed lip and countenance, on which 'thought sat sedate,' awaited, cold and determined, the approach of coming events. I opine that many a bowie and revolver were hastily examined and adjusted, of which the passer-by had no thought or knowledge, which, in an emergency, might have been made useful.

"It was a spectacle of true courage to see these federal officers, clothed with important duties, stand up and assert their rights, when they knew but too well that this 'request' upon the part of the meeting and the Committee had a far more grave significance, if that request were not complied with.

"They have been called on by a number of citizens and gentlemen since the visit of the Committee, and have received but one expression of opinion as to what has passed; and that is, that the proceedings throughout were an outrage, and only intended to get rid of men who cannot be used against the interest of the General Government, and whose fidelity to duty makes them alike hated and feared by the Mormon leaders."

The following, from the same correspondence, will show the conduct of Young during this emergency: —

"While the objects of all this wrath pursue the even tenor of their way, and sleep soundly, with scarce a casement barred, unmindful of the threatened storm without, yet not so with him, 'the Lord's Anointed,' who appears to dream dreams and see visions, that to his distempered fancy seem to foreshadow the 'handwriting on the wall,' at the great day of his judgment which is to come. Like unto the great magician, the famous Fakir, who upon a time, by his incantation, raised a demon which he could not control, which would not 'lay' at the conqueror's command, and from which he fled in dismay; so, in the present instance, the 'Lion of the Lord' is sorely affrighted at the hideous aspect of the devil ('of a muss') he has raised, which, he has the sagacity to see, may not 'down' at his bidding, but may return to plague the inventor.

"There is abundant evidence to show that he is alarmed at his own creation, and foreseeing that he has provoked justice, incensed mercy, seeks to guard against the retribution which he knows the offended majesty of loyalty and law should visit upon him.

"The night succeeding the action of the mass meeting, some fifty armed sentinels or guards were on duty, in and about Brigham's premises, which number has since been augmented to several hundreds, a portion of whom serve as pickets, or night-patrol, on the different streets leading toward Camp Douglas. It has been currently reported that orders have been issued to arrest Brigham and his counsellors, and hence these precautionary measures to guard against any sudden inroad of troops from Col. Connor's command. . . .

"On the 8th inst., the Sabbath succeeding the date of the mass meeting, Brigham delivered a very treasonable and violent harangue in the Tabernacle, to an immense audience, which filled almost to suffocation that capacious structure. . . . 'We have always,' he said, 'done everything in our power to show our loyalty. Is there anything that could be asked that we would not do? Yes; let the present Administration ask us for a thousand men, or even five hundred, and I'd see them damned first, and then they couldn't have them! What do you think of that?

[Loud cries of "Good, good!" and great applause.] We have liars, murderers, and thieves among us, who are watching us, to report something against our loyalty. Their object is to send another army here to "wipe us out"; but let me tell them that cannot be done; "they can't come it," — putting his thumb to his nose, and making the peculiar gyrating movement with the fingers, so very expressive among rowdies and shoulder-hitters. At this antic, a long, and loud, and universal shout and laughter went up from all parts of the house, joined with clapping of hands, and stamping of the feet, in one general din and uproar.

"' It was said that we were disloyal because we burned some seventy government wagons, at the time Johnston's army came here. Well, let me ask, *what the devil were they doing out here?* Coming here to destroy, and wipe us from the face of the earth; and we only took and destroyed some of their good things, so that they had to *gnaw mules' bones*, and eat cattle which had frozen to death; that's what they did.

"' I swear some, my brethren and sisters; but it is always in the pulpit, — never anywhere else.'

"Following Brigham came 'brother Heber,' a large, gross man, bald-headed, and with a harsh and disagreeable voice, and apparently fast approaching the age of 'the lean and slippered pantaloon.' His remarks were in the main but a re-hash of those made by Brigham, save in one or two noticeable points, as follows:—'They say I am a secessionist, *but that's a lie.* Then they say I have more than one wife; well, I *have* several wives, and lots of children, and by the help of the Lord I'll have many more of them!'

"Speaking about anticipated trouble with the General Government, he said: — 'The entire power of the United States cannot destroy us, for the Lord will fight our battles.'

"*Brigham fears Arrest.*

"Yesterday Col. Connor rode into the city, and called on Judge Waite at his residence, and made a stay of perhaps an hour or so. Immediately after his departure, a signal of distress was hastily thrown to the breeze, from a small flag-staff on Brigham's 'Lion House.' . . . Immediately a commotion was seen, and soon armed men began to pour along the different streets, and the report was carried, as on the wings of lightning, to the uttermost parts of the city, that an order was being made out for the arrest of Brigham and his counsellors, and that Col. Connor had been down to make arrangements for enforcing the writ. Men with muskets and rifles, — some few with antiquated swords, — of all ages, from the brawny youth to the old white-haired sexagenarian, came pouring along, singly and in groups, by twos, by threes, and the half-dozen or more, pressing hurriedly on towards Brigham's premises, zealous, and ready to yield up life, if need be, in defence of the 'Prophet of the Lord.' Altogether some two thousand 'citizen soldiery' collected, and stood guard during the watches of the night, over the beloved Brigham and his harem. Verily, 'The wicked flee when no man pursueth.'"

That Brigham really feared arrest at this time, and believed that a movement was on foot for that purpose, is evident from the following, taken from the "Latter Day Saints' Millennial Star," published in London. It is a portion of a letter written for that magazine by David O. Calder, a clerk in the tithing-office: —

"AMERICA. GREAT SALT LAKE CITY, March 13th, 1863.]
"*President G. Q. Cannon:*

"Dear Brother, — You of course have learned through the New York press of our 'expected collision between the military and citizens of Utah,' and will learn through Capt. Hooper, (he being just informed by telegraph to write to you,) that comparative peace is restored. I shall now give you some details of the trouble.

"As you are aware, we have been of the opinion that the mission of the troops despatched from California last year was not altogether to be confined to the guarding of the mail and telegraph lines, and the protection of the California emigration, and consequently have been watchful of their proceedings; the more so, that they made their winter-quarters within the city limits, and on one of the most commanding benches above the city, instead of being distributed at the several posts along the line of travel.

"We also have been made acquainted with the doings of **Governor Harding, and Judges Waite and Drake**; that they were corresponding with the authorities at Washington, and moving everything that could be moved to bring the army here in contact with the people, and to have the War Department send on two or three thousand more troops.

"These and other movements compelled the citizens to be on their guard, and prepared for any emergency. On Monday last, a reliable person overheard Colonel Connor and Judge Waite in conversation. The Colonel says, 'These three men must be surprised.' The Judge replied, 'Colonel, you know your duty.' In half an hour after, from a signal given, which was previously understood, about one thousand citizens were armed, and on duty, and in another half hour another thousand men were on duty. This sudden demonstration proved to them that their secret was known, and that we were fully prepared for them. In the mean time our 'outside' friends in this city telegraphed to those interested in the mail and telegraph lines, that they must work for the removal of the troops, Governor Harding, Judges Waite and Drake, else there would be difficulty, and the mail and telegraph lines would be destroyed. Their moneyed interest has given them great energy in our behalf. They have placed their line at the disposal of President Young, to be used to Washington, or New York. We fully expect the Colonel, Governor, and Judges will be recalled."

Here, it will be noticed, is the same covert threat contained in Brigham Young's speech, that the mail and telegraph lines would be destroyed, if the federal officers should be retained at their posts. It is to be regretted that this standing menace should so far have had its effect, as to induce the President, some two or three months afterward, to recall Governor Harding from his position. It is true, by transferring him to the Chief Justiceship of Colorado Territory, his removal was disconnected with any censure of his administration. It still remained, however, a substantial yielding to the arbitrary demands of Brigham Young, and as such, had a direct tendency to encourage him in his lawless proceedings, and to postpone for years the solution of the Utah problem.

Judges Waite and Drake had, immediately after the demonstration of the 3d of March, written to the President, giving it as their opinion that the laws were nugatory, and the Organic Act entirely inoperative in the Territory, and declining to hold any terms of the District Court in their respective districts until they should be properly supported by the military power of the Government; at the same time giving it as their opinion, that such a support should be at least five thousand men, well armed, equipped, and provided.

The failure to furnish this force, and the subsequent change in the governorship of the Territory, satisfied them that the Government was not then prepared to meet the questions which had arisen in such a manner as the dignity and honor of the nation required, and accordingly all effort to further counteract the evil effects of this intolerant theocracy were, for the time, abandoned.

Judge Waite, after holding, with his associates, in July, 1863, a term of the Supreme Court, *at which there was not a single case on the docket*, left the Territory in disgust, and established himself in the practice of his profession in Idaho City, Idaho Territory. He resigned his office, and was succeeded, in the spring of 1864, by Judge McCurdy, the present incumbent.

Governor Harding was succeeded, in May, 1863, by James Duane Doty, who, at the time of his appointment, was Superintendent of Indian Affairs. Governor Doty is a man of sound judgment, and of large experience in public affairs; and does as well as any man could in his embarrassing position. But his governorship is merely nominal. With the form and semblance, he lacks all the substance of power; and where he should *order*, he must satisfy himself with request and expostulation.

Judge Drake still remains in Utah, and with all the talent, energy, and experience necessary to fill his position to the great benefit of the people, he is obliged to remain entirely inactive, and goes through the forms of holding court, with scarcely an attempt to administer justice to the whole people, so well persuaded is he that all such attempts are futile in the present condition of affairs.

Gen. Connor also remains, and, considering the small force at his command, has accomplished wonders. By his bold and fearless vindication of the rights and interests of the Government, guided, at the same time, in all his acts by great discretion and moderation, he has compelled some show of respect for the federal authority.

Neither **Gen. Connor nor** Judge Waite had the slightest intention of arresting Brigham Young at the time alluded to in March, 1863. The astute leader of the Mormons had a spy listening to the conversation of those gentlemen, and the spy aforesaid heard some things, and thought he heard others. He reported to headquarters the supposed result of his discoveries, and it must be admitted that those who had been placed under this insulting espionage took no great pains to correct the impression which prevailed, and which so quickly and so thoroughly developed the disloyal sentiments which the people had imbibed under the infamous teachings of Brigham and his corrupt priests, apostles, and bishops.

Mark the language used by Mr. Calder. "On Monday last, a reliable person overheard," &c. Here the infamous system of espionage maintained over the federal officers by Young, stands plainly confessed. But the fact was well known, and he reaped no great benefit from it.

So thoroughly was he frightened, that, to save himself the ignominy and humiliation of a public and forcible arrest, he went privately to his friend, Chief Justice Kinney, and gave his bonds for his appearance at Kinney's court, to answer to any indictment that *might be* found against him for polygamy.

The grand jury, of course, found no indictment, and the incident is only worth mentioning as curiously illustrative of the extent to which he was operated on **by his** fears on that occasion.

A brief notice of the federal officers stationed and residing in Utah, while the writer was living in that Territory, will close the present chapter.

Hon. Stephen S. Harding, who was Governor from the spring of 1862 for about one year, is from Milan, Indiana. He is about fifty years of age; is a sound lawyer, and a man of extraordinary energy and decision of character. These traits are modified, in some degree, by considerable ambition, and great love of approbation. In his administration of Utah affairs, so far as he was governed by this feeling, he labored for the respect and approval of the great body of the American people, rather than of the masses by whom he was immediately surrounded.

That he possesses much personal courage is evidenced by many of his official acts, some of which he had reason to believe would subject him at once to personal danger. The presence of the military in the immediate neighborhood was sufficient to prevent any open outbreak; still there were many ways in which his personal safety might be jeopardized, without subjecting the perpetrators of the acts to punishment.

So well is this understood in Salt Lake, that it requires a high degree of moral courage to enable one to do any act offensive to " the powers that be " in the Holy City.

Every attempt was made to seduce him from the path of duty, not omitting the same appliances which had been brought to bear upon Steptoe and Dawson, but all in vain.

His family remained at Milan, except his son, Attila, who was with the Governor at Salt Lake, and acted as his private secretary.

Hon. James Duane Doty, the successor of Harding, and the present Governor of the Territory, was, for nearly two years previous to receiving the appointment of Governor, Superintendent of Indian Affairs for the Territory. He was appointed to succeed Harding in April or May, 1863.

James Duane Doty, Governor of Utah, was born at Salem, in the County of Washington and State of New York, on the 5th day of November, A. D. 1799, the last year of the last century.

He emigrated to Detroit, Michigan, where he was admitted to the Supreme Court, and settled in the practice of the law in the year 1818, and was one of the earliest emigrants to that State.

The next year he was elected Clerk of the Common Council of the City, and appointed Secretary to the Legislature, which was then composed of the Governor and Judges of the Supreme Court; and was also appointed a Notary Public, and soon afterwards Clerk of the Supreme Court of the Territory by the Judges of that court.

In 1820 he accompanied Governor Cass, as Secretary, in his expedition to the sources of the Mississippi, travelling a distance of over four thousand miles through the Indian Country in a birch-bark canoe, from the 20th of May to the 20th of November.

In this year he revised the laws of the Territory, which were published by the authority of the Legislature.

In 1821 he was admitted an attorney of the Supreme Court of the United States at Washington.

In 1823 the country north of lakes Huron and Michigan, and west of lakes Michigan and Superior, was made by Congress a judicial district, and he was appointed by James Monroe its Judge, with the title of "an additional Judge of the Territory of Michigan." He performed the duties of this office until the year 1832, — having married, and fixed his residence at Green Bay, then the largest settlement in the country north or west of Detroit.

In 1832 he was appointed by the Secretary of War a Commissioner to locate Military Roads from Fort Howard, at Green Bay, to Fort Crawford on Prairie du Chien, and to Fort Dearborn at the mouth of Chicago Creek, now the site of the city of Chicago, — between which points there were then scarcely twenty white inhabitants.

In 1834 and 1835 he served in the Legislative Council of Michigan, having been elected by the voters west of the Lake ; and introduced the measure of a State government, which was adopted by the Council.

He contended for the right of the people to form a government for themselves, under the provisions of the Ordinance of 1787.

By this measure a territorial government was obtained for Wisconsin, and a permanent separation from Michigan of the country west of Lake Michigan, which had been attached to that Territory in 1818, when Illinois was admitted into the Union. It had been sought in vain of Congress from the year 1825, — the application having been successfully opposed by the party averse to laying the foundation of new non-slaveholding States.

In 1837 he was elected Delegate to Congress from Wisconsin, and continued to serve in that office by reëlection until the year 1841, when he was appointed Governor and Superintendent of Indian Affairs in that Territory; and as Commissioner held treaties at Oeyoowurah, on Minnesota River, with the Dakotahs, and with the bands of that nation on the Mississippi River.

It was in 1837 that he laid out the town of Madison, and succeeded in making it the seat of government, — one of the most valuable services which he ever rendered that State. It is now considered one of the most beautiful sites for a town. When selected by him there was not a white settler within forty miles, and it was occupied by Winnebago Indians.

He was elected and served as a member of the Convention to form a State Constitution in 1846 for Wisconsin.

In 1849 he was elected in the Third District of Wisconsin a Representative in Congress, and was reëlected in 1851, — serving on several committees. It was during his first term as a member that he was declared an Abolitionist — now no longer a term of reproach — by Father Ritchie and the Southern leaders, because he declined to vote for a repeal of the duty on lead.

In 1861 he was appointed Superintendent of Indian Affairs in the Territory of Utah; and in 1862 was appointed a Commissioner to negotiate treaties with the Shoshonees, — which were held by him in 1863. These were the first treaties ever made by the United States with this nation of Indians.

In May, 1863, he was appointed Governor of the Territory of Utah. During his long public service he has had the acquaintance, and enjoyed the friendship, of most of the eminent men connected with the Government of our country. Of those who were on the stage when he entered public life, it is believed that but one is now living, — Gen. Cass, who was his generous patron in boyhood, and has been his friend during this long period of an eventful life.*

Hon. Thomas J. Drake, Associate Justice, is from Pontiac, Michigan, where he had resided from early manhood. He is now over sixty years of age. He has a thin, wiry frame, dark hair, and a nervous, bilious temperament.

His mind is vigorous and clear, and his virtue and integrity of the old Roman order. Of blameless life and manners, all the shafts of his accusers fall harmless at his feet.

The wrongs and iniquities he has witnessed, added to personal ill-treatment, has engendered an intense hatred of the despots who sit enthroned over the people of Utah, but he has the most kindly feelings toward the great body of the people.

Lacking all adequate power, he is obliged to sit quietly by, and see wrongs perpetrated, which he is utterly unable to redress.

Judge Waite, the Associate of Harding and Drake, was from the State of Illinois, where he had resided since the year 1840.

---

* Since writing the above we have to record the death of Gov. Doty, who departed this life at Salt Lake City, full of years and honors, and was accompanied to his temporary resting place by all the Federal Officers, and a large concourse of citizens, by whom he was respected and loved as a father.

At the time of his appointment, in February, 1862, he was thirty-eight years of age. He was then living near Chicago, in which city he had resided and practised law since 1853. He had previously practiced his profession at Rock Island, Illinois, where he was admitted in 1847. After leaving Utah, in 1863, he resumed his practice in Idaho, where he resided three years, during a portion of which time he was District Attorney of the Third Judicial District of Idaho, embracing Boise County. In the fall of 1866 he returned to Illinois, and again took his place with the Chicago Bar.

Hon. John Titus, who succeeded Kinney, and is the present Chief Justice of the Territory, is somewhat past fifty years of age, — a gentleman of much dignity and urbanity of manners. He is large and well formed, and has an active temperament. He still occupies the position of Chief Justice, which he has filled with integrity and ability.

Chief Justice Titus was appointed from the Philadelphia bar.

Dr. Frank Fuller was Secretary of the Territory about two years, and was succeeded by Mr. Reed, in the fall of 1863.

Dr. Fuller is from New Hampshire, and a dentist by profession and practice. He was attentive and obliging in his official intercourse with all parties. He is a polished gentleman also in social intercourse.

He was one of the few federal officers in Salt Lake at that time who was so fortunate as never seriously to offend Brigham Young. Doubtless his position brought him less in collision with that gentleman than was the case with other officers. If he saw any difficulties approaching, by a little shrewd management he carefully avoided them. If in thus steering between Scylla and Charybdis he did not always meet the approbation of his fellow-officers, he managed at least to avoid any open differences, and thus kept up the appearance of friendship with all.

He enjoyed for a long time the confidence and apparent respect of Brigham, to a greater degree, perhaps, than Kinney himself.

From Salt Lake he went to San Francisco, where he engaged in dealing in mining stocks.

From the time of Dawson's hasty departure in the fall of 1861, until Governor Harding's arrival in July, 1862, he acted as Governor of the Territory, and his administration gave general satisfaction to the Mormons.

Amos Reed, Esq., who succeeded Dr. Fuller as Secretary in 1863, and who now holds that position, came into the Territory with Governor Doty from Wisconsin.

During the winter of 1863–64, while Governor Doty was absent in Washington, Reed was the acting Governor, and as such evinced a high order of administrative talent. The affairs of the Territory were, during that time, conducted with much discretion and judgment, and so far as was in his power, the rights and interests of all classes were respected.

General P. Edward Connor was born in County Kerry, Ireland, and migrated to the United States, with his parents, at a very early period of life.

Having reached the age of manhood, he enlisted in the regular army of the United States, and served an honorable term, as private, for five years, on the frontier.

At the breaking out of the Mexican War, he raised a company of Texas Volunteers, and as captain, led them with distinguished success and heroism at the battle of Buena Vista. He was mentioned in official dispatches, with high encomiums for bravery. At this battle he was severely wounded, and received a pension from the Government. At the close of the war he settled upon the Pacific coast.

Captain Connor resided in Stockton, California, for ten years, prior to the rebellion, engaged in private business, wherein he attained a handsome competence.

He was married at Stockton, and now has two children living. During his residence in Stockton, Captain Connor took an active interest in military affairs, and commanded a uniform company.

At the breaking out of the present rebellion, he was tendered the appointment of Colonel of the Third Regiment of Infantry, California Volunteers. With the expectation that his regiment was to be sent East, he promptly raised and organized it.

The exigencies of the service, however, required his presence in Utah, and in the summer of 1862 he led the 3d Infantry, and part of the 2d Cavalry, Cal. Vol., across the Plains, in a most successful, though arduous march, and established his camp where it would command the City of the Saints.

Amid the snows and storms of the winter of 1862-63, he planned and prosecuted a successful campaign against hostile Indians, and on the 29th of January, 1863, fought the hard battle of Bear River, defeating and almost annihilating the savages, under the leadership of Bear Hunter and Lehigh.

For the brilliancy of this action, Col. Connor was promoted by the President to be Brigadier-General of United States Volunteers, which rank he now retains.

He is a man of strong common sense, excellent and quick judgment, invincible energy and determination, firmness almost amounting to obstinacy, and the strictest integrity.

His administration in Utah has been eminently successful. By Brigham Young he is at once hated and feared. He is but little past forty years of age.

CHAPTER VII.

BRIGHAM AS PRESIDENT OF THE CHURCH.

Organization of the Mormon Church. — Functions of the various Officers. The Two Priesthoods. — Mode of Treating Dissenters or "Apostates." — Divisions in the Church. — The Gladdenites. — History of the Morrisites. — The Josephites. — Return to the true Mormon Church.

IN his capacity as President of the Church of Jesus Christ of Latter Day Saints, Brigham Young possesses and wields despotic power over "this people," and rules them by his single will, in all their affairs, both spiritual and temporal.

This is owing, not to any peculiarity in the church organization. Any organization which should recognize him as the absolute head of the church, and dispense with every system of checks and balances, would answer the same purpose. Once admit the necessity of a spiritual head, and fail to require from him any responsibility, and all that remains is, to establish a grade of agents and mediums for the transmission of his will and wishes to the masses, and the system is complete.

Such a grade is fully established under the Mormon system.

First, — *The First Presidency.* This consists of three, chosen from those who hold the high-priesthood and apostleship, and its office is to preside over and direct the affairs of the whole church. It consists of a President and two Counsellors. The President is also Seer, Revelator, Translator, and Prophet. He rules in all spiritual and temporal affairs.

Secondly, — *The Apostles.* These are to build up, organize, and preside over churches, administer the ordinances, etc.

Thirdly, — *The Seventies.* The Quorums of the Seventies are to travel in all the world, preach the gospel, and administer its ordinances and blessings. There is, also, the Patriarch, whose duty is to bless the fatherless, to prophesy what shall befall them, etc.

Fourthly, — *High-Priests and Elders.* The High-Priest is to administer the ordinances, and preside over the *Stakes* of the church; that is, over the churches established abroad.

The Elders are to preach and to baptize; to ordain other Elders, also Priests, Teachers, and Deacons. All the foregoing officers are of the Melchisedec Priesthood.

Fifthly, — *The Aaronic Priesthood,* which includes the offices of Bishop, Priest, Teacher, and Deacon.

The *Bishop* presides over all the lesser offices of the Aaronic Priesthood, ministers in outward ordinances, conducts the temporal business of the church, and sits in judgment on transgressors.

The *Priest* is to preach, baptize, administer the sacrament of the Lord's Supper, and visit and exhort the saints.

The *Teacher* is to watch over and strengthen the church, etc.

The *Deacon* is to assist the Teacher.

There is also a High Council, consisting of Twelve High-Priests, with a President. The office of the Council is to settle all important difficulties.

The Priesthood comes direct from Heaven, and was lost to man, until the keys of both orders of the Priesthood were given to Joseph Smith, by an angel from Heaven, in 1829. After the death of Smith, they came into the hands of Brigham Young.

From this *resumé* of the church organization, it will be seen that it is sufficient for the purpose. All these officers are but mediums for the transmission of the will of the President. Nor is it confined to spiritual affairs. Under the form of a church organization, this system absorbs not only the religious, but all the civil and political liberty of the individual member. The High Council forms an apparent check on the power of the President; but when it is considered that this body is composed of persons nearest the President, and under his immediate influence and control, in other relations in the same organization, — as High-Priests, etc., — it will be seen that the check is only nominal, and forms no real protection to the rights of the people.

The orders of the Priesthood, to which these officers are respectively attached, are thus distinguished: —

The Melchisedec Priesthood hold the right of Presidency, receive revelations from Heaven, for the guidance of the church, and hold the keys of all its spiritual blessings.

The Aaronic Priesthood hold the keys of the ministering of angels, and have the right to administer in outward ordinances. This Priesthood must be filled by lineal descendants of Aaron.

It will be seen that the mission of all the officers of the Melchisedec Priesthood — the Apostles, High-Priests, Seventies, and Elders — is to propagate the gospel, and make converts; while the government of the church and of the people is committed to the Aaronic Priesthood.

Of these the chief is the Bishop, who is accordingly the civil and religious magistrate of the ward in which he resides.

There are other civil magistrates, whose duties are bu little more than nominal, except in Salt Lake City, where the occasional large influx of "gentiles" who will not submit to this spiritual government, renders necessary an approximation to the forms of civil proceedings to which they have been accustomed.

The "saints" themselves are not expected to go before other than the ecclesiastical magistrates. When brought unwillingly before a civil magistrate, the same being a Mormon, the case receives a favorable consideration.

Rare exceptions may be cited where, from motives of policy, this rule is relaxed or departed from. For instance, in the winter of 1863-64, Jason Luce, a Mormon, was tried, convicted, and shot, for the murder of a gentile in Salt Lake City. But the murder was of the most cruel and unprovoked character, the crime was perpetrated on the street, and the evidence was open and abundant. Much indignation existed among the miners, many of whom were congregated in Salt Lake City at the time.

If this had not been the first instance in the history of Utah of the execution of a Mormon, under judgment of a Mormon court, for the murder of a gentile, it might be taken as evidence of an intention to do justice to all. As it is, it should be marked to their credit; and it is only to be hoped that subsequent events may not prove it to have been an act of policy merely.

The machinery of the Mormon Church, through which the people are governed in all their affairs, civil as well as religious, is well described in the following extract from the Salt Lake Correspondence of the "Chicago Tribune" of May, 1863:—

"The machinery of the church consists of Brigham, who is greatly pleased and flattered by the blasphemous title of the 'Lord's Anointed,' the Second and Third Presidents, College of Twelve Apostles, Patriarchs, Quorums of Seventies, Counsellors, Presidents of 'Stakes,' Bishops, Elders, and Teachers; and last but not least, the Danites, or 'Destroying Angels,' who are scattered throughout the Territory, and who superintend the temporal and spiritual affairs of the people in every city, village, 'stake,' and hamlet in the same.

"These various organizations and persons, from the Second President to the red-haired Danite, who is simply the employed assassin of the Great Head, are the shafts, driving-wheel, cog and spur-wheels, belts and pulleys of the great machine called the Church, and as such are made to perform their various functions with a precision and fitness of things that is wonderful indeed.

. . . "Brigham, like a skilful engineer, stands on the platform of his locomotive, with hand placed upon the lever, **sheltered in the caboose, with peep-holes in front, on the right and on the left, and the crook of** whose finger causes the whole train to move forward **or** back, **or to** switch off on the track of some new dogma, to which **he lures on the** unsuspecting passengers and precious freight, with the catchpenny whistle of 'Revelation!' which **is** most persistently sounded when **he hears the** restive murmurings of those who may catch but **a premonitory** glimpse **of** the awful precipice to which he is **hurrying them on, as to a** terrible **and** eternal destruction."

The motive-power **is** religious **delusion, which is constantly** applied by Brigham, who **thus drives along the** whole combination with fearful power.

"And in that train may be **found** all that makes up the hopes and fears, the joys and sorrows, the love and hatred, of that 'moral and physical phenomenon,' the Mormon Church, — not only here, but scattered throughout all Europe, and the 'Isles of the Seas,' who have ventured their all — their lives and fortunes, their bodies and souls — on the solution of that dearest of all problems to their minds, the ultimate **triumph** of the 'Church of Jesus Christ of Latter Day Saints' **(as it is blasphemously** called) **over all governments, powers, and principalities of earth!"**

In reference to the organization of the church, and the functions of the respective priesthoods, **the** following is Brigham's own explanation of the whole matter. In this exhibit will be seen how little importance he attaches to the High Council.

Speaking of laying the corner-stones of the Temple, **he** says: —

"I am not a visionary man, **neither am I given much to prophesying.** When I want any of that done **I call on Brother Heber,**— he is my prophet; he loves to prophesy, and **I** love to hear him.

"Now, who do we **set,** in **the** first place, to lay the chief, **the** South-East corner-stone? We begin with the First Presidency, and the Apostleship. Who comes next in the church? The Bishop is the next standing authority in the Kingdom of God; therefore we set the Bishop at the second corner-stone **of the** building. The Melchisedec Priesthood, with the altar, fixtures, and furniture, belonging thereto, is situated on the East, and the Aaronic Priesthood belongs on the West; consequently the Presiding Bishop laid the second corner-stone.

"The High-Priests' Quorum, do they come next in order? No, not any more than the Elders, nor the Elders any more than the High Council, nor the High Council any more than the Teachers, Deacons, or Priests. The High-Priests' Quorum is a standing quorum, abiding at home. So is the Elders' Quorum. But the place of the Bishop is in the temporal affairs of the church. So, then, what shall we say? Why, out of due respect to the High-Priesthood, which is nothing more than right and reasonable, we say to the High-Priests, 'Lay the third corner-stone.'

"We started at the South-East corner, with the Apostleship; then the lesser, Aaronic Priesthood, laid the second stone; we bring them in our ranks to the third stone, which the High-Priests and Elders laid; we take them under our wing to the North-East corner, which the Twelve and Seventies laid, and then again join the Apostleship. It circumscribes every other priesthood, for it is the Priesthood of Melchisedec, which is after the order of the Son of God." *

But all this arrangement and subordination does not suffice to prevent disaffection in the church. This will arise, and results in differences, schisms, and divisions.

Not to notice smaller matters of difference, three systematic and organized attempts have been made by large bodies of Mormons, since their arrival in Utah, to throw off their allegiance to Brigham Young. They have all been met and treated by him with a fierce bitterness, indicating how thoroughly he is alarmed by such movements.

The third of these is now in progress, and promises to be successful.

The first of the "apostasies," as they are called by the Mormons, was headed by Gladden Bishop, in 1852-53, and his followers were called "Gladdenites."

Some idea of the manner in which they were met by

* April 6, 1863. *Journ. of Dis.*, Vol. I. p. 135.

Brigham, and of his mode of dealing with apostates generally, may be gathered from the following extracts from a sermon preached by him in March, 1853: —

"I will ask, What has produced your persecutions and sorrow? What has been the starting-point of all your afflictions? They began with apostates in your midst; those disaffected spirits caused others to come in, worse than they, who would run out and bring in all the devils they possibly could. That has been the starting-point and grand cause of all our difficulties, every time we were driven. I am coming to this place, — I am coming nearer home. . . . Do we see apostates among us now? We do.

"When a man comes right out like an independent devil, and says, 'Damn Mormonism and all the Mormons,' and is off with himself to California, I say he is a gentleman by the side of a nasty, sneaking apostate, who is opposed to nothing but Christianity. I say to the former, 'Go in peace, sir, and prosper if you can.' But we have a set of spirits here, worse than such a character. When I went from meeting last Sabbath, my ears were saluted with an apostate, crying in the streets here. I want to know if any one of you who has got the spirit of Mormonism in you, the spirit that Joseph and Hyrum had, or that we have here, would say, 'Let us hear both sides of the question. Let us listen and prove all things.' What do you want to prove? Do you want to prove that an old apostate, who has been cut off from the church thirteen times for lying, is anything worthy of notice? I heard that a certain picture-maker in this city, when the boys would have moved away the wagon in which this apostate was standing, became violent with them, saying, 'Let this man alone; these are saints that you are persecuting.' [Sneeringly.]

"We want such men to go to California, or anywhere they choose. I say to those persons, 'You must not court persecution here, lest you get so much of it you will not know what to do with it. Do NOT court persecution.' We have known Gladden Bishop for more than twenty years, and know him to be a poor, dirty curse. Here is sister Vilate Kimball, brother Heber's wife, has borne more from that man than any other woman on earth could bear; but she won't bear it again. I say again, you Gladdenites, do not court persecution, or you will get more than you want, and it will come quicker than you want it.

"I say to you, Bishops, do not allow them to preach in your wards. Who broke the roads to these valleys? Did this little nasty Smith, and his wife? No. They stayed in St. Louis while we did it, peddling ribbons, and kissing the gentiles. I know what they have done here,—they have asked exorbitant prices for their nasty, stinking ribbons. [Voices, 'That's true.'] We broke the roads to this country.

"Now, you Gladdenites, keep your tongues still, lest sudden destruction come upon you. I say, rather than that apostates should flourish here, I will unsheathe my bowie-knife, and conquer or die. [Great commotion in the congregation, and a simultaneous burst of feeling, assenting to the declaration.] Now, you nasty apostates, clear out, or 'judgment will be laid to the line, and righteousness to the plummet.' [Voices generally, ' Go it, go it.'] If you say it is all right, raise your hands. [All hands up.] Let us call upon the Lord to assist us in this and every other good work." *

In the same discourse he commanded the Bishops to "kick these men out of their wards," and warned the apostates themselves that "they were not playing with shadows," but "it was the voice and the hand of the Almighty they were trying to play with, and they would find themselves mistaken if they thought to the contrary."

In accordance with this bloody teaching, many unfortunate apostates who were unwilling or unable to leave the country, "bit the dust." They felt the literal edge of the bowie-knife thus from the pulpit unsheathed for their destruction. Many of the murders committed during the succeeding six or seven years were fully authorized by these instructions; and yet Brigham, unable to deny that they had been committed, has openly boasted that his enemies have been unable to trace any of them to him, and fasten them upon him.

He unsheathes the bowie-knife, and issues a general mandate; but when the murder of some individual dissenter is brought to his door, he turns away and says, "Thou canst not say, I did it."

* March 27, 1853. *Jour. of Dis.*, Vol. I : 82.

The second organized opposition to Young was made by Joseph Morris and his followers.

The rise and progress and subsequent history of the people called "Morrisites," is as follows:—

On the 19th of November, 1860, a man dressed in ordinary working-clothes wended his way on foot from Slatersville, a settlement in Weber County, north of Salt Lake, to the Holy City. This was Joseph Morris, and the object of his visit was to deliver to Brigham Young two letters which he had written, under the supposed influence of the Spirit.

It seems that for some reason the life of Morris had been threatened, and having been driven from the place where he had been living, he was now going to appeal to the President in person for protection. Morris had received, previous to this time, many revelations, some of which looked to a purification of the church,—all of which he had communicated to Brigham and the Apostles.

On his way to Salt Lake he met John Cook, brother of Richard Cook, at that time a Mormon Bishop, presiding at South Weber. To him Morris communicated his views and projects, and made so favorable an impression that both the Cooks soon afterward espoused his cause, and became his zealous supporters.

Morris delivered his letters to the President at his residence, but received no reply.

He then proceeded to the house of Mr. Cook, on the Weber River, about thirty miles northward from the city.

Not only the Cooks, but a number of their neighbors, now began to entertain favorable opinions of the claim of their new acquaintance to inspiration.

Others who conceived that the divine right of Brigham was being endangered or infringed upon, determined to put Morris to death, or drive him from their midst. But Bishop Cook stood in the way.

In this emergency President Young was appealed to, who sent two high ecclesiastics, Messrs. John Taylor and Willford Woodruff, both Apostles, to investigate the matter. They appointed a general meeting at South Weber, and invited the Bishops of the surrounding settlements, with as many of their people as possibly could, to attend.

The meeting convened on the 11th of February, 1861, and the delegates commenced their court of inquiry by demanding whether there was a man in the ward who professed to be a prophet? And whether there were any individuals who entertained him, or professed faith in his claims?

To the astonishment and consternation of the Mormons, seventeen of the believers, with Bishop Cook at their head, arose and declared that they would enjoy and defend the right of conscience, by adhering to their new faith, though it should bring upon them the most bitter persecution, and the loss of their lives. An old man named Watts arose, and in an inflammatory speech, recommended that the adherents of the new Prophet should be "cut off under the chin," and laid away in the brush; at the same time accompanying his words with a motion of the hand, drawing it across his throat. This, he said, was what ought to be done, according to his understanding of the laws of the church.

After some further discussion, in which Watts was boldly rebuked by Cook for the utterance of such sentiments, the question was put to the parties on trial, whether they believed that Brigham Young was a Prophet, Seer, and Revelator. They all answered in the negative. Mr. Taylor testified that he knew Brigham to be such, and said those who believed to the contrary must be excommunicated from the church. They were then subjected to the process of excommunication.

It will be noticed that the right of Brigham to preside over the church as its temporal head, was not questioned by Morris or his followers.

From this time the followers of Morris increased in numbers with wonderful rapidity.

On the 6th of April, 1861, five persons were baptized into

the new church in the Weber River. On the same day of the same month, thirty-one years previous, the Mormon Church had been instituted by the baptism of six persons. Encouraged by this augury, a church was organized, and the work commenced in earnest. Converts flocked to them from all parts of the Territory.

In three months the new church numbered about three hundred persons. Its highest number did not exceed five hundred.

In the mean time difficulties arose between them and the surrounding Mormons. The Morrisites refused to train as militia. Heavy fines were imposed in consequence, and much property sold on execution for their payment.

These fines and exactions were increased until the Morrisites refused longer to submit to them. A number of fines of $60 each had been imposed. When the sheriff appeared and proposed to arrest those who would not or could not pay, he was resisted. Further proceedings were then suspended for the present.

In the spring of 1862 a team, consisting of two yoke of cattle, which had been sent to mill from the Morrisite settlement, was, together with a load of flour, seized and retained by one William Jones, who threatened in like manner to retain all that should be sent until some difficulties between him and them should be settled to his satisfaction. The Morrisites, standing in immediate need of the flour, sent a *posse* of men, and took not only the flour, but Jones and two associates prisoners.

Application was now made to Chief Justice Kinney, who immediately issued writs for the arrest of the leading Morrisites, and writs of *habeas corpus* for the Mormons held in custody.

These writs being disregarded, a *posse* of several hundred men, headed by Robert T. Burton, sheriff of Salt Lake County, well armed and equipped, and having several pieces of cannon, were sent to execute the writs, and enforce obedience. This force was augmented on the way by volunteers, and additional arms, until they approached the settlement of the Morrisites, with a force of about a thousand well-armed men, and five pieces of artillery.

Early on the morning of the 13th of June, some of the *posse* appeared on the heights above South Weber settlement, and took possession of the Morrisites' cow-herd, killing such as they desired for beef. During the morning, Sheriff Burton sent a proclamation to the leaders within the Morrisite "fort," — for such they had constructed, — calling upon them to come out and deliver themselves up, according to the requirements of the writs in his hands, and warning them of the consequences, if they refused.

This not being responded to, about an hour later the *posse*, most of whom had been hitherto out of sight, commenced to defile over the bluffs, and to occupy a prominent position commanding the camp.

Morris now called a meeting of those within the fort. Scarcely had they assembled, when a cannon-ball came into the congregation, killed two women, and wounded a girl. From this time cannonading and musketry fire was continued with but little intermission.

The camp consisted of a few houses built of willows, like basket-work, and plastered, and of tents, and covered wagons. Still the fight was kept up by these deluded people for three days, during all which time, fighting with the energy of desperation, they held this immense force at bay. On the evening of the third day, a white flag was raised, and the whole camp surrendered. The Morrisites stacked their arms, under guard of a detail from the *posse*, who had by this time entered the fort.

Amidst much confusion, the men and women were separated, and large numbers of the men were placed under arrest. Morris, and a leader by the name of Banks were shot in cold blood; also two of the women. All these were killed after the Morrisites were unarmed, and their arms in the possession of the sheriff. The *posse* had two men killed. The Morrisites ten in all.

After the Morrisites had been taken prisoners, their houses were searched and plundered, and property, consisting of watches, jewelry, clothing, &c., taken, to the amount of many hundreds of dollars.

The prisoners were taken to Salt Lake City, and placed under bonds by Judge Kinney for their appearance at his court. They were afterwards tried, and large numbers of them were fined and imprisoned. All of those imprisoned were afterward pardoned and released by Governor Harding.

Thus ended "the Morrisite War." The Morrisites were now "scattered and peeled," and so remained until May, 1863. At that time Gen. Connor established a military post at Soda Springs, a beautiful place at the northern bend of Bear River, about 175 miles north of Salt Lake City. Before starting with his expedition, Gen. Connor gave notice that all persons wishing to go up and form a settlement at that point, would be furnished by him with transportation. The result was, that about eighty families, consisting of over two hundred persons, nearly all Morrisites, availed themselves of this offer, — removed, with their goods and household gods, and established themselves at Soda Springs.

This settlement continues to exist and flourish, and may now be looked upon, it is to be hoped, as a permanent point where the weary emigrant may pause and rest on his long journey over the Plains, and be free from the whims, exactions, and dangers of Mormonism. The place is now in Idaho Territory, and returned eighty-one votes at the territorial election of 1864.

Although the court and juries were fast to bring to punishment those who had resisted the writs, yet Burton, the leader of the *posse*, who shot four persons after they had surrendered, was not even indicted by a Mormon grand jury. The evidence was laid before them, but without avail.

The following affidavit of a man of much respectability, now residing at Soda Springs, shows what was the conduct of Burton on the occasion alluded to: —

"United States of America, } ss.
Territory of Utah.

"Alexander Dow, of said Territory, being duly sworn, says:

"In the spring of 1861, I joined the Morrisites, and was present when Joseph Morris was killed. The Morrisites had surrendered, a white flag was flying, and the arms were all grounded and guarded by a large number of the *posse*.

"Robert T. Burton and Judson L. Stoddard rode in amongst the Morrisites. Burton was much excited. He said, 'Where is the man? I don't know him.' Stoddard replied, 'That's him,' pointing to Morris. Burton rode his horse upon Morris, and commanded him to give himself up in the name of the Lord. Morris replied, 'No, never, never.' Morris said he wanted to speak to the people. Burton said, 'Be d—d quick about it.' Morris said, 'Brethren, I've taught you true principles,'—he had scarcely got the words out of his mouth before Burton fired his revolver. The ball passed in his neck or shoulder. Burton exclaimed, 'There's your Prophet.' He fired again, saying, 'What do you think of your Prophet now?'

"Burton then turned suddenly and shot Banks, who was standing five or six paces distant. Banks fell. Mrs. Bowman, wife of James Bowman, came running up, crying, 'Oh! you blood-thirsty wretch.' Burton said, 'No one shall tell me that and live,' and shot her dead. A Danish woman then came running up to Morris, crying, and Burton shot her dead also. Burton could easily have taken Morris and Banks prisoners, if he had tried. I was standing but a few feet from Burton all this time. And further saith not.

"Alexander Dow.

"Subscribed and sworn to before me, this 18th day of April, A. D. 1863.

"Charles B. Waite,
"*Associate Just., U. T.*"

This Burton is the same man who is now the Collector of Internal Revenue for Utah Territory!

The next movement, and one which promises seriously to

interfere with the schemes of Brigham Young, is under the auspices of the Mormon Church East, or the "Josephites," as they are called, in contradistinction to the "Brighamites."

Joseph Smith, the son of the Prophet, resides at Nauvoo, in Illinois, near where his father was put to death. He claims to be the head of the true Mormon Church, and of course repudiates Young for the same position. He is opposed to polygamy, is loyal to the Government and laws of the United States, and is said to be a good and worthy citizen.

For several years there have been indications of a "breaking up" among the followers of the Pretender, Brigham, and a rallying around the standard of the legitimate House of Joseph. In the States, those who have gone back to their first love are to be numbered by thousands.

In Utah the progress of disintegration, and of secession from the church as there organized, is slower, and accompanied by more danger.

But in July, 1863, the "fulness of time" having come, the movement was commenced in earnest, and a system of proselyting inaugurated, which has already drawn hundreds of deluded people back to their duty to themselves and their country, and which even now threatens the power of Brigham so strongly that it seems almost tottering to its fall.

During the latter part of the month mentioned, E. C. Briggs and Alexander McCord, two missionaries, sent by the Church East, for that purpose, arrived in Salt Lake, and announced themselves as harbingers of a better gospel,—as messengers of the true Church of Christ on earth. Taking their lives in their hands, they had crossed the Plains alone, and the Lord had protected and sustained them.

It may be supposed that their arrival caused considerable excitement at Salt Lake City.

Briggs called on Young and acquainted him with the nature of his "mission." The Prophet became very angry; refused him the use of the Tabernacle, or any other building

Joseph Smith

in the city; forbade him preaching to the people, and said if he remained in the city, he (Young) would not be responsible for his personal safety. Briggs declined to avail himself of this polite hint to leave; and notwithstanding these thunders from the Vatican, he went boldly to work, and "daily ceased not to teach and preach Jesus Christ."

He talked with the people, visited them at their houses, prayed with them, and sang with them.

The effect was electrical. Singly, by dozens, and by scores, the people began to fall off from the great apostasy, and to return to the mother-church. Persecution commenced from the first day of his labors. He and McCord were forbidden all the houses of the city, by an order of Brigham which none dared to disobey. One house, that of a gentile, was still open to them, and there they held their meetings, which were well attended.

Before spring their numbers had increased to over three hundred. About half of that number returned across the Plains in the spring of 1864, and so strong was the excitement, and so bitter the persecution and enmity of the "saints" toward this comparatively handful of seceders from Brigham's authority and dominions, that Gen. Connor deemed it necessary and advisable to send a strong escort with them as far as Green River, about 145 miles.

Besides this number who departed for the region of the rising sun, large numbers of the westward-bound emigration were stopped, and having their eyes opened by missionaries of the same stamp, were induced to withhold their steps, at least until another season.

The Josephites in Salt Lake, although the subjects of bitter and unrelenting persecution from the Mormons, found favor and protection from Gen. Connor and the military under his command.

They will doubtless continue to flourish and increase, and it is possible that in this way Utah may be brought to loyalty and good citizenship, without bloodshed or commotion. It is but a possibility, however, as Brigham will not see himself thus undermined without desperate efforts to prevent it.

In Europe whole churches have already changed, or "gone over," from the apostasy of Brigham to the old church, with Joseph at its head.

Briggs is President of the Twelve Apostles, and is admirably fitted for the work before him. He is a man of great energy and heroism, and takes hold of his mighty task as though it were but the work of a summer day. Nowhere can be found a better exemplification of the self-sacrifice and sublime heroism of the Christians of the Middle Ages.

The following are the Articles of Faith of the Church of Jesus Christ of Latter Day Saints, under the presidency of Joseph Smith, son of Joseph the Martyr:—

"We believe in God, the Eternal Father, and his Son Jesus Christ, and in the Holy Ghost.

"We believe that men will be punished for their own sins, and not for Adam's transgressions.

"We believe that through the atonement of Christ, all mankind may be saved by obedience to the laws and ordinances of the gospel.

"We believe that these ordinances are: 1st. Faith in the Lord Jesus Christ; 2d. Repentance; 3d. Baptism by immersion for the remission of sins; 4th. Laying on of hands for the gift of the Holy Spirit; 5th. The Lord's Supper.

"We believe that men must be called of God, by inspiration, and by laying on of hands by those who are duly commissioned to preach the gospel, and administer in the ordinances thereof.

"We believe in the same organization that existed in the primitive church, viz.: Apostles, Prophets, Pastors, Teachers, Evangelists, &c.

"We believe in the powers and gifts of the everlasting gospel, viz., the gift of faith, discoursing of spirits, prophecy, revelation, visions, healing, tongues and the intrepretation of tongues, wisdom, charity, brotherly love, &c.

"We believe the word of God recorded in the Bible; we also believe the word of God recorded in the Book of Mormon, and in all other good books.

"We believe all that God has revealed, all that he does now reveal, and we believe that he will yet reveal many more great and important things, pertaining to the kingdom of God and Messiah's second coming.

"We believe in the literal gathering of Israel, and in the restoration of the ten tribes; that Zion will be established upon the Western Continent; that Christ will reign personally upon the earth a thousand years; and that the earth will be renewed, and receive its paradisaical glory.

"We believe in the literal resurrection of the body; that the dead in Christ will rise first, and that the rest of the dead do not live again until the thousand years are expired.

"We believe in being subject to kings, queens, presidents, rulers, and magistrates; *in obeying, honoring, and sustaining the law.*

"We believe in being virtuous, chaste, temperate, benevolent, and in doing good to all men.

"*We believe that the church in Utah, under the presidency of Brigham Young, have apostatized from the true order of the gospel.*

"*We believe that the doctrines of polygamy, human sacrifice, or killing men to save them, Adam being God, Utah being Zion, or the gathering place for the saints, are doctrines of devils,* instituted by wicked men, for the accomplishment of their own lustful desires, and with a view to their personal aggrandizement.

"*We believe in being true and loyal to the Government of the United States,* and have no sympathy or fellowship for the treasonable practices or wicked abominations indorsed by Brigham Young and his followers."

CHAPTER VIII.

BRIGHAM AS TRUSTEE IN TRUST FOR THE CHURCH.

Nature of the Trusteeship. — The Tithing System. — Brigham's Private Speculations. — The Emigration Fund. — The Hand-Cart Company.

> — "He was a man
> Who stole the livery of the Court of Heaven
> To serve the Devil in; in virtue's guise
> Devoured the widow's house and orphan's bread;
> In holy phrase, transacted villanies
> That common sinners durst not meddle with."

As Trustee in Trust for the Church, Brigham Young is in his element. Here his genius shines preëminent, giving him the character, at home and abroad, of a good, as he certainly is a successful, financier.

But here, upon the outset, let no one be misled by the words employed to designate the capacity in which he handles and manages the funds of the church. It is called a "*trust*," because he is supposed to use the money for the benefit of the church.

But this *Trust* is very general and indefinite in its character. It has no prescribed duties or conditions. It has no guards or limits. *It has no prescribed nor acknowledged mode of accountability.*

Many years ago, attempts were made at the General Conferences, to exhibit a balance-sheet of receipts and disbursements. These were confused and unsatisfactory; and lest they should be too closely examined, they have of late years been entirely abandoned, — the increasing faith of the saints in their leader rendering it entirely unnecessary that any explanation should be made of the disposal of their funds.

Again: a corps of clerks are employed in the tithing-office, and are paid out of the public tithing-fund salaries ranging from $1000 upwards. They are supposed to keep a complete system of accounts, showing all the receipts from this net-work of fiscal veins, and all the disbursements through the various arteries of the religious body. But beyond the receipt and deposit of moneys, and the keeping of the tithing account with individual members of the church, the duties of these clerks are merely nominal. Each has another part to perform. The reader will smile to be informed that these clerks are really the principal stock actors in the Salt Lake Theatre. Having but little office business, their time is thus turned to a good account, reading novelettes and newspapers, a plentiful supply of which may be found in their several offices. The theatre is the private property of Brigham, and the proceeds go into his own pocket, disconnected with any real or imaginary embarrassment arising from the relation of Trustee. Hence it will be seen to be good "financiering" for the tithing-clerks, under pay of "the church," to perform for the benefit of "Brother Brigham." Should they fail to comply with his wishes, he has only, as "Trustee in Trust," to dispense with their services. This may be mentioned as a notable instance of the "shrewd financiering" of Brigham Young.

These clerks simply keep the accounts with individuals, and receive and deposit the money and property paid in to the tithing-fund. They also keep the accounts of laborers on the temple and other public works.

It is needless to say they are entirely under the control of Brigham. According to the Mormon creed, the temporal affairs of the kingdom should be entirely directed and controlled by the Aaronic Priesthood. The presiding Bishops of this priesthood are agents to perform the will of the head of the order, who is the President himself.

To keep the public mind quiet and satisfied, it is stated from the pulpit that the accounts of Brigham Young, as an individual, and those which he keeps as trustee for the church, are entirely separate and distinct, and that not a dollar of church money goes to the private use of the President or his family, without being duly charged and accounted for. But these public declarations are all the assurance the people have that such is the fact. The system of book-keeping by double entry is entirely ignored as an invention of the gentiles; and if an investigation of the accounts should be instituted, it would be conducted under great disadvantages, and could have no certainty in its results.

Notwithstanding these protestations so frequently made from the pulpit, there is a growing conviction among the masses that the increasing evidences of the individual wealth of Brigham, notwithstanding his immense outlays, can only be accounted for in one way, — by the gradual absorption and assimilation of the funds of the church with his own private moneys. Indeed he does not hesitate to affirm, boldly, that if he wishes to build a grist or a saw-mill, or to engage in any other enterprise, he borrows from the tithing or other public funds the necessary means, paying it back by instalments when convenient, or turning in some other property that he has no immediate use for. In these private arrangements and trades, between himself *in propria persona* and himself in his fiduciary capacity, it is not to be supposed that he would make them to his own disadvantage, or that he would voluntarily assume losses which he could just as well throw upon the church at large. With this scape-goat upon which to throw his unfortunate speculations, and with a large revenue derived from legislative gifts, in the shape of timber canyons, herding-grounds, ferries, and other franchises, it is not strange that his worldly store should be constantly and largely augmented. He boasts that he takes no thought how to make money or get rich, and yet riches constantly flow to him. He has said, he can "drop dollar for dollar with any monarch in Europe." He looks after the Lord's interests, and the Lord looks after his interests!

The following are some of the principal Legislative Acts in favor of Brigham Young, passed by the Legislative Assembly of Utah:—

An Act in relation to City Creek Canyon, approved December 9, 1850. This gave Young the sole control of City Creek and Canyon, for which he was required to pay into the treasury the sum of $500. Under this grant Brigham exacts from those getting wood in the canyon, every third load; and as this is the only wood within fifteen miles of the city, this alone is the source of an immense revenue. Besides, he has built upon City Creek two or three mills,— he having the exclusive use of the water. It is estimated that Young's income from this canyon alone is $10,000 per annum.

An Act passed February 5th, 1852, granting to Brigham Young the waters from the channel of Mill Creek.

January 20, 1854. An Act providing that all property left by any deceased or absconding person, to which there is no claimant, shall pass into the Perpetual Emigration Fund. Brigham is President of this Society, and custodian of the fund. This Act adds largely to the income of the Trustee President.

January 19, 1855. An Act appropriating to Brigham Young $2500 for building an Academy in Salt Lake City. The Academy was never built.

December 18, 1855. An Act granting to Brigham Young exclusive right of herd-ground known as Kansas Prairie.

Same date. An Act granting to Brigham Young the whole of Cache Valley for a herd-ground. This valley is fifty miles long, and more than ten miles in width, and the richest and most productive valley in the Territory.

December 27, 1855. An Act granting to Brigham Young all of Rush Valley, except the United States Reserve, for a herd-ground. Another extensive tract of country.

January 4, 1856. An Act granting to Brigham Young exclusive right to establish a ferry over Bear River.

January 5, 1856. **An Act** granting to Brigham Young a ranch and herd-ground in Lone Rock Valley.

January 12, 1856. An Act granting to Brigham Young exclusive right to control the road and coal-beds in Coal Canyon, San Pete County.

Same *date. An Act making an appropriation to Brigham Young of* $1000 *from the Territorial Treasury, to enable him to pay for a share in the Deseret Iron Company.*

January 22, 1864. **An Act** authorizing Brigham **Young** to establish a toll on the **Tooele Road.**

After reading all these donations and munificent franchises, one can appreciate the point of the joke perpetrated by Brigham, when he says "he takes no thought how to get rich, and yet riches constantly flow to him."

The Tithing System.

The object of tithing, as stated in the "Book of Doctrines and Covenants," is to exalt the poor, and humble the rich,— taking from where it is not wanted the surplus property of the church, and placing it where it is needed. The law of tithing, as originally instituted, calls for one tenth of the annual increase and gains, after providing for the wants of the family. When the poor were amply supplied, the residue was to be used for purchasing inheritances for the saints, building houses for public worship, etc.

Of late years, however, tithing assumes an entirely different form, and is much more comprehensive in its scope and exacting in its demands. The "saints" in Utah, Europe, and throughout the world, are required to pay one tenth of their income, without any reference to their ability to meet the demand. Thus the laboring man in Utah, who receives but one dollar and fifty cents per day,— not enough to support his family comfortably,— is assessed tithing to the amount of about forty-five dollars per annum.

But this is not all. Every emigrant and new-comer is expected to pay one tenth of his entire possessions. Upon this point much strictness prevails. On the arrival of the faithful in Zion, they are visited by a bishop and clerk, and inventories of all their property taken. One tenth of everything must then be sent to the tithing-office, not even excepting household furniture, cooking utensils, or clothing: Should the party be in possession of a little money, he is urged to pay the tithing all in cash.

A very good idea of the extent to which this tithing system is carried may be formed from the following tithing-song, sung at a meeting of one of the quorums, and published in the " Deseret News," No. 6, Vol. V.: —

"TITHING-SONG.

[*Air.* The King of the Cannibal Islands.]

"Come, Mormons all, attention pay,
Whilst I attempt to sing my say;
I've chosen for my text to-day,
'Come forward, and pay up your tithing.'
These may not be the very words,
Which ancient Holy Writ records;
But Malachi, I think, affords
A verse which with the sense accords.
It seems that he had cause to scold
The saints, or Israelites of old;
In fact, they needed to be told,
'Come forward, and pay up your tithing.'

Chorus.

"Then if to prosper you desire,
And wish to keep out of the fire,
Nay, if you to be saints aspire,
Come forward, and pay up your tithing.

"Just as it was in the olden times,
With ancient saints in other climes,
The call is *now*, 'Bring out your dimes,' —
'Come forward, and pay up your tithing.'

Our Prophet says, 'When Elders preach,
The law of tithing they should teach;
Pay up themselves, and then beseech
All those who come within their reach.'
This makes me now entreat of you
To follow counsel; right pursue;
And whilst all evil you eschew,
'Come forward, and pay up your tithing.'

Chorus.

"Then if to prosper, etc.

"Now, male and female, rich and poor,
Who wish to keep your standing sure,
That you salvation may secure,
'Come forward, and pay up your tithing.'
A tenth, that is, and nothing less,
Of all you do or may possess,
In flocks and herds, and their increase,
With pigs and poultry, ducks and geese:
A tenth, indeed, of all your toil,
Likewise the produce of the soil;
And if you've any wine or oil,
'Come forward, and pay up your tithing.'

Chorus.

"Then if to prosper, etc.

"HENRY MAIBEN.

"GREAT S. L. CITY, 1855."

Not only the extent of this exaction, but the penalty for non-payment, is fully set forth in this song, to wit, exclusion from the church, and deprivation of all spiritual blessings. What greater penalty can be placed before a true Mormon?

The administration of the law of tithing has been excessively cruel in Europe. Many of the saints in England, who, from infirmity, age, or incapacity to labor, have been supported by the parish, receiving one, two, or three shillings per week, have been anathematized and cut off from the church, because they could not pay their tithing out of their parish allowance, and support life from the remainder!

From the European Mission alone, over $500,000 of British gold has found its way into the pockets of Brigham Young. No account has ever been made of this vast amount, nor is there any public work or project requiring expenditure of church-money, which has not been more than provided for by the home tithing-fund.

The poor in Utah suffer severely from this exaction. You may see families barefooted, women and children nearly naked, destitute of even the necessaries of life, the husband making every effort to meet the day of tithing, fearful of losing his soul's salvation should he fail. Cases of extreme destitution have not been, in former years, comparatively numerous; but as the rich become richer and the poor poorer, by the operation of this system, these cases become more marked and frequent, and already a rumbling of discontent is heard among the masses, which occasionally reaches the throne, and which will soon break forth in loud peals of thunder, demanding justice for a long oppressed and outraged people.

Again, there is a standing tithing-price which must be paid for flour and other necessaries, by those who are engaged upon the public works, or who are obliged to work for their richer brethren. These always pay their laborers in produce at tithing-prices. But these prices are usually far beyond the cash value of the same article in the market. In 1862–63, the tithing-office price of flour was $6 per hundred. The wages of workmen were nominally $2 per day. But if a poor saint worked for his more affluent brother, as in most cases he was obliged to do, he uniformly received his pay in flour at $6. It was not uncommon to see a laboring man going home at night, with his sack of flour, the result of his day's work, or of the labor of two or three days. At the same time the market-price of flour did not exceed $3 per hundred. If the poor man, who was obliged to take all his pay in flour, wished to purchase some sugar or groceries for his family, he must exchange for the same his flour, at half the price paid for it. Thus did the dignitaries of the church " grind the face of the poor."

The masses were induced to submit to this state of things, by the assurance that flour would rise to a price much greater than $6, and when it should do so, the balance would be upon the other side, and the poor would be the gainers, as they should never pay more than that sum.

In the winter of 1863–64, flour rose rapidly, owing to the new markets opened up in Idaho and other mining regions. Now the time had come when the predictions and prophecies concerning the rise of flour had been fulfilled. But the church authorities, notwithstanding the solemn promises which had been made to the people, raised the tithing-price of flour to $12 per hundred. This was "the last straw that broke the camel's back," and came near producing a revolution. One day a workman in the "church" (*alias* Brigham's) blacksmith shop, called at the "tithing-store" for his flour, as was customary, the same being his wages for work for a stated period. At the store the flour was weighed out, and he was given a ticket at $12 per hundred. This was the first time he had been charged over $6. The blacksmith left his bag of flour at the store, and proceeded, fired with indignation, to the President's office. Inquiring for him, he was told the President was out, and he could not see him. He replied he must see him, and should remain until he did. After some time the President appeared. " Brother Brigham," said the excited workman, " you are a liar and a hypocrite." This caused a great excitement at once. The clerks sprang instantly from their places, some surrounding Brigham, others the blacksmith. The latter proceeded : " Have you not repeatedly given the people your solemn promise that they should never be charged by the church over $6 per hundred for flour? You with your wives and families are rolling in wealth, surrounded with everything the heart can wish. But go with me, and I will show you cases of destitution and suffering which will cause your soul, if you have one, to shudder with horror."

The clerks were here ordered to put him out of the office, which was done immediately, but the enraged man, now that his lips were unsealed, continued to talk in a loud tone of voice, until a number of people, attracted by curiosity, gathered around him. To them he explained the cause of the difficulty, and inveighed in unmeasured terms against those who were living in luxury and extravagance upon the industry and hard-earned savings of the poor.

The crowd was finally dispersed, and one of the clerks sent to the outraged blacksmith to inform him that he could have the flour at $6. He replied that he would die of hunger ere he would ever taste of it or touch it. The next day Brigham drove down to the poor man's house, taking the flour in his carriage, and induced him to accept it, and the same day the tithing-price of flour was reduced to $6 per hundred.

The best articles of everything paid in for tithing — the choice hams and beef, the best butter, cheese, etc. — are laid away until the families of the first Presidency, the clerks, and a few of the elect are supplied. The balance is served out to the mechanics and laborers. Thus the church dignitaries literally live off of "the fat of the land." Often when butter, or some other article not quite so abundant as usual, is called for by the workman, he is told "there is none in the store," while at the same time large quantities are stowed away; and scarcely is he out of sight, before some member of higher standing in the church visits the same store, and his wants are amply supplied.

As Brigham is not scrupulous on the subject of appropriating the means of the "church," that is, of the people, minor officers, as Bishops of settlements, do not hesitate to speculate upon their own account. This is more or less tolerated, according to the faithfulness of the party to the interests of the heads of the church, and his diligence in "attending to counsel," or, in other words, in obeying orders. It is notorious that the Bishops all become quickly wealthy. Appoint a man Bishop of a settlement, and in two or three years his fortune is made; and he who previously lived in a log-cabin, with barely the necessaries of life, is soon in possession of a fine house, with carriages, horses, &c., at his command. Every Bishop is expected to "build up the kingdom" by having numerous wives. If he has less than half a dozen, he is scarcely considered as "doing his duty to the church," and at once exposes himself to remark, if not to censure.

Many incidents might be mentioned illustrative of the manner in which property is accumulated by the Bishops. When the army under Col. Johnson was located at Camp Floyd, a Bishop of one of the southern settlements sold to the officers at the camp, at fifty cents per pound, all the butter which had been paid in for tithing, and accounted for it at the general tithing-office, at the tithing price,—twenty-five cents per pound.

Frequently the people would in this way be deprived of luxuries which had been sold, and the proceeds of which had gone into the pockets of the Bishops and other officers of the church. On one occasion Kimball alluded in his sermon to the complaints of the people, that they could not get butter or anything else to eat on their bread. In response he told them, if their bread was hard and dry, "dip it in City Creek."

On the departure from the Territory of the army under Col. Johnson, Brigham bought a large quantity of bacon at one cent per pound, selling it again to the laborers on the public works at twenty-five cents. The large contracts of purchase are usually awarded to him, partly because he has more money with which to fulfil them, and partly because men of lesser means do not wish to cross his path, by interfering with his financial operations. A large quantity of condemned crackers were purchased at the same time, at a nominal sum, many of which were afterward dealt out to the laborers on the public works, at fifteen cents per pound.

Soon after the arrival of the saints in Utah, their attention was especially directed to the building of a temple. Promises were made to them, that upon its completion, the Saviour, together with angels, would enter therein, and minister unto those who remained faithful. There they were to receive blessings that could be obtained in no other place. This has been held out as a strong inducement for the payment of money. Over $100,000 has been paid for the accomplishment of this object by the British saints alone. Not a dollar of this money has been used for that purpose, as all that has been done upon the temple has been more than paid for by the people of Utah.*

The work upon the temple has proceeded very slowly, and the foundation is but little above the surface. Many of the saints are dissatisfied with its progress, and ask each other why more has not been accomplished during the fifteen years that have rolled away since its commencement; and especially while such ample means have been constantly on hand, — the tithing system furnishing an immense revenue, and no other public work on which to expend it? And why it is that $200,000 should be expended by Brigham Young upon a theatre for his own benefit, and nearly as much more upon a hotel now being built, and house added to house and building to building in his own enclosure, while the temple is neglected? These questions have much significance, and doubtless the day is not far distant when the people will insist upon an answer more satisfactory than they have yet received.

The immense fund realized from the tithing system, and which is constantly at Brigham's disposal, enables him to im-

---

* Persons who are known to possess property, are called upon to pay for seats in the temple. A lady residing in one of the northern settlements, was cajoled into paying £50 for that purpose. The good lady, upon arriving in Utah, found that the famous temple, in which she had purchased a seat, was scarcely above its foundations.

prove many opportunities that are offered for private speculations. These he is not slow to perceive, nor does he permit any advantage of that kind to escape him. A very common speculation is to send a brother who is doing well, and accumulating a handsome property, upon a foreign mission. The call to go upon a mission is considered a trial of the brother's faith, and he is not expected to decline. Should he desire to sell his house or other possessions, rather than to leave them in the hands of agents, brother Brigham stands ready to purchase them at a reduced price. In this way a large amount of property falls into his hands. If the missionary returns at all, he comes nearly impoverished, and commences anew to acquire property.

In 1862 there were two distilleries in Salt Lake City, the owners of which, Moon & Bradley, were rapidly increasing in wealth. Brigham professed much indignation, telling them "they should welter in hell for manufacturing the intoxicating draught to destroy their brethren." As a sort of expiatory act for their offence he sent them upon a mission to raise cotton in Southern Utah. As soon as they were gone, he opened a distillery himself, in the name and under the sanction of the city council, under pretence of regulating the traffic by law. Thus he managed to monopolize the large profits from the manufacture of ardent spirits, an immense quantity of which is used in Salt Lake City and throughout the Territory.

Among the various inducements held out to the poor saints in Europe, has been the promise to each of a city lot in Salt Lake, of one acre and a quarter, upon the payment of the cost of survey, $1.25. On their arrival, they find to their astonishment, although there are plenty of vacant and unfenced lots, that they have to pay to Young or Kimball $100 or $150 for a lot. On one occasion a poor Dane having purchased a lot upon credit, built a small house upon it, but his wife falling sick he was unable to pay for the lot at the time agreed upon. Kimball compelled him to pull down the house and remove the material; and the Dane was obliged, in consequence, to pass the winter, with his family, in his covered wagon. Fortunately the winter was a mild one, or they might have perished.

The saints are fond of dancing, and in the winter season social parties for that purpose are numerous. Each ward has a commodious house, built by taxation, which is used for schools and public meetings. But for dancing their use is forbidden, and the people are obliged to pay Brigham $100 per night for a building called the "Social Hall." Yet this hall was built from the proceeds of tithing paid in by the very people who are thus obliged to pay for the rent of it!

Mr. Taussig, a simple and unpretending man, had succeeded in establishing a substantial tannery well stocked with leather. By some designing persons he was induced to refuse the payment of his taxes, on the ground that they were exorbitant, and the Territorial Collector sold the property, which was bought by one of Brigham's agents, and the poor man reduced to poverty.

In the fall of 1857, Brigham called a mass meeting in the Tabernacle, and after dilating upon the disadvantages the people were laboring under in being without a currency, established a bank, calling upon the faithful to bring in all their gold and silver, and receive the new paper currency in exchange. This was done. In a few months the bank was suspended, and depositors were paid in labor tithing, for the currency held by them, in exchange for their gold and silver.

One Mr. Tennant, a gentleman residing in Lancashire, England, embraced Mormonism. His property was estimated at over $70,000. He was soon marked as a victim. By appliances and representations brought to bear with much assiduity, he was induced to purchase of Brigham Young a house in Salt Lake, which he had never seen, and pay for the same the sum of $20,000; about four times its value. In addition to this, large sums of money were obtained from him by the Elders, under pretence of his becoming a shareholder and partner with Young in grist-mills, sugar machinery, iron-works, &c., solemnly assuring him in relation to its safe investment and future profits. Mr. Tennant died while crossing the Plains, leaving a wife, with a young child. On arriving in Salt Lake, **Mrs. Tennant,** instead of being comfortably installed in the house purchased by her husband, found herself placed in lodgings, the carriage, horses, and other property seized upon, and herself placed under the control of a guardian. This, together with the loss of her husband, so worked upon her mind, that she became insane. Afterward Brigham gave her in marriage to Daniel Spencer, as his fourth or fifth wife, and thus completed the wrongs for which the poor woman will call him to account in the day of judgment. She now lives upon a miserable pittance doled out from the tithing-office.

A Mr. Williams, well known to the writer, became a Mormon in England. He was a man of considerable property, and while on his way crossing the Plains, was induced to invest $15,000 in an iron company formed for working the iron mines in Southern Utah. The money was paid over, and invested by the Elders, in goods, in St. Louis. The goods were duly transported across the Plains, and unloaded within the enclosure of Young, in Salt Lake City. Mr. Williams received, in St. Louis, a receipt for his money, stating that the same would entitle him, upon his arrival in Utah, to certificates of stock in the company. But he never was able to get any stock or other equivalent for his money, nor any statement of the affairs of the company. Indeed, the dignitaries of the church, after one or two conversations upon the subject, refused to converse with him further in relation to it. Soon after, the Legislature of Utah, composed in good part of the same men, repealed the Act incorporating the company, and thus the whole thing "vanished into thin air." In 1862, which was several years after the money had been paid, Mr. Williams took legal advice, and was told he could file a bill in chancery, against all persons implicated in the transaction, requiring them to answer under oath. He hesitated to do so, giving as a reason that he thought "the time had not yet come," and that such a course would imperil his life.

This mode of getting money by the Elders from the wealthy saints, and the retaining the same, is not only excused, but openly justified and encouraged by Brigham. The following extract from one of his published sermons will show his views upon these questions, and the character of his morality and financial integrity:—

"I wish to impress another thing on your minds. An Elder who is willing to preach the gospel, borrows a hundred or a thousand from you, and you never breathe a word of complaint against him, until you come home to this valley; but after you have been here for a few days, you follow me round and fill my ears with complaints against this brother, and ask me what he has done with your money? I say 'I do not know.' Thus you are distressed, and in misery all the day long, to get it back again. If an Elder has borrowed from you, and you find he is going to apostatize, then, you may tighten the screws upon him; but if he is willing to preach the gospel without purse or scrip, *it is none of your business what he does with the money he has borrowed from you. If you murmur against that Elder, it will prove your damnation.* . . .

"No man need judge me. You know nothing about it, whether I am sent or not; furthermore, it is none of your business, only to listen with open ears to what is taught you, and serve God with an undivided heart." *

Stephen Goddard owned a store on Main Street, Salt Lake City, which he desired to sell. He was offered its value by a gentile, but before selling, consulted "Brother Brigham." The President said he wanted the store, and would give him $8,000 for it. To this Goddard demurred, as the sum was less than half what he had been offered. Young said when the Lord wanted his property, that should be the end of it, and the price was none of his business. Goddard and Bishop Woolley, who was present, retired outside and talked the matter over. The Bishop remarked, "He thought when a

* *Jour. of Dis.*, Vol. I. p. 340.

man had worked hard to accumulate property for the benefit of his family, he should be permitted to sell it for a fair price." This was overheard by a spy, and reported to headquarters. The Bishop was sent for and sharply reprimanded. He was told that he was in a spirit of apostasy. Goddard, afraid to do otherwise, sold the store to Young for $8,000.

Besides the property acquired through the machinery of the tithing system, a large amount is obtained under the "law of consecration." Under this law, those saints who can be induced to do so, place their whole property in the hands of the President, as trustee in trust for the church, to be used when the necessities of the church require it. The object is to guard against apostasy. Brigham Young says:—

"The rulers of Great Britain have tried to make every capitalist identify his interest with the Government that has sustained the kingdom. Brethren, do you wish this heavenly kingdom to stand? . . . Imitate the policy of that earthly kingdom; identify our interest with the kingdom of God, so that if our hearts should ever be weaned from loyalty to the sovereign, all our earthly interest is bound up there, and cannot be taken away. . . .

"If a man has the purse in his pocket, and he apostatizes, he takes it with him; but if his worldly interest is firmly united to the kingdom of God, when he arises to go away, he finds the calf is bound, and, like the cow, he is unwilling to forsake it. If his calf is bound up here, he will be inclined to stay."*

THE EMIGRATION FUND.

The published object and design of this fund is to emigrate the poor saints from Europe and other foreign countries to Utah, the Zion of the church. In those foreign countries there is a continual weekly subscription paid in for that purpose.

Every emigration season, each Conference is permitted to send persons at the rate of one for every £10 sterling so subscribed. Each one so emigrating, is required to enter into obligations, before leaving Liverpool, for the repayment

* *Jour. of Dis.* Vol. I. p. 202.

of the same, as soon as possible after his arrival in Salt Lake City. Parties in Utah, also, wishing their relations brought over, must pay the required amount, before they are sent for, unless in some special cases, where notes are accepted in payment. The sum of £4 10s. is required to pay the transportation of each person to the first American port, and the remaining £5 10s. thence to Salt Lake City. The emigrants are stowed away like cattle, on the freight cars and on the decks of the boats and vessels, and thus by having them conveyed in the cheapest manner possible, considerable of the amount paid for transportation is saved, making a large sum in the aggregate, all of which goes into that "treasury of the church," — the pocket of Brigham Young.

Again: as *all* are obliged to pay their passage-money, either in advance or after their arrival in Utah, and as a large portion of the sum is previously raised by contribution, of course the amount, in thousands of cases, is duplicated, and paid twice into the same treasury.

The transportation across the Plains costs the church nothing at all, except a slight diminution of the tithing-fund *prospective*. The teams are furnished, so many from each ward and settlement, and the owners are given credit for the use of the same in tithing account. Large quantities of provisions are furnished and sent out to meet the incoming saints, but these, although donated and sent by their friends, are all charged to them by the careful priests and elders.

Before starting across the Plains, meetings are held, and the saints are counselled to give up all their money and valuables, so that they may be preserved on their journey. One man, in obedience to this "counsel," gave up his money, together with a valuable gold watch and chain. Afterwards, remembering that he had not provided any tobacco for the journey, he asked for a dollar back, to purchase some, which was refused him.

Much cruelty is exercised on the Plains for the slightest disobedience. A young man, brother of Walter Sanders, of

Salt Lake, was whipped nearly to death for being unable to travel as required.

Several years since, Brigham, with the view of saving still more from the emigration fund, projected the plan of bringing the saints across the Plains in hand-cart companies. Under this arrangement, every person, male and female, was expected to assist in drawing a hand-cart; each cart being drawn by three persons, and containing a certain quantity of provisions, clothing, &c.

One of the companies, under the lead of Franklin D. Richards, was detained on the frontiers until common prudence should have dictated their remaining until another year. In consequence of the lateness of the season, before the journey was half performed, winter was upon them, and their sufferings beggar all description.

Mrs. Chapman, a very intelligent English lady, who crossed the Plains in this company, related to me many incidents of this dreadful journey.

They started from the frontier very late, sometime in October, I think; and to allay the fears and forebodings of the saints, Richards prophesied, in the name of Israel's God, that the elements should be controlled; and that the winds and snows of winter should be stayed until the faithful arrived in Zion. Entirely unacquainted with the country and the route before them, they were reassured, and went boldly forward, trusting in their leader.

In order to lighten their loads and facilitate their progress, every article of clothing that they could possibly spare, was left behind; barely sufficient being taken to prevent them from freezing.

It may be supposed that only the very poor were subjected to this terrible ordeal. Not so. Many families of means made the journey in this way, being assured that this sacrifice would add to their exaltation in the eternal world. They had not proceeded far when the snow began to fall, and many became sick from want and exposure. When a river was to be crossed, they were driven into the water,— men, women, and children,— and were told, if they had sufficient faith, they should, like the Israelites of old, go over dry shod. Many of the men carried their wives and children over the streams, as long as they were able. If any were unable longer to drag their carts, they were obliged to lighten them by throwing away clothing, cooking utensils, and even provisions,— thus necessitating a reduction from their daily allowance of food. Fuel was scarce, and it was often necessary to go into the snow, waist-deep, to procure it. Mrs. Chapman's husband, a strong, athletic man, formerly a member of the Queen's Guards, from constant exertion and exposure, at length fell sick, and though there were a few wagons for the sick and feeble to ride in, they were not admitted into them so long as they were able to walk.

The poor man continued to grow worse, and it soon became evident that he must die. One morning, when the train was ready to start, the Captain came to the tent of the sick man, and finding him dying, said to Mrs. Chapman, " Your husband must die; leave him in the hands of God, and proceed on your journey." " What!" said the heart-stricken woman, " leave my husband on this barren waste, a prey to wolves? No; while there is breath in his body, I shall remain by his side, and share his fate. Leave us if you will, for the wild beasts of the desert cannot be more cruel than you have been." In five minutes more, he breathed his last; and throwing him into a hole dug in the sand, they dragged the weeping wife and children from all they held dear on earth. In a few days the same woman left her baby, too, on the sands of the desert, a prey to wolves. She says, " I never see Franklin D. Richards, but I feel hand-carts from the crown of my head to the sole of my feet."

One day, as they approached their Mecca, an old white-haired saint said to the Captain, in a weak voice, — " Captain, I feel as if I should die, drawing in this hand-cart; can't I ride a little while?" — " Draw till you die then," replied the

hard-hearted wretch, "for I'll be d——d if you can ride."
"Oh, well," said the old man, "I suppose I shall draw till I
die." He took out his watch. "A quarter of four. It will
soon be over. Ten minutes. Oh dear; oh, my God! Five
minutes to four,— four;"— and the old man fell down in his
place,— he was dead.

Every day witnessed the death of large numbers by cold
and starvation. Those who survived were more like walking skeletons than human beings. They were covered with
vermin, and loathsome to behold. Some were so badly frozen
that their flesh fell from their bones. Many remained disabled for life.

"Oh Religion! what crimes are perpetrated in thy name!"
When Mormons speak of the hand-cart company, they shudder and grow pale. All this suffering was the result of an
attempt, on the part of the leaders of the church, to save a
still larger sum from the emigration fund. It was a speculative experiment, which was never repeated. These people
bought their carts with their own money; but on their arrival in Salt Lake, the carts were claimed by Brigham, in
behalf of the church, and were afterwards sold from the
tithing-office at five dollars each.

CHAPTER IX.

BRIGHAM AS PROPHET, SEER, AND REVELATOR.

Brigham's Position as Head of the Church. — Mormon Theology. — Brigham's Theology, or Utah Mormonism. — Adam as God. — Brigham Young as God. — Human Sacrifice. — Introduction of Polygamy. — Polygamy no part of the original Mormon Religion. — The Revelation, or Celestial Marriage. — The Ceremony of Sealing. — Consequences and Incidents of the Doctrine. — Incest. — Summary of the Mormon Religion.

NOT only is Brigham Young the temporal head of the church, its chief business agent, and the sole custodian of its funds, but he is the spiritual head, the established fountain, in whom is gathered from on high all spiritual blessings, and from whom they are expected to flow through the various officers of the priesthood, and thus be distributed to the faithful among the masses. Standing in this capacity between the people and the Supreme Being, he is at once Prophet, Seer, and Revelator. As Prophet and Seer, he sees and foretells to the people what is to befall them, as the result of certain courses of action. As Revelator, he reveals and translates, to the comprehension of the people, the hidden will of God concerning them.

An acknowledgment of this relationship of Brigham with the Divine Being is made a test of fellowship; as in the case of the Morrisites, who, although they admitted his right to preside over the church as its temporal head, denied him the attributes of prophet and revelator. Hence they were cut off from the church.

Acting in this capacity, he not only prescribes a course of conduct for his followers, but promulgates, from time to time, doctrines, to be received, believed, and advocated. Thus the theology or creed of the church changes, from time to time, to suit the changing opinions, the whims and caprices, or the passions and lusts, of its head and leader. What is here said, therefore, of the Mormon religion, must be understood in reference to the received doctrines and tenets of the church in former years,—many of which still remain, but incorporated with new dogmas, and any part or all of which are liable at any time to be changed, modified, or entirely overthrown.

Mormon Theology.

There are many Gods, and they are of both sexes. But to us there is but one God,—the Father of mankind, and the Creator of the earth.

Men and women are literally the sons and daughters of God,—our spirits having been literally begotten by God, in the heavenly world, and having been afterwards sent to the earth, and invested with these tabernacles.

God is in the form of man. He has a body, composed of spiritual matter. There is no difference between matter and spirit, except in quality. Spirit is matter refined.

God is omnipotent, but not personally omnipresent. He is everywhere present by his Holy Spirit. His personality is generally expressed by the phrase, "He has body, parts, and passions." He resides in the centre of the universe, near the planet Kolob. This planet revolves on its axis once in a thousand of our years, and one revolution of Kolob is a day to the Almighty.

Jesus Christ was the Son of God, literally begotten by the Father, and had the Spirit of God in the body of a man. After his resurrection, he had a body of flesh and bones only, typical of man's resurrected body. He differs in nothing from the Father, except in age and authority,—the Father having the seniority, and consequently the right to preside.

The Holy Spirit is a subtle fluid, like electricity. It is

the subtlest form of matter, and pervades all space. By its agency all miracles, so called, are performed. Miracles are simply the effects of the operation of natural laws. But they are laws of a higher character than those with which we are acquainted. This Holy Spirit is communicated by the laying-on of hands by one of the properly authorized priesthood, and the recipient is then enabled to perform wonderful things, according to his gift, — some having the gift of prophecy, some of healing, some of speaking in unknown tongues, etc.

There are three heavens, — the telestial, the terrestrial, and the celestial.

The *telestial* and *terrestrial* heavens are to be occupied by the various classes of persons who have neither obeyed nor rejected the gospel. The telestial is typified by the stars, — the terrestrial, by the moon.

The *celestial*, or highest heaven, has for its type the sun, and is reserved for those who received the testimony of Jesus, and believed on His name, and were baptized by one having authority from Him, and who afterwards lived a holy life.

The earth, as purified and refined, after the second coming of Christ, is to be the final habitation of those entitled to the glories of the celestial kingdom. Jerusalem is to be rebuilt, and Zion, or the New Jerusalem, is to be built in Jackson County, Missouri, whence the saints were expelled in 1833.

There is a fourth class of persons, not entitled to either of these heavens. They are those who sin against the Holy Ghost; that is, those who apostatize after receiving the Holy Spirit. These go into everlasting punishment, to remain with the devil and his angels.

The gospel, which people are called upon to obey, in order to gain a place in the celestial kingdom, is, — *First*, They must believe in Jesus Christ as the Son of God, and in His authorized priesthood. *Secondly*, They must repent of their sins; *Thirdy*, They must be baptized by immersion for the remission of their sins; and, *Fourthly,* They must receive the laying-on of hands for the gift of the Holy Ghost.

God, having become nearly lost to man, revived His work, by revealing himself to Joseph Smith, and conferring upon him the keys of the everlasting Priesthood,—thus making him the mediator of a New Dispensation, which is immediately to precede the second coming of Christ. All those who recognize the divine authority of Smith, and are baptized by one having authority, are the chosen people of God, who are to introduce the Millennium, and to reign with Christ, on earth, a thousand years.

Previous to the year 1852, it was also an orthodox principle of the Mormon religion, that a man should have but one wife, to whom he should be true and faithful.

Those who have any curiosity to pursue the subject further, will find these views and doctrines fully explained and illustrated in the religious writings of the Mormons,—of which the following are some of the principal: Book of Mormon; Book of Doctrine and Covenants; Works of Orson Pratt; Key to Theology, by P. P. Pratt; The Only Way to be Saved, etc., by L. Snow; Pearl of Great Price; Voice of Warning, by P. P. Pratt; Catechism for Children, by John Jaques; Deseret News, 14 vols.; Journal of Discourses, 6 vols.; Latter-Day Saints' Millennial Star, London, 26 volumes.

Brigham's Theology; or Utah Mormonism.

The doctrines taught and practised by the present head of the Mormon Church differ so much from the previously established tenets of the church, that they require a separate consideration.

One of the most important innovations upon the established doctrines of the church, is in relation to the Godhead. In April, 1852, Brigham put forth the startling doctrine that Adam is God, and to be recognized and honored as such! This announcement created some consternation among the

Mormon theologians, and some of them had the courage to oppose it. The following is the "Revelator's" own exposition of this doctrine:—

"When the Virgin Mary conceived the child Jesus, the Father had begotten him in his own likeness. He was not begotten by the Holy Ghost. And who is the Father? *He is the first of the human family;* and when he took a tabernacle, it was begotten by his Father in heaven, after the same manner as the tabernacle of Cain, Abel, and the rest of the sons and daughters of Adam and Eve. . . . It is true that the earth was organized by three distinct characters, namely: Elohim, Yahovah, and Michael, [Adam;] these three forming a quorum, as in all heavenly bodies, and in organized element perfectly represented in the Deity, as Father, Son, and Holy Ghost.

"When our Father Adam came into the garden of Eden, he came with a celestial body, and brought *Eve, one of his wives,* with him. He helped to make and organize this world. He is Michael, the Archangel, the Ancient of Days. *He is our Father and our God, and the only God with whom we have to do.* . . . Jesus, our elder brother, was begotten in the flesh by the same character that was in the garden of Eden, and who is our Father in heaven." *

It is manifest that Young is not so much at home in theology as when engaged in financial schemes and money speculations. So disgusting and blasphemous are these ideas, and so unacceptable were they, even to Mormons, who were not prepared to see the basis of their religion thus rudely overthrown, that Brigham finally felt compelled to caution the Elders not to preach the new doctrines concerning Deity, until the people should be better prepared to receive them.

Mahomet is the great exemplar and prototype whom Brigham Young aims to imitate, and doubtless he took from the Koran his ideas about the deity of Adam. Thus in chapter two of the Koran, we have the following:—

"And when we said unto the angels, 'worship Adam,' they all worshipped him, except Eblis, [Lucifer,] who refused."

From the following affidavit of John Stiles, father of Judge

* *Jour. of Dis.* Vol. I. p. 50.

Stiles, formerly one of the United States Judges in Utah, a man of much probity of character, and well known in Salt Lake City as " Father Stiles," it appears that the blasphemous pretensions of Brigham Young do not stop with Adam, but that, among the brethren, he has encouraged a doctrine, which he dare not put in print; — no less than *to arrogate to himself the attributes of Deity.*

"Territory of Utah, } ss.
Great Salt Lake City.

"In the spring of 1856," John Stiles says, "I resided in the 11th Ward of Great Salt Lake City, in the Territory of Utah. I was appointed by the quorum to which I then belonged, as a Missionary High-Priest for the said Ward. My duty was to look after the morals of the people of the Ward, and especially to see that there was no false doctrine taught there. I subsequently found that there were not only immoralities, but also false doctrines among some of the people, as I supposed at the time. Many people believed and taught the doctrine, that Brigham Young was all the *God* that we were amenable to. I found by opposing that doctrine, that I gave offence to the authorities of the Ward, and was consequently called to answer for my opposition before the Bishop of the Ward, although he had no jurisdiction over me. As a High-Priest I was amenable to a higher authority, but not to him.

"In a public assembly he wished me to state my views on the question, whether *if Brigham Young was not God, who was?* I told him I would do so. I rose and stated that my idea of the being of God was expressed in a passage of Scripture, and I need only repeat the passage to explain the idea. The passage was :

To us there is but one God, *the Father*, of whom are all things, and we in Him, and one Lord Jesus Christ, by whom are all things, and we by Him.' I subsequently, in explanation, cited this passage of Scripture : ' **This is life eternal**, that we might know thee, the only living and true God, and Jesus Christ whom thou hast sent.' I then sat down, and the Bishop rose and said : 'Brethren, we perceive that Father Stiles runs round Brigham.' I replied, ' Yes; I do not mention Brigham Young on the same day with God, as of the same Godhead.' His (the Bishop's) First Counsellor, then moved that Father Stiles be cut off from the church. This was seconded by the Second Counsellor. This was proposed to the assembly as a question by the Bishop, and I was cut off accordingly. I subsequently discovered that by my opposition and explanation, I gave offence to the authorities of the Mormon Church, and was cut off from the church and dismissed from the place of Missionary High-Priest of that Ward. I have never been restored as Missionary High-Priest.

(Signed,) JOHN STILES.

"Sworn to and subscribed before me at Great Salt Lake City, this April 26th, 1864.

"JOHN TITUS,
" Ch. Justice of Utah."

Another doctrine of a startling character, promulgated by one of Young's counsellors and endorsed by him, is that of *human sacrifice for the remission of sins.*

It was first announced by Jedediah M. Grant, Second Counsellor to the President, in the following language:—

"Brethren and sisters, we want you to repent and forsake your sins. And you who have committed sins that cannot be forgiven through baptism, *let your blood be shed, and let the smoke ascend,* that the incense thereof may come up before God as an atonement for your sins, and that the sinners in Zion may be afraid." *

Again:—

"We have been trying long enough with this people, and I go in for letting the sword of the Almighty be unsheathed, *not only in word, but in deed.*" †

In accordance with such bloody teaching, it is said that an altar of sacrifice was actually built by Grant, in the temple block, upon which these human sacrifices were to be made. On the 21st of September, 1856, Grant said:—

"I say there are men and women here that I would advise to go to the President immediately, and ask him to appoint a committee to attend to their case; and then let a place be selected, and let that committee shed their blood." ‡

---

* *Deseret News,* October 1, 1856.   † *Ibid.*
‡ *Ibid.* Vol. VI. p. 235.

This horrible proposal to immolate upon the altar of sacrifice the erring saints, was fully endorsed by Brigham Young as follows:—

"There are sins that men commit for which they cannot receive forgiveness in this world, or in that which is to come; and if they had their eyes open to see their condition, *they would be perfectly willing to have their blood spilt* **upon the** *ground*, that the smoke thereof might ascend to Heaven as an offering for their sins, and the smoking incense would **atone for their** sins; whereas, if such **is not** the case, they will stick **to them, and remain upon them in** the spirit-world.

"I know, when you hear my brethren telling about cutting people off from the earth, that you consider it is strong doctrine. It is to save them, not to destroy them. I will say further, I have had men come to me, and offer their lives to atone for their sins. **It** is true that the blood of the Son of God was shed for sins, through the fall, and those committed by man, yet men can commit sins which it can never remit. As it was in ancient days, so it is in our **day**; and though the principles are taught **publicly** from this stand, still the people do not understand them; yet the Law is precisely the same. There are sins that can be **atoned for** by an offering upon the altar, as in ancient days, and there **are sins that the blood of a lamb, of a calf, or of** turtle-doves cannot remit, *but they must be atoned for by the blood of the man*. That is the **reason** why men **talk to you** as they do from this stand. They understand the doctrine, and throw out a few words about it."*

But the greatest change of all **in the** Mormon religion, made by Brigham Young, was the introduction and **establishment of** polygamy.

This was **no part of** the Mormon system of **religion as** originally established. **On the** contrary, it was expressly repudiated by **all the Mormon** writers and speakers, previous **to** 1852, **and in** Europe for some years afterward.

The Mormon religion **was** founded by Joseph Smith and his coadjutors, and the principles and doctrines of the religion

---

* Sermon by Brigham Young, published in the *Deseret News*, October 1st, 1856.

were, in the first instance, such as they established. The Book of Mormon is the historical foundation, corresponding with the Old Testament of the Christian Bible. Afterward, a volume of revelations to Smith and others was collected and published, called the Book of Doctrine and Covenants. This corresponds to the Christian's New Testament. It may be safely asserted, therefore, that previous to the innovations of Young, the Mormon religion was embodied in these two volumes. Their authority in the church is universal and unquestioned.

Let us examine these volumes, and see whether they teach or countenance polygamy.

The Book of Mormon nowhere contains a word in favor of it. On the contrary all of its principal characters were monogamists. Such was Lehi, the patriarch of Mormon history. Such also were Ishmael and Nephi.* That the people of Zarahemla were monogamists, is evident from what is said concerning them on page 146.

But we are not left to inference as to the testimony of this volume concerning this practice. On page 119 we have the following:—

"Behold the Lamanites, your brethren, whom ye hate because of their filthiness and the cursings which hath come upon their skins, are more righteous than you; for they have not forgotten the commandment of the Lord, which was given unto our fathers, that they should have, save it were one wife; and concubines they should have none; and there should not be whoredoms committed among them. And now, this commandment they observe to keep; wherefore, because of this observance, in keeping this commandment, the Lord God will not destroy them, but will be merciful unto them; and one day they shall become a blessed people." †

Again:—

"And it came to pass that Riplakish did not do that which was right in the sight of the Lord, for he did have many wives and concubines, and did lay that upon men's shoulders which was

---

* *Book of Mormon*, pp. 3, 12, 33, 43. † *Ibid.* p. 119.

grievous to be borne; yea, he did tax them with heavy taxes and with the taxes he did build many spacious buildings." *

And again: —

"And he [Noah] did not walk in the ways of his father. [Zeniff.] For behold, he did not keep the commandments of God, but he did walk after the desires of his own heart. And he had many wives and concubines. And he did cause his people to commit sin, and to do that which was abominable in the sight of the Lord. Yea, and they did commit **whoredoms** and all manner of wickedness. And he laid a tax of one fifth part of all they possessed." . . . "All this did he take to support himself, and his wives and his concubines; and also his priests, and their wives and their concubines; **thus he had** changed the affairs of the kingdom." †

"And it came to pass that he placed his heart upon his riches, and he spent his time in riotous living, with his wives and his concubines; and so did also his priests spend their time with harlots." ‡

As if to place this matter beyond any question, we have the following still more explicit testimony, on pages 115 and 118: —

"And now it came to pass that the people of Nephi, under the reign of the second king, began to grow hard in their hearts and indulge themselves somewhat in wicked practices, such as like unto David of old, desiring many wives and concubines, and also Solomon his son." . . .

"The word of God burdens me because of your grosser crimes. For behold, thus saith the Lord, this people begin to wax in iniquity; they understand not the Scriptures; for they seek to excuse themselves in committing whoredoms, because of the things which were written concerning David, and Solomon his son. Behold David and Solomon truly had many wives and concubines, which thing was abominable before me, saith the Lord; wherefore, thus saith the Lord, I have led this people forth out of the land

---

* *Book of Mormon*, p. 535. 5th sec. of 4th chap. of Book of Ether.
† *Book of Mormon*, p. 167.
‡ *Ibid.* p. 168.

of Jerusalem, by the power of mine arm, that I might raise up unto me a righteous branch from the fruit of the loins of Joseph. Wherefore, I the Lord God, will not suffer that this people shall do like unto them of old. Wherefore, my brethren, hear me, and hearken to the word of the Lord; for there shall not any man among you have, save it be one wife; and concubines he shall have none; for I, the Lord God, delighteth in the chastity of women. And whoredoms are an abomination before me; thus saith the Lord of Hosts." *

Here it is stated as coming from God himself, that the polygamy and concubinage of David and Solomon were abominable before the Lord. And yet we every day hear David and Solomon, as well as Abraham, Jacob, and others, cited by those practising polygamy, as their illustrious prototypes, whose example is worthy of all imitation.

Orson Pratt, the ablest writer on Mormon theology, is compelled to admit that the Book of Mormon is opposed to polygamy. He says:—

"Do you believe that the Book of Mormon is a divine revelation? We do. Does that book teach the doctrine of plurality of wives? It does not. Does the Lord in that book forbid the plurality doctrine? He forbid the ancient Nephites to have any more than one wife." †

Elder Pratt then endeavors to blunt the force of this testimony in the following manner:—

"Why were the ancient Nephites restricted to the one-wife system? Because, first, the number of males and females among them, at the time the command was given, was about equal. Secondly, there was no probability that judgments, wars, or any other calamities which were to befall their nation, would produce a disproportionate number of males and females. Thirdly, this small remant of the tribe of Joseph, were, at that time, about equally righteous; and one was about as capable of raising up a family in

---

* *Book of Mormon*, pp. 115, 118. 1st and 2d chapters of the Book of Jacob.
† Article on Celestial Marriage, in *The Seer*, Vol. I. p. 30.

righteousness as another. And, lastly, the Lord himself informs them, in the same connection with the quotation which I have just made, that if He would have them practise differently from what He had previously taught them, it must be by His command." *

Thus, in the attempt to weaken the force of the evidence furnished by the Book of Mormon against polygamy, Pratt acknowledges, in the most explicit manner, the validity of the argument against it, founded upon the equality in the numbers of each sex. Two of the four reasons why the Nephites were to retain monogamy, relate to the equality in the numbers of the sexes. But there is a substantial equality in the numbers of the sexes, not only in the United States, but in Utah Territory. (See U. S. Census.)

Let us now turn to the Book of Doctrine and Covenants, and see if we can find in that volume any authority for polygamy. The following passages will determine the question: —

"Thou shalt love thy wife with all thy heart, and shalt cleave unto her, and none else; and he that looketh upon a woman to lust after her, shall deny the faith, and shall not have the spirit; and if he repents not he shall be cast out." †

Again. In 1845, the year after Smith's death, an Appendix was authoritatively added to the Book of Doctrine and Covenants, containing the following, which is extracted from the section entitled "Marriage": —

" 2. Marriage should be celebrated with prayer and thanksgiving; and at the solemnization, the persons to be married standing together," etc., "he [the person officiating] shall say, calling each by their names, 'you both mutually agree to be each other's companion, husband and wife, observing the legal rights belonging to this condition; that is, keeping yourselves wholly for each other, and from all others, during your lives.' And when they have an-

---

* *The Seer*, Vol. I. p. 30.
† *Doctrine and Covenants*, p. 125.

swered 'yes,' he shall pronounce them 'husband and wife,' in the name of the Lord Jesus Christ, and by virtue of the laws of the country, and authority vested in him. . .

"4. . . . Inasmuch as this church of Christ has been reproached with the crime of fornication and polygamy; we declare that we believe that one man should have one wife; and one woman but one husband, except in case of death, when either is at liberty to marry again." *

Can anything be more explicit than this? Polygamy is not only expressly repudiated by the church, but is classed by the side of fornication as a crime.

Thus we find that polygamy is contrary to both books of the Mormon Bible. That it is, in fact, strongly condemned in those volumes.

It is, therefore, no part of the Mormon religion, as given to the world by Joseph Smith.

But polygamy is practised in Utah. Whence did it arise, and upon what foundation does it rest?

Like slavery, and all other great social evils, it had its origin, doubtless, in an abuse of the passions of man.

It was first publicly announced and recommended in Utah Territory on the 29th of August, 1852, by Orson Pratt and Brigham Young, at a politico-religious meeting, held in Great Salt Lake City.

On that occasion, President Young said:—

"You heard Brother Pratt state, this morning, that a Revelation would be read this afternoon, which was given previous to Joseph's death. It contains a doctrine a small portion of the world is opposed to; but I can deliver a prophecy upon it. Though that doctrine has not been preached by the Elders, this people have believed in it for years.

"The original copy of this Revelation was burnt up. William Clayton was the man who wrote it from the mouth of the Prophet. In the mean time it was in Bishop Whitney's possession. He wished the privilege to copy it, which Brother Joseph granted. Sister Emma (wife of Joseph Smith) burnt the original. The rea-

---

* *Book of Doctrine and Covenants,* pp. 330, 331.

son I mention this is, because that the people who did know of **the** Revelation, suppose it was not now in existence.

"The Revelation will be read to you. The principle spoken upon by Brother Pratt this morning, we believe in.

. . . "Many others are of the same mind. They are not ignorant of what **we are doing in our social** capacity. They have cried out proclaim it; but it would not do a few years ago; every**thing must come in its time, as there is** a time to all things. **I am** now ready to proclaim it.

"This Revelation has been in my possession many years; and who has known it? None but those who should know it. I keep a patent lock on my desk, and there does not anything leak out that should not." *

The Revelation, so called, which was read at the close of this sermon, purports to have been given to Joseph Smith, July 12, 1843. It is very lengthy, consisting of twenty-five sections **or** paragraphs. It is published in full, in Burton's "City of the Saints," and in various other publications. The following synopsis exhibits all that is essential of this extraordinary Revelation.

THE REVELATION.

Section 1. "Verily, thus **saith the Lord unto** you, my servant **Joseph, that** inasmuch **as you have** inquired of my hand **to know and** understand wherein **I, the** Lord, justified my servants Abraham, Isaac, and Jacob, as also Moses, David, and Solomon, my servants, as touching the principle and doctrine of their having many wives and concubines: Behold, and lo, I am the Lord thy God, and will answer thee as touching this matter." [The balance of this section is prefatory, declaring that **a** new law and everlasting covenant is about to be revealed, and that he who abides not that covenant shall be damned.]

Sec. 2. All covenants, contracts, vows, etc., not made and

* Sermon of Brigham Young, published in the *Deseret News*, Extra, of September 14, 1852.

sealed by the Holy Spirit of promise, of him who is anointed (Joseph Smith) both as well for time and for all eternity, are of no efficacy or force after the resurrection.

Sec. 3 represents the necessity of having everything sanctioned by the Almighty.

Secs. 4 and 5. Persons married for life only, or for time and eternity, but not by the proper authority, not bound to each other after this life.

Sec. 6 provides that if a man marry a wife by the law of God, and by the new and everlasting covenant, and if they abide in the covenant, and do not shed innocent blood, then the covenant shall be binding throughout time and eternity, "and they shall pass by the angels, and the gods which are set there, to their exaltation and glory in all things."

Sec. 7 declares that such shall be gods in the eternal world.

Sec. 8 states that none can receive such exaltation except those who receive and abide the law of God.

Sec. 9. "Verily, verily I say unto you, if a man marry a wife according to my word, and they are sealed by the Holy Spirit of promise according to mine appointment, and he or she shall commit any sin or transgression of the new and everlasting covenant whatever, and all manner of blasphemies, and if they commit no murder wherein they shed innocent blood, yet they shall come forth in the first resurrection, and enter into their exaltation, but they shall be destroyed in the flesh, and shall be delivered unto the buffetings of Satan unto the day of redemption, saith the Lord God."

Sec. 10 explains that shedding innocent blood, and assenting unto the death of Christ, is the blasphemy against the Holy Ghost, which shall not be forgiven in the world nor out of the world.

Secs. 11 and 12 refer to Abraham as the father of the faithful, and him to whom the promises were made. "This promise is yours also, because ye are of Abraham, and the promise was made unto Abraham." "Go ye, therefore, and do the works of Abraham; and enter ye into my law, and ye shall be saved."

SEC. 13 intimates that Sarah acted in accordance with the command of God in giving Hagar to Abraham.

SEC. 14 refers to the concubines which Abraham received, and says, "they bare him children, and it was accounted unto him for righteousness." The latter part of the section is as follows: "David also received many wives and concubines, as also Solomon, and Moses **my** servant; and also many others of my servants, from the beginning of creation until this time; and in nothing did they sin save in those things which they received not of **me.**"

SEC. 15. "David's wives and concubines were given unto him, **of** me, by the **hand** of Nathan, my servant, and others of the prophets who had the keys of this power; and in none **of** these things **did he sin** against me, save in **the** case of Uriah and his wife; and therefore he hath fallen from his exaltation, and received his portion; and he shall not inherit them out of the world; for I gave them unto another, saith the Lord."

SEC. 16 prescribes certain regulations concerning **those who commit adultery, and provides** that in **case the husband commits adultery, and the wife** is innocent, and the fact is revealed by God to Joseph, the wife shall be given by Smith to one who has not committed adultery, "but hath been faithful, for he shall be made ruler over many."

SEC. 17. "And verily, verily I say unto you, that whatsoever you seal on earth shall be sealed in heaven; and whatsoever you bind on earth in **my** name and by my **word,** saith the Lord, it shall **be eternally** bound in the heavens; and whosoever sins you remit on earth shall be remitted eternally in **the heavens;** and whosoever sins ye retain on earth shall be retained in heaven."

SEC. 18. "And again, verily I say, whomsoever you bless **I will** bless, and whomsoever you curse I will curse, saith the Lord; for I, the Lord, am thy **God.**"

Sec. 19. "And again, verily I say unto you, my servant Joseph, that whatsoever you give on earth, and to whomsoever you give any one on earth, by my word, and according to my law, it shall be visited with blessings, and not cursings, and with my power, saith the Lord, and shall be without condemnation, on earth and in heaven." Then follows a declaration to the effect that Smith has found favor with God, and that he will forgive his sins, etc.

Sec. 20 commands Emma Smith "that she stay herself, and partake not of that which I commanded you to offer unto her; for I did it, saith the Lord, to prove you all," etc., and continues as follows: " And let mine handmaid, Emma Smith, receive all those that have been given unto my servant Joseph, and who are virtuous and pure before me; and those who are not pure, and have said they are pure, shall be destroyed, saith the Lord God; for I am the Lord thy God," etc.

Sec. 21 commands Emma Smith, wife of Joseph, to abide and cleave unto Joseph and none else, under penalty of destruction. She is also exhorted to forgive Joseph his trespasses.

Sec. 22 forbids Joseph putting his property out of his hands.

Sec. 23 touches upon the law of the priesthood, and says of any one who is called of God, as was Aaron, "if he do anything in my name, and according to my law, and by my word, he will not commit sin, and I will justify him." Joseph is to be justified, etc.

The last two sections are as follows: —

Sec. 24. "And again, as pertaining to the law of the priesthood: if any man espouse a virgin, and desire to espouse another, and the first gives her consent; and if he espouse the second, and they are virgins, and have vowed to no other man, then he is justified; he cannot commit adultery, for they are given unto him; for he cannot commit adultery with that that belongeth unto them, and to none else; and if he have ten virgins given unto him by this law, he cannot commit adultery, for they belong to him, and they are given unto him; therefore is he justified. But if one, or either of the ten virgins, after she is espoused, shall be with another man, she has committed adultery, and shall be destroyed; for they are given unto him to multiply and replenish the earth, according to my commandment, and to fulfil the promise which was given by my Father before the foundation of the world, and for their exaltation in the eternal worlds, that they may bear the souls of men; for herein is the work of my Father continued, that he may be glorified."

Sec. 25. "And again, verily, verily I say unto you, if any man have a wife who holds the keys of this power, and he teaches unto her the law of my priesthood as pertaining to these things, then shall she believe, and administer unto him, or she shall be destroyed, saith the Lord your God; for I will destroy her; for I will magnify my name upon all those who receive and abide in my law. Therefore it shall be lawful in me, if she receive not this law, for him to receive all things whatsoever I, the Lord his God, will give unto him, because she did not believe and administer unto him, according to my word; and she then becomes the transgressor, and he is exempt from the law of Sarah, who administered unto Abraham according to the law, when I commanded Abraham to take Hagar to wife. And now, as pertaining to this law: Verily, verily I say unto you, I will reveal more unto you hereafter; therefore let this suffice for the present. Behold, I am Alpha and Omega. Amen."

Such is the foundation upon which is built the superstructure of Utah polygamy. And the system itself, what is it in its theory and practical application? The mode of its institution has been shown. Its ceremonials, and many facts illustrative of its tendency and effects, will be given; and it is for our readers to determine how much it is better than promiscuous intercourse, and to discover, if they can, its redeeming features, as distinguished from such a state of society.

No man who has a wife already, has any right to make propositions of marriage to a lady, until he has consulted the President of the whole church, and through him obtained a revelation from God upon the subject. If the revelation be favorable, he must next obtain the approbation of the parents, and *thirdly*, he is to consult the lady herself.

It is also necessary that the first wife be consulted. If she refuses her consent, however, the lover husband may take an appeal to the President; and unless the wife can give to the President satisfactory reasons why her consent is withheld, the husband may proceed to introduce another wife into the family, against her will. The plan is, either to divorce the first wife, and damn her eternally, or to torment her daily, until, with a broken heart and a crushed spirit, she goes to the altar, and there gives another to her husband. Thus the semblance of her approbation is obtained.

The exquisite cruelty of this abominable practice will appear most vividly from the marriage ceremony.

"When the day set apart for the solemnization of the marriage ceremony has arrived, the *bridegroom* and the *wife*, and also the *bride*, together with their relations, and such other guests as may be invited, assemble at the place which they have appointed. The scribe then proceeds to take the names, ages, native towns, counties, States, and countries of the parties to be married, which he carefully enters on record. The President, who is the Prophet, Seer, and Revelator over the whole church, throughout the whole world, and who alone holds the keys of authority in this solemn ordinance, calls upon the *bridegroom* and his *wife*, and the *bride*, to arise, which they do, fronting the President. The wife stands on the left hand of her husband, while the bride stands on her left. The President then puts this question to the wife: 'Are you willing to give this woman to your husband, to be his lawful and wedded wife, for time and all eternity? If you are, you will manifest it by placing her right hand within the right hand of your husband.' The right hands of the bridegroom and the bride being thus joined, the wife takes her husband by the left arm, as if in the attitude of walking. The President then proceeds to ask the following questions of the man: 'Do you, brother, (calling him by name) take sister (calling the bride by name) by the right hand, to receive her unto yourself, to be your lawful and wedded wife, and you to be her lawful and wedded husband, for time and for all eternity, with a covenant and promise on your part, that you fulfil all the laws, rites, and ordinances pertaining to this holy matrimony, in the new and everlasting covenant, — doing this in the presence of God, angels, and these witnesses, of your own free will and choice?' The bridegroom answers, 'Yes.' The President then puts the question to the bride: 'Do you, sister, (calling her by name) take brother (calling him by name) by the right hand, and give yourself to him to be his lawful and wedded wife, for time and for all eternity, with a covenant and promise, on your part, that you will fulfil all the laws, rites, and ordinances pertaining to this holy matrimony, in the new and everlasting covenant, — doing this in the presence of God, angels, and these witnesses, of your own free will and choice?' The bride answers, 'Yes.' The President then says: 'In the name of the Lord Jesus Christ, and by the authority of the Holy Priesthood, I pronounce you legally and lawfully husband and wife, for time and all eternity; and I seal upon you the blessings of the holy resurrection, with power to come forth in the morning of the first resurrection, clothed with glory, immortality, and eternal lives; and I seal upon you the blessings of thrones, and dominions, and principalities, and powers, and exaltations; together with the blessings of Abraham, Isaac, and Jacob; and say unto you, be fruitful and multiply, and replenish the earth, that you may have joy and rejoicing in your posterity, in the day of the Lord Jesus. All these blessings, together with all other blessings, pertaining to the new and everlasting covenant, I seal upon your heads, and enjoin your faithfulness unto the end, by the authority of the Holy Priesthood, in the name of the Father, and of the Son, and of the Holy Ghost. Amen.'"

The scribe then enters the *marriage* on the records, and the parties retire. The wedding is then celebrated with a feast at the husband's house, and a "Mormon dance." The new wife is assigned a room, — if indeed the happy husband's domicil contains two rooms, — and her exper'ence in "plurality" begins.

In well-regulated Mormon families, the first wife stands at the head of domestic concerns. She carries the keys of the storehouse, makes the purchases for the family, and deals them out to the plural wives, in much the same manner as other housekeepers do to their cooks. The husband's will is law, and from it there is no appeal, except in extreme cases, when the Bishop may be consulted.

If a husband has lost his wife by death, before he had the opportunity of attending to this holy ordinance, and securing her as his lawful wife for eternity, then it is the duty of the second wife, first, to be sealed or married to the husband, for and in the name of the deceased wife, for all eternity; and, secondly, to be married for time and eternity herself, to the same man. Thus, by this holy ordinance, both the dead and the living wife will be his in the eternal worlds. But if, previous to marriage for eternity, a woman lose her husband by death, and marry a second, and if her first husband was a good man, then it is the duty of the second husband to be married to her for eternity, not for himself, but in the name of her deceased husband, while he himself can only be married to her for time; and he is obliged to enter into a covenant to deliver her up, and all her children, to her deceased husband, in the morning of the first resurrection.

Thus, by these refinements, a religious veil, captivating to the fancy, is thrown over the institution to hide its deformity. The same distinctions are carried through all the various relations of life; hence in case a widow is married to a widower, three ceremonies are necessary, in order fully to establish the eternal relations of all the parties.

Incest is the practical result of some of the branches of this new-fangled system of sealing and marriage. It has already been shown, by the report of the Committee on Territories in the United States Senate, and the Message of Gov. Harding, that a mother and her daughters (by a former husband) all live together, as wives of the same husband.*

* The marriage of brothers and sisters was at one time openly encour-

A still more revolting relation is sometimes maintained. It is called "heirship," and is plainly enough sanctioned by Young, as follows: —

"The text is, the right of heirship. I will, however, make an addition to the scripture, before I proceed further with my remarks, and say, 'the right of heirship in the Priesthood.'"

After asserting that the right of heirship belongs to the first-born son, he says: —

"There are sisters in the church that have been bereaved of their husbands, who died full of faith in the Holy Gospel, and full of hope for a glorious resurrection to eternal life. One of them is visited by a High Priest, of whom she seeks information touching her situation, and that of her husband. At the same time the woman has a son, twenty-five years of age, who is an Elder in one of the Quorums of the Seventies, and faithful in all the duties connected with his calling. She has also other sons and daughters. She asks this High-Priest what she shall do for her husband, and he very religiously says to her, 'You must be sealed to me, and I will bring up your husband, stand as proxy for him, receive his endowments, and all the sealing, keys, and blessings, and Eternal Priesthood for him, and be the father of your children.' Hear it, ye mothers! The mother that does that, barters away the sacred right of her son. Does she know it? No. But you that will hear, and be made to understand the true principles that govern this matter, go from this place, and do hereafter as has been done in by-gone days; instead of the children being robbed of their just rights, the woman shall lose her children, and they shall yet stand in their place, and be put in possession of their rights. Let mothers honor their children. If a woman has a son, let her honor that son." *

aged by President Brigham Young. George D. Watt, reporter for the *Deseret News*, married his half-sister, and lived with her as a wife, for about twelve years. She passed as the wife of Young, for several years, owing to the presence of gentiles and the prejudices of the saints. She has since been convinced of her error, and joined the "new organization," and with her three children returned to the States.

* April 8, 1853, *Deseret News*, Vol. III. No. 12.

But we will not pursue these disgusting details further.

Capt. Robert Burton, the famous English traveller, **thus epitomizes the Mormon faith:** —

"In the Tessarakai Decalogue above quoted, we find syncretized the Shemitic Monotheism, the Persian Dualism, and the Triads and Trinities of the Egyptians and the Hindoos. The Hebrews also have a personal Theos; the Buddhists, avataras and incarnations; the Brahmins, self-apotheosis of man by prayer and penance; and the East generally holds to quietism, — a belief that repose is the only happiness, and to a vast complication of states, in the world to be.

"The Mormons are like the Pythagoreans, in their procreation, transmigration, and exaltation of souls; like the followers of Leucippus and Democritus in their atomic materialism; like the Epicureans in their pure atomic theories, their *summum bonum*, and their sensuous speculations; and like the Platonists and Gnostics in their belief of the Æon, of ideas, and of moving principles in element. They are Fetichists in their ghostly fancies, their *evestra*, which became souls and spirits. They are Jews in their theocracy, their ideas of angels, their hatred of gentiles, and their utter segregation from the great brotherhood of mankind. They are Christians, inasmuch as they base their faith upon the Bible, and hold to the divinity of Christ, the fall of man, the atonement, and the regeneration. They are Arians, inasmuch as they hold Christ to be 'the first of God's creatures,' a 'perfect creature, but still a creature.'

"They are Moslems in their views of the inferior status of womankind, in their polygamy, and in their resurrection of the material body. Like the followers of the Arabian Prophet, they hardly fear death, because they have elaborated 'continuation.' They take no leap in the dark; they spring from this sublunary stage into a known, not into an unknown world; hence also their worship is eminently secular, their sermons are political or commercial, and — religion being with them not a thing apart, but a portion and parcel of every-day life — the intervention of the Lord in their material affairs becomes natural, and only to be expected.

"Their visions, prophecies, and miracles are those of the Illuminati; their mysticism that of the Druses, and their belief in the Millennium is a completion of the dreams of the Apocalyptic sects.

Masonry has evidently entered into their scheme; the Demiurgus whom they worship is 'as good at mechanical inventions as at any other business.'

"With their later theories, Methodism, Swedenborgianism,— especially in its view of the future state,— and Transcendentalism are curiously intermingled. And, finally, we can easily discern, in their doctrine of affinity of minds and sympathy of souls, the leaven of that faith which, beginning with the Mesmer, and progressing through the Rochester Rappers, and the Poughkeepsie Seer, threatens to extend wherever the susceptible nervous temperament becomes the characteristic of the race." *

According to this learned author, Mormonism is a conglomeration of all the *isms* from Adam to the present time.

The predominant characteristics of Mormonism are, the concentration of power in one individual,— the entire unity of church and state,— and the united efforts of the people and their leaders to establish and maintain a kingdom, spiritual and temporal, which shall spread over the whole earth, and result in the complete subjugation and subordination of all other kingdoms, principalities, and powers.

The establishment of polygamy among such a people, was no difficult matter. It was but an easy step from materialism to sensualism. Here the passions and lusts harmonize with the love of power and dominion.

The following toasts were given at a celebration on the 24th of July,† 1856. Therein the Mormons speak for themselves.

"*Mormonism.* A plurality of worlds, a plurality of gods, and a plurality of wives, with all truth in all eternity."

"*President Brigham Young.* With the keys of heaven and earth to open and shut, and all Israel to sanction."

* *City of the Saints,* pp. 397, 398.

† The 24th of July, 1847, was the day when the first Mormons arrived in Salt Lake Valley. The 24th of July is therefore celebrated by them as the 4th is by gentiles.

CHAPTER X.

BRIGHAM AS LORD OF THE HAREM.

Brigham's Block. — The Lion House. — The Tithing-House. — The Beehive House, Office, etc. — Description of the Harem. — Plan, Rooms, etc., of each Floor, and who occupies the same. — Life at the Harem. — Brigham at Home.

BRIGHAM'S BLOCK consists of about twenty acres, situated in the northern part of the city, and on the "first bench." These "benches" are level plateaus, or ridges running along at the base, and parallel with the mountain sides, and rising one above another, in regular succession. They are supposed to have been formed by the action of water, which doubtless at one time, covered the whole country, half way to the mountain tops. These benches overlook the city, which is mostly built on the flats, or bottom lands of the Jordan River. From Brigham's Bench the view is particularly beautiful, including the lake spread out in all its grandeur to the westward, with mountains rising in and beyond it, and mountains bounding the horizon in every other direction.

The grounds are surrounded by a wall from eight to ten feet in height, built of pebble-stones, cemented with mortar, and strengthened and supported by semicircular buttresses, at equal distances. The main entrance faces south, and the gateway is surmounted by a huge eagle carved in stone, which sits in a very uncomfortable position, and looks as though desirous of soaring to his native hills, or of making a descent upon some of the denizens of earth. His business is to watch and see who enters this sacred precinct, and to see that every third load of wood brought from City Creek (or

Brigham's) Canyon, which leads into this enclosure from the north, is deposited at the Prophet's door. The only entrance into this canyon is *through* this gate, and the canyon itself contains the only wood within fifteen miles of the city. The gold also, which it is well understood lies embedded in City Creek Canyon, is thus pretty well guarded.

The grounds are regularly laid out by William C. Staines, one of Brigham's adopted sons. The Prophet himself is very fond of fruit, and has carried its culture to a considerable degree of perfection. Large numbers of apple, pear, peach, and apricot trees, have been set out, and are producing every year. Grape culture also has not been neglected. It is a custom here to present the President with a specimen of every new variety of fruit and vegetable raised, and he receives very graciously anything presented, from a barrel of brandy to an umbrella, and is sure to think more of the donor, ever afterward.

Everything bears the mark of utility, and nothing is expended for show, or merely to gratify taste. No expensive flower-garden or green-house is to be seen, and this is perfectly characteristic of the Prophet, who is thoroughly utilitarian in all his views and tendencies.

On the southwest corner, and fronting the temple block, stands the tithing-store and office, and the Deseret printing-office. A description of the tithing-office and store, with its concomitant system, is given elsewhere. Back of the tithing-office, is a cattle-yard and barn, and numerous other buildings connected with tithing operations. Also a long row of buildings for various mechanical purposes: a carpenter's shop, shoe-shop, etc., with a blacksmith's shop in the rear. A number of small tenements are scattered over the premises, in which some of the employees reside.

The next large building, east of the Deseret store and printing-office, is the "Lion House," or Harem.

Further to the east, and connected with the Harem by a covered passage-way, is Brigham's general business office.

This is a large room, with three desks on either side; those to the left on entering, being appropriated to the clerks of "Brigham Young, Trustee in Trust for the Church," and those to the right, used by the clerks of "B. Young & Co." At the end opposite the door is a large platform railed off, and a gallery runs round the upper wall. The bookcases are of the yellow box elder-wood, highly polished. A business-like air pervades the room, and all is neat and clean.

Still further east and connected by another passage-way, is the private office of the "President." This is a plain, neat room, about twenty-five feet square. A large writing-desk and money-safe, tables, sofas, and chairs, and a "store" carpet, make up the furniture of the room. Back of, and adjoining this, is the *sanctum sanctorum;* the Prophet's own private bedroom. Few, even of the family, are permitted to enter this room without special invitation. Here is the "veil," behind which the Prophet receives his "revelations." Here he consults on his most private and important matters. He usually occupies this room alone, and when he desires the company of one of his wives, sends a message to that effect. When he is sick, he designates one of them to attend upon him.

The next building to the eastward is the Bee-Hive House, so named from models of bee-hives, on the top and in front of it. The honey-bee is the Mormon symbol, as according to "Reformed Egyptian," *Deseret* means "the honey-bee." As yet, however, the term applies only by faith, to Utah, as that industrious insect is almost an utter stranger to her borders.

The Bee-Hive House is a large, handsome adobe building, excellently plastered on the outside, and dazzlingly white. It is a two-storied tenement, and balconied from ground to roof. On the top is an observatory, surmounted by a bee-hive. Its cost was about $65,000, and it is the best edifice in the Territory.

Eastward still, and farther back from the road, stands the school-house, a white building, with green blinds, and a cupola. Here the children of the Prophet, about fifty in number, are educated. Though not an educated man himself, nor a patron of learning, among the people he employs good teachers, and takes considerable pains in the education of his children.

Farther to the right, upon an eminence, stands the "White House," occupied by Mrs. Young, the first wife, and her children. This is a very lonesome-looking old house, just such a one as you might fancy to be haunted. It was the first one built by Young, and glass being then very expensive, the windows are few and small.

These, with other smaller buildings, make up the improvements on the Prophet's Block, and constitute a small town of themselves.

THE HAREM.

The "Lion House" is a three-storied building. First, a basement, built of stone; then the main building, of wood, with peaked gable, and narrow-pointed Gothic windows, and steep roof. This house cost over $30,000, and would have cost more, but for the economy of the owner. It was completed, ready for the shingles, and the shingles were waiting. At a meeting in the Tabernacle on Sunday, he announced that he had a mission for all the carpenters, and asked if they would accept it. They raised their hands, and were then coolly told to "shingle the Lion House in the name of the Lord, and by the authority of the Holy Priesthood." A large lion, carved in stone, is placed upon a pillared portico, in front of this edifice, "resting, but watchful."

The following is the inside plan of the Lion House:—

Principal Story.—No. 1. Parlor. You enter the parlor from the left, and find a long, narrow room, with a large window in front, and four on the side, all heavily curtained. A beautiful Brussels carpet—design, a large bouquet of flowers, a rose, surrounded with other flowers and leaves, with a light ground—covers the floor. Two centre-tables, of solid

PLANS OF THE LION HOUSE.

BASEMENT STORY.

PRINCIPAL STORY.

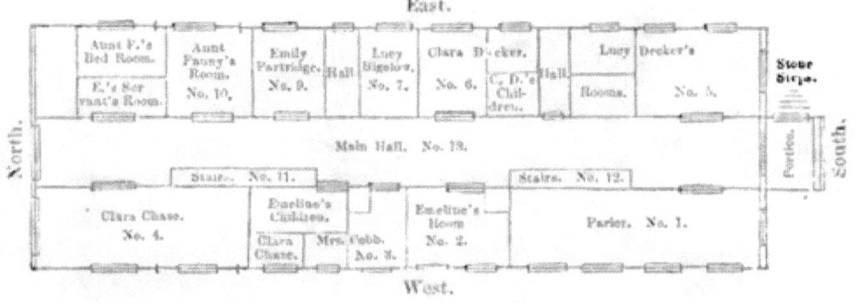

UPPER STORY.

mahogany, are placed at equal distances from the ends of the room. An elegant rose-wood piano sits at the lower end of the room. Between the windows hangs a large mirror, under which is a melodeon. A large sofa, upholstered with dark crimson velvet, occupies the opposite side, and near this is a bureau, with silver candlesticks and other ornaments. The chairs are painted to represent mahogany, and gilded. The room is painted and gilded in the same manner. A large stove in the corner, near the door, completes the furniture of the drawing-room of the Harem.

The family meet in this room, every morning and evening, at the ringing of the bell, to attend family prayers. The favorite wives, Emeline, Lucy, and Clara Decker, receive their company in the parlor, while the less favored ones entertain theirs in their rooms.

There are said to be underground passages from Brigham's houses to Kimball's on the north, and Wells's on the south. Also apartments under the Lion House, where he secretes his wealth and punishes his refractory wives. I cannot vouch for the truth of this assertion, but give it as a rumor. I am credibly informed, however, that all the carpenters and masons who worked on the lower story of this building have disappeared.

The three favorite wives before named, receive and entertain the friends of the Prophet, who visit at the Lion House. He very seldom introduces here any outside the church. Gentile visitors are usually entertained at the Bee-Hive.

No. 2 is Emeline's room, just back of the drawing-room. She formerly occupied No. 4, but was removed to No. 2, because Brigham, in going to her room, was obliged to pass several other rooms, thus creating remark and jealousy among the other women. He therefore had a hall, No. 8, prepared, leading from his office to No. 2, to which room he removed his favorite wife. Here he formerly spent much of his time. She dressed his artificial curls, petted and caressed him, and worshipped him alternately as her God. The furniture in Emeline's room consists of a three-ply carpet, mostly red, a high post bedstead, with white and red curtains, sofa, table, chairs painted to resemble oak, a large square mirror, oil-shades, wardrobe, and fireplace.

No. 3. Mrs. Cobb formerly occupied this room, but now resides in a neat cottage outside the walls. A three-ply carpet, red and yellow, common bedstead, standing in a recess, fall-leaf table, chairs painted oak, oil-shades with white curtains, a small mirror, also a small closet and a fireplace, constitute the furniture of this room. This was the home of a woman who had lived in a comfortable and commodious house in Boston, as its mistress and head, with a large and interesting family around her. All this she left for the ridiculous delusion called Mormonism. To what extremes will not religious fanaticism and mistaken zeal lead its devotees!

No. 4 is a large, pleasant room, with bedroom attached. This was occupied by Clara Chase and her children, before her death. She was once a favorite with Brigham, which will account for her superior accommodations. This room is furnished as follows: a carpet similar to Emeline's, common bedstead placed in a recess, common table, nice large gilt mirror, red and white curtains, wardrobe, and fireplace.

No. 5. This room, opposite the parlor, belongs to Lucy Decker, the first wife in plurality, and is rather plainly furnished. Rag-carpet, common bedstead, stand, mirror, oak chairs, wardrobe, small cupboard and a fireplace, curtains of the prevailing colors red and white. A sitting-room and two bedrooms are allowed Mrs. Lucy Decker, as she has a number of children.

No. 6. In Clara Decker's room stands a beautifully carved bedstead, arched overhead with heavy damask curtains, chairs like parlor, stand, settee, Venetian blinds, and oil-shades. Brigham's portrait in oil, half size, hangs on the wall, also a large mirror. A rag-carpet covers the floor. A bedroom and recess are attached to this room, and from its superior furniture it is easy to infer that its occupant is a woman fond of show, as well as a favorite with the Prophet.

No. 7. Lucy Bigelow's room contains a common bedstead, three chairs, a stand, wardrobe, carpet, mirror, and white curtains.

No. 8. Hall leading to Emeline's room.

No. 9. Emily Partridge, one of the "proxies," occupies this room. A common carpet, calico curtains, a fall-leaf table, bedstead, and the usual quota of chairs, make up the furniture of this woman's home.

Formerly a tin pail and tin wash-dish constituted the toilet set of most of the wives, but since the Prophet has had so many fat government contracts, and his purse has become plethoric with public money, and from the continued inflow of tithing, he has indulged his "women folks" with crockery ware. As Uncle Sam is rich, and a good easy-going soul, why should he not furnish "Harems" for his "loyal and law-abiding citizens?"

No. 10 is Aunt Fanny Murray's room. Her furniture consists of a red and yellow carpet, home-made bedsteads, oak chairs, a fall-leaf table, and oil-shades. A sitting-room and a small bedroom belong to Aunt Fanny. But you ask, Who is Aunt Fanny? She was in her young days, Fanny Young, and had a great awkward brother, called Brigham. She married a Mr. Murray, to whom she was devotedly attached. She was a gentle, kind creature; and when her husband died, she became dependent on her brother. She had long been a believer in Mormonism, and was with the Mormons at Nauvoo. After the death of her husband, she was, by the earnest persuasion of her brother Brigham, induced to be sealed to another. She protested at the time, and said it would break her heart. And in relating the story to a young friend, years afterward,—"Bessie," said she, "my poor, poor heart is breaking now;" and laying her hand on her heart, she wept aloud. Aunt Fanny has gone to her rest. She has suffered want and privation, mental anguish and bodily pain, for her religion. Who shall say that her dear heavenly Father, whom she so blindly worshipped, will not reward her with a crown of glory in His kingdom above, when she shall rejoin the partner of her youth, free from the shackles of tyranny and superstition?

Nos. 11 and 12 are staircases.

No. 13. Main Hall, extending the whole length of the building; it is lighted from a large window at the further end.

This completes the principal story of the Lion House.

The Basement Story. — No. 14. General cellar, where all kinds of vegetables and provisions are stored.

No. 15. Ash-house.

No. 16. Weaving-room. The wives spin, color, and prepare the yarn, and a man is kept employed in weaving. A large quantity of cloth is made at the Harem every year. Brigham's motto is, " No drones in the hive."

No. 17 is the coachman's room.

No. 18. Pantry. Milk, pies, cake, bread, and cooked provisions, are kept in this place.

No. 19. Back Hall.

No. 20 was formerly occupied as a school-room and dancing academy for the Youngs.

No. 21. Wash-room.

No. 22. Kitchen.

No. 23. Dish-room.

No. 24. The Dining-room is about fifteen by forty feet. Two tables extend its whole length, allowing only a passageway at each end. A third table extends two thirds of the length of the room. Also a side-table, and chairs of different sizes, to accommodate the various ages of the family group.

Each wife has her seat at the table, and her children sit with her. The wives who have children are seated at the heads of the tables in the order in which they came into the family, — they taking the preference over those who have no children. This is the case in every well-regulated Mormon family. Among Mormons, the title of mother includes that of queen, and is consequently the highest distinction a woman can attain. If a woman has no children, she is miserable, and her position in society a very unpleasant one. She can only redeem herself by urging her husband to take more wives. Many women do this, and afterward labor incessantly for the new mistresses and their children.

Lucy Decker, the first "plurality" woman, presides at one of the long tables. At the head of the short table, Brigham always presides, when he takes his meals at the Harem. On his right sits Clara Decker, with her children, and on the left, Emeline, with hers. This order is strictly observed. This preference causes much unhappiness on the part of other wives less favored.

No. 25. Main Hall.

Nos. 26 and 27 are staircases.

No. 28. Small side Hall.

Third Story. — This floor is divided in the centre by a wide hall, and ranged on either side are ten small rooms, of nearly uniform size, with one door and window each. These rooms are about twelve by fifteen feet, and are occupied principally by those of "the women" who have no children. The windows are of the Gothic style.

No. 29 is occupied by "Twiss," and has a carpet, common bedstead, three oak chairs, a little toilet-stand, small mirror, and plain white curtains.

All these rooms are similarly furnished. All are neat and clean. Harriet Cook, Ellen Rockwood, and Twiss, display more taste than the others in the arrangement of their little cages.

In addition to these articles, Harriet Cook has mahogany chairs, instead of oak, and a large cupboard, painted to represent mahogany. All the rooms are furnished with stoves, except three, which have fireplaces.

No books, except the Book of Mormon, Book of Doctrine and Covenants, and Mormon Hymn-Book, will be seen in any room except Eliza Snow's; she being a woman of considerable literary taste, and withal a writer,—having made a number of contributions to Mormon literature,—her room is indicative of the same, being well supplied with books and papers.

What the Women do.

The internal arrangement of affairs at the Harem is very similar to that of a young ladies' boarding-school. Each woman having her own room, her affairs are all centred there. The culinary department is under the control of such of the wives as Brigham from time to time appoints. She is the stewardess, and carries the keys. A cook is employed, — generally a man, — and several servants besides, who are all under the control of the stewardess.

When the meals are prepared and ready, the bell rings, and each woman, with her children, if she have any, files down to the dinner-table, and is seated as before stated.

Each, on rising, has her children to attend to, and get ready for breakfast; this over, she commences the business of the day, arranges her rooms, and sits down to her sewing or other work, as the case may be.

A sewing-machine is brought into requisition, and one of the number appointed to use it. For the benefit of those who want a sewing-machine, it may be well to state how this one was procured. One day a man from St. Louis came to offer one for sale, stating that his price was ninety dollars. Brigham bought it, promising to pay the man whenever he should call. He being poor, called in a few days. He did not get his pay. He called again, a number of times, with the same result. One of the wives became quite indignant, and said,—" If I was in his place, I never would ask it from one so high in the priesthood. He had better give it to him than to ask pay of him." The poor man never received his money, and as soon as he could get the means, left the Territory. This is the manner in which the Prophet becomes possessed of much of his property.

Most of the women spin and make their every-day clothing, doing their own coloring. They are quite proud of the quantity of cloth manufactured in their establishment every year. All work hard, and take but very little out-of-door exercise. Parties and the theatre are the favorite amusements. At the theatre, Brigham and one or two of the favored wives sit together in " the King's box," but the remainder of the women and the children sit in what is called " Brigham's corral." This is in the parquette, about the centre of the area. The Prophet goes down once or twice during the evening to the corral, and chats for a few moments with one and another, but in a short time he can be seen beside his " dear Amelia " again.

At the Mormon parties, much gayety prevails. Appearances are maintained, somewhat, by paying more respectful deference to the first wives, on such occasions. Gentiles, with whom the saints are on good terms, are well received and kindly entertained at these parties, and all join in giving themselves up to the influences of mirth and festivity. Dancing is not only a favorite amusement, it is more; it is cultivated to such an extent that it becomes a passion.

Brigham's women, though better clothed than formerly, still work very hard. They are infatuated with their religion, and devoted to their husband. If they cannot obtain his love, they content themselves with his kindness, and endeavor to think themselves happy. As religion is their only solace, they try to make it their only object. If it does not elevate their minds, it deadens their susceptibilities, and as they are not permitted to be *women*, they try to convince themselves that it is God's will they should be *slaves*.

A music-master, a dancing-master, and a teacher of the ordinary branches of an English education, are employed in the family school. Also a teacher of French. His children have much better advantages than any other in the Territory. Dancing and music are the leading accomplishments, and everything else is made subordinate to these.

Brigham at Home.

Much interest naturally attaches to the inner life of such a man as Brigham Young. His time is much occupied. He rises early, calls the whole family together; they sing a hymn; he prays fervently, and they separate for the duties of the day. In past times, he ate at the Harem. His fare is very simple, usually consisting of a bowl of milk, covered with cream, and dry toast or bread.

His next duty used to be, to "see the women folks," to whom he was friendly and kind, but no more. He is not Brigham the husband, but Brigham the Prophet and Seer. The women fear and reverence him as their God, watch his countenance as he gives them counsel, and look upon every word he utters as the "key" to some great mystery. He pays much less attention to them now than formerly, but is kind and considerate in his conduct toward them.

This duty done, he next proceeds to his office, to receive his visitors, and to transact any business that may be there awaiting his attention. His counsel is sought upon all subjects, even in the minutest domestic affairs of the people. So numerous are these applications for advice and assistance, that many are turned away with a very brief answer, while some are denied access entirely.

Theoretically, no one but he can "seal" or give plural wives in marriage, and such at first was the practice. But in later years, this power has been delegated to Kimball and others, and to the Bishops of distant wards. The divorces of such can only come from him; and from this source alone he derives a handsome revenue. He once said from the pulpit to the people, that "the divorce money which he received through their d——d foolery, furnished him with plenty of spending money."

No speculations are entered upon, no enterprises begun, without consulting "Brother Brigham." This he encourages and commands. "If you do not know what to do, in order to do right, come to me at any time, and I will give you the word of the Lord on the subject."

This mode of directing the people, though laborious and perplexing, has its advantages. Their secret thoughts and plans are thus laid open to his view, and facts are sometimes brought to his knowledge very important and essential to be known, having a direct bearing upon the permanent maintenance of his rule and authority. The people, too, by such frequent consultations, are led to believe that their prosperity, happiness, and safety, are all dependent upon the favor and assistance of their leader. If any one becomes contumacious and troublesome, he has the earliest information of the fact, and soon devises means to be rid of the annoyance.

It is a common expression among the people at Salt Lake, "When I obey counsel, I am prospered in everything; when I neglect it, I prosper in nothing."

Years ago, Brigham was kind and fatherly toward his followers. If he met one of them in the street, he gave him a cordial greeting and a hearty shake of the hand, with an inquiry concerning his family and prospects. But of late, the Prophet, having become rich, has grown haughty and proud, and as he rides along in his fine carriage, surrounded by his courtiers and sycophants, the toiling, hard-handed brethren, who receive no friendly recognition, sometimes shake their heads and mutter sentiments strangely discordant with those generally expressed in conversation.

The feeling of dissatisfaction at the distance placed by the Prophet between himself and his followers, has grown, as that distance became more perceptible, until it has become quite universal among the poorer classes. The poverty-stricken saint, as he takes home upon his back or his wheel-barrow a sack of flour, or piece of meat, obtained with difficulty by his daily toil, beholds his Prophet, his spiritual guide, clothed in fine raiment, seated in a splendid carriage, by his side a courtesan, a so-called wife. He sees the smile and kind word, which should be given to his suffering and down-trodden people, lavished upon a harlot. He turns in disgust, and with a weary and troubled spirit, seeks temporary rest in his own humble home. Here kind poverty has protected him from the vices of his leaders, and he thanks God inwardly, after all, that he has not yet abandoned the wife of his youth. To such, the new preachers sent by the "Josephites," to bring the people back to virtue, to loyalty, and to the original Mormon religion, appear as angels from heaven, and hence the ready assent given to their teachings, and the rapid defection from the established church.

CHAPTER XI.

THE WIVES OF BRIGHAM YOUNG.

Mary Ann Angell Young, the first wife. — Her Family. — Lucy Decker Seely, the first wife in Plurality. — More of "My Women": Clara Decker, Harriet Cook, Lucy Bigelow, Twiss, Martha Bowker, Harriet Barney, Eliza Burgess, Ellen Rockwood, Susan Snively, Jemima Angell, Margaret Alley, Margaret Pierce, Mrs. Hampton, Mary Bigelow, Emeline Free, or the Light of the Harem. — Proxy Women: Miss Eliza Roxy Snow, Zina D. Huntington, Amelia Partridge, Mrs. Cobb, Mrs. Smith, Clara Chase, the Maniac. — Amelia, the last love. — The Prophet in Love the Thirtieth Time.

Mrs. Mary Ann Angell Young.

THIS lady is the first living and legal wife of the Prophet. She is a native of New York, and is a fine-looking, intelligent woman. She is large, portly, and dignified. Her hair is well sprinkled with the frosts of age; her clear, hazel eyes and melancholy countenance indicate a soul where sorrow reigns supreme. She has been very much attached to her husband, and his infidelity has made deep inroads upon her mind. Her deep-seated melancholy often produces flights of insanity, which increase with her declining years.

Bereft of her husband's society, she naturally clings to her children, of whom she has five: Joseph, Brigham A., John, Alice, and Luna. They all reside with her. She formerly occupied "the Bee-Hive House," but as the number of her husband's wives increased, it became necessary that additional accommodations should be furnished the "plural" portion of the family. The first wife was obliged to vacate her residence for the benefit of new comers. She was removed to a great barn-like house on the hill. This building looks more like a penitentiary than anything else. It was the first house built upon the premises, and, as before stated, is very deficient in the number and size of its windows.

Mrs. Young seldom receives guests, and her husband himself scarcely ever pays her a visit.

When I looked upon this poor, suffering woman, as she sat at church, surrounded by her husband's mistresses, I seemed for the first time fully to realize the true character of that " institution " which has crushed the hearts of many noble women.

She is very kind to her children and dependents, and is much beloved by them. She has not succeeded so well in gaining the affection of "the wives." With them she is very unpopular, and by some of them she is often mocked and upbraided. It is said, "one hates whom he has injured." This may account for much of this feeling among the " plurals."

Joseph, or " Joe Young," as he is familiarly known in Utah, is a fast young man. He has been on a " mission," travelled in Europe, smokes, chews, gets drunk, swears, preaches the gospel, has three wives whom he whips and otherwise shamefully abuses, and is a good Mormon, in full fellowship in the church. While at a fashionable watering-place, at Great Salt Lake, in the summer of 1863, he insulted a gentile lady. The gentleman who accompanied her, being an officer, promptly knocked him down, and this not seeming to be satisfactory, afterwards challenged him. Joseph's friends interfered, and obtained a settlement of the difficulty.

Brigham A. is more respectable. He has also been on a "mission." This is equivalent to saying that he has been wild and reckless, as it is the Mormon custom to send all who are unruly and hard to manage, or who have committed crimes, on a mission. It is thought that by " bearing the pure vessels of the Lord" to such poor wicked wretches as the gentiles, they will perchance themselves become purified.

John, being the youngest, has not developed his tastes so fully. He seems inclined to seek after the loaves and fishes of office. He was Sergeant-at-Arms of the Council in the winter of 1863-64, and will doubtless be one of its members when he is old enough, should his father then reign in Utah.

Mrs. Alice Clawson is the oldest daughter. Rather amiable, with fair hair, blue eyes, and of *petite* stature. She is one of the performers in her father's theatre. As an *artiste* she is "flat, stale, and unprofitable." But being Brigham's daughter, and good looking, she is applauded to the echo. She is one of three wives of Hiram B. Clawson, who is the Prophet's chief business agent and manager. Quick, shrewd, and unscrupulous, he is a fit instrument with which to accomplish the purposes of such a man.

In the year 1851, a Mr. Tobin came to Salt Lake with Capt. Stansbury. While there, he met Miss Alice, fell in love with her, and they were engaged to be married. Mr. T. had occasion to leave Salt Lake on business, and did not return until 1856. He then renewed his engagement with Alice, but afterward, for reasons satisfactory to himself, broke it. This subjected him to the vengeance of her father, which never slumbers. Tobin and his party were followed, attacked in the night, on Santa Clara River, 370 miles south of Salt Lake City. Several of the party were severely wounded. They lost six horses, and were compelled to abandon their baggage, which was completely riddled by bullets. During Tobin's absence, Alice had been engaged to another, who had been sent off to the Sandwich Islands, by her watchful father. Hiram B. Clawson, the confidential clerk of the President, next appeared as a candidate for the young lady's hand. He had already one wife, but was anxious to secure a second.

A little incident in their courtship, will illustrate the manner of obtaining No. 2.

"Good-morning, sister *Clawson*," said a young friend whom she met in walking.

"What do you wish me to understand?" said Alice.

"Nothing more than that your father gave his consent

this morning, in my presence, to your marriage with Hiram Clawson."

"There, Alice," said brother Clawson, who at this moment made his appearance, " did I not **tell** you? You would not believe me."

" This matter begins to **be** serious," said Alice, **" now that** my father has given me away to a man that has **one** wife already, and is courting another beside me, both of them much handsomer than I am."

Hiram was nettled, for it was true that **he was** courting a third wife, and of the three Alice was the least beautiful. She then proposed, playfully, to elope with an old gentleman, a friend of the family. " I would do so," she said, " before I would be given away **like** an old mule, to a man who already has one wife, and is seeking for others."

Yet Alice, though doubtless **giving expression at this time** to the sentiments of her heart, was afterward prevailed upon, and consented to become No. 2 in the harem of Hiram B. Clawson. Hiram, having commenced at a much earlier age than his father-in-law, may, if unchecked in his career, **yet rival him** in the number **of his wives** and the extent **and** magnificence of his " plural " establishment.

Luna Young is a *character.* She is very wilful and headstrong. She always governed her sister Alice, and even her father could not control this wayward child.

She is the fourth daughter, **by** the first wife, two having died. She has light hair, blue eyes, and a fair complexion. She is very haughty and beautiful. Slender as the gazelle, and free and joyous as **a** bird, brooking no control, she **was** the light, and often **the** annoyance **of** her father's house in her girlish days. She is now married, and very likely will become amiable and docile, under Mormon discipline.

Lucy Decker Seely.

This is the first wife in " plurality," — or the **second** **" woman."**

Lucy Decker was married to Isaac Seely, and had two children. She afterward became a Mormon, and went to Nauvoo to reside. Her husband, Seely, was somewhat dissipated, but treated her well. She, however, saw Brother Brigham, and loved him. He visited her, told her that Seely could never give her an "exaltation" in the eternal world; that he, being "high in the priesthood," could make her a queen, in the first resurrection.

She yielded to these inducements and the promptings of her inclination, left her husband, and was "sealed" to Brigham Young.

Lucy Decker has brown hair, dark eyes, small features, a fair skin, and of short stature; but quite *en bon point*. She would strongly remind you of a New-England housewife, "fat, fair, and forty." In common with nearly all the inmates of the Harem, she is of very ordinary intellect, and limited education.

Her first child, after marrying Young, was named Brigham Heber, and was the first-born in Mormon polygamy. He is now a lad of about eighteen years of age.

Lucy Decker is still one of the favorite wives. She lives in the "Bee-Hive," and keeps a sort of boarding-house for the work-hands. She has had eight children by Brigham, all of whom are living. A story is told which illustrates well the disposition and character of these polygamous children. "Brigham Heber" was in the habit of playing while the family were at breakfast. One morning, after breakfast was over, this boy, then only ten or twelve years of age, went into the kitchen, and undertook to help himself to anything he could find. Mr. Smith, the cook, would not permit it. Brigham Heber seized a fork, and with oaths that would put a pirate to shame, swore he would stab the cook. Smith caught him, wrenched the fork from his hand, and pushed him into the hall. He and Oscar, son of Harriet Cook, swore they would kill Smith the first time they should catch him out.

More of " My Women."

Clara Decker, sister of Lucy Decker, is a short, thick-set person, very much like Lucy in appearance. She is much more intelligent and agreeable than her sister, and in every way her superior.

She is also quite a favorite with the Prophet; has three or four children, and is much attached to her "husband."

Harriet Cook was early in plurality; having been sealed to Brigham, at "Winter Quarters," on the Missouri River, while the Mormons were on their way to Utah. This was five years before polygamy was publicly proclaimed in Utah as a divine institution. Harriet is very tall, has light hair, blue eyes, a fair complexion, and sharp nose. She is rather slender, but has much power of endurance, and a look of determination.

When all is going on smoothly, she is as calm and serene as a May morning; but let Brigham or any one else in the establishment cross her path, and the blue eyes at once light up, and give evidence of a coming storm. When irritated and aroused, she denounces the whole Mormon religion, including polygamy, and says, " the whole thing is a humbug, and may go to the devil for aught she cares." Brigham, though a stern disciplinarian, makes good his escape, at such times, and the "women" all keep at a respectful distance.

When she is in a religious mood, which is seldom the case, she says: " I don't profess to know much, but there is one thing I *do* understand, and that is Mormonism. Whenever Brother Brigham (all the wives call him Brother) goes behind the veil, I make him tell me what he sees and hears there. I mean to know all about it." She is the "smartest" of all the women. She has one son in plurality, named Oscar. He is a wild, ugly boy, and curses his mother *ad libitum*. Brigham cares nothing for this woman, and avoids her as much as possible.

Lucy Bigelow is of middling stature, has dark brown hair, blue eyes, aquiline nose, and a pretty mouth, and is very pleasant and affable. She is very pretty and ladylike in the ball-room, but does not appear to so good advantage in the nursery and kitchen. She is the one who was the subject of a well-turned repartee at the anniversary ball in Salt Lake City, on the 24th of July, 1863. Governor Harding, on that occasion, having danced with several of the wives of "Governor" Young, became somewhat enthusiastic and extravagant in his compliments. Among other fine sayings, he remarked to one of the wives, upon leading her on to the floor, — "The President has introduced several of his wives to me as 'Mrs. Young,' 'Mrs. Young,' 'Mrs. Young.' As well might the astronomer point me to the stars of heaven, without giving me their names." "Governor, I understand your compliment, and appreciate it. The name of this particular star is Lucy."

She has but little influence over Brigham, and he seldom visits her.

Twiss has sandy hair, inclined to curl, round features, blue eyes, low forehead, complexion fair, face somewhat freckled. She is short and stout. This woman makes a good servant, and is always ready to wait on her lord and master. She prepares his linen, and is content. She has no children.

Martha Bowker is low in stature, with black hair and eyes. She is very quiet. Is plain and sensible; neither showy nor interesting. Very neat in dress, very ordinary in intellect and acquirements. She is of few words, and rather quick-tempered. Very little influence over the Prophet.

Harriet Barney. — This lady is tall, slender, and graceful. She has hazel eyes, light-brown hair, mild, sweet expression of countenance, and is indeed a beautiful woman. Her character is as lovely as her face, and the suffering and sorrowing always find a friend in her. She is patient and forbearing, and would rather suffer wrong than do wrong. Her kind and sympathetic nature, and excellent character, place her far above all the other inmates of the Harem.

Believing in polygamy, she left her husband, and became one of the plural wives of the President of the church in which she believed. She loves, with all the intensity of her nature, him for whom she has sacrificed everything. Of course, she deeply feels his neglect, but, like a true woman, complains not. Having sacrificed her happiness upon the altar of her faith, she continues to love, to endure, and to suffer.

She had three children by her first husband; none since.

Eliza Burgess. — Her parents resided in Manchester England, and came to Nauvoo in the early days of Mormonism. Soon after, they both died, leaving Eliza an orphan. She was thrown upon the cold charities of the world, and Brother Brigham, ever the friend of *youth* and *beauty*, took her into his family. She served seven years, and then desired to marry another. She applied to Young for his consent, but the Prophet had other projects inconsistent in their nature with the proposed marriage. "Eliza," he said, "you have been so long in the family, that I need you. I wish to marry you myself. Will you not be my wife? Brother S. is a very good man, but I can give you a greater exaltation. I can make you a queen." This argument was conclusive, and Eliza gave up her lover, and married Brigham Young.

In person Eliza is small, with large dark eyes, dark hair, and dark complexion. She is quick-tempered, and is of the class — English serving-girl. She is the only one of the Prophet's women who is not American. She has several children.

Ellen Rockwood is of medium size, slender, with light hair, light-brown eyes, and fair complexion. She is the daughter of the warden of the penitentiary, who is a "regular down-east Yankee." Ellen is rather quiet, even-tempered, but quite narrow-minded. Her health is poor, and she spends most of her time in embroidery and needle-work. She has no children, and, per consequence, very little influence with her husband. He calls upon her in her little room, about once in six months.

Susan Snively. — A middle-aged woman, of medium size, dark hair, light eyes, dark complexion, and expressionless face; the plainest of all the women. She is good and kind in her nature, quiet and retiring. She spins and colors yarn, and is a good housewife, of the type — New-England farmer's wife. Having no children, she adds nothing to the kingdom and glory of her husband, and is estimated accordingly.

Jemima Angell is the sister of Mary Ann, the lawful wife. She is an elderly lady, with dark hair, gray eyes, and pensive countenance. Of low stature, but quite robust. Her first husband died out of the church, and she is merely sealed to Young, for her exaltation in another state. She lives in a little house by herself, and seldom receives a visit from her spiritual husband.

Margaret Alley. — Short and small; light hair and eyes, rather lengthened features, but mild expression of countenance. Being much neglected by her husband, she became very melancholy. She died in 1853, leaving two children.

Margaret Pierce. — Of medium height, light hair, and blue eyes, sharp nose, and very variable in temper. She has several children, but not much influence with her husband.

Mrs. Hampton. — This woman is very tall, and noble in appearance, has round features, large lustrous eyes, dark hair, and fair complexion. She was early married to Mr. Hampton, by whom she had six children. They removed to Nauvoo, where Hampton died. Mrs. Hampton was afterward sealed to Young.

When the Mormons were driven from Nauvoo, Mrs. Hampton was, for some reason, left behind. She then married a Mr. Cole, by whom she had one daughter, named Vilate. When this child was about four years old, Cole went to California. Young then sent for Mrs. Hampton to come and live with him. She obeyed, and became, a second time, one of his plural wives. During this time Cole wrote letters frequently, and sent her his likeness.

About this time, Feramorz Little, one of Young's nephews, married Julia Hampton, daughter of Mrs. H., and half sister to Vilate Cole. Mrs. Hampton lived at the Harem about eight years, and superintended the culinary department. Some misunderstanding having arisen between her and the Prophet, he again cast her off. It is said that she was unwilling to be sealed over the altar for eternity to Young, preferring her first husband in the eternal world. Her son, Nephi Hampton, provided a house for her at Ogden, a pleasant town forty miles north of Salt Lake, where she now resides.

Vilate is now about fourteen years of age, beautiful and accomplished. She and Brigham Heber, now about twenty years old, were engaged to be married, but his father disapproved the match, and laid a plan to defeat it. In the fall of 1863, Feramorz Little sent for Vilate to come down to the city, and proposed to have her board with him and attend school. His real object was to secure her for his fourth wife and at the same time prevent her marrying the son of the President. During all this time the girl frequently inquired, with much anxiety, about her father.

In 1863 Cole enlisted in the 2d Regiment of Infantry, Nevada Volunteers, and came to Salt Lake City expressly for the purpose of finding his daughter. After much inquiry he ascertained where his wife and child were living, and wrote a letter to Vilate. The mother received the letter, read it, and put it in the fire. Thus the matter rested, until Vilate came to the city. One day she said to her sister Julia, (Mrs. Little,) "Would it not be strange if my father was among the soldiers?" Said Julia, "He is. Did n't you know it? Nephi told me all about it." This gave her new courage, and thenceforth she made every effort to see her father. For some time she was closely watched, and Cole, who had found where she was, was denied admission to her;

but the girl's resolution remaining firm, Little, fearing she would leave him, finally permitted an interview. The happy meeting of the father with his only child, after an absence of eleven years, who shall describe? Cole still remains in Utah, devoted to his daughter, whom he visits frequently, and is not without hope of getting her away from her unfortunate associations. The task is a delicate and difficult one, and in his efforts to accomplish it, he has the sympathy of every father.

Mary Bigelow. — I can give no description of this woman. She was sealed to Young at "Winter Quarters," and came on with him to Utah. After a time she left the Harem, and what became of her is unknown to me.

Emeline Free, or the Light of the Harem.

>―― "O Nourmahal!
>Thou loveliest, dearest of them all;
>The one whose smile shone out alone
>Amidst a world, the only one
>Whose light, among so many lights,
>Was like that star, on starry nights,
>The seaman singles from the sky,
>To steer his bark forever by!"

Emeline is tall and graceful; with mild, violet eyes, fair hair, inclined to curl. She has long been the favorite of the Prophet, — the light of his eyes, and the joy of his heart.

Mr. and Mrs. Free, her father and mother, were opposed to polygamy, and Brigham went one day to convince them of their error. The beautiful Emeline was the first he sought to win, and he argued and expounded the new doctrine with wonderful zeal and fervor. At length the parents were convinced. The Prophet of the Lord stepped up to Emeline, laid his saintly hand upon her shoulder, and said, in fervid accents, "Emeline, will you be my wife?" "Yes, sir," was the reply. This was their courtship. She at once became the favorite, and many a heart grew sad when she became an inmate of the Harem.

Brigham distinguished her in every way; gave her better rooms than the rest, and servants to wait upon her. She grew to love him, and obtained a powerful influence over him. There is no weapon so powerful as a woman's tears. This Emeline believed, and often acted upon, to bring back her truant lover, when she thought too much attention was paid to others. Finally, so great became the jealousy of the other wives, that the husband of these contending fair ones constructed a private hall leading from his office to Emeline's room, that he might visit her without observation or constraint. He devoted himself to her exclusively, and she reigned supreme over the sisters. She received her company in the grand saloon; she occupied the seat of honor at the table, at the right hand of her husband. In short, she was the mistress of the Harem.

At that time the most of the women did their own work, and stayed in their own rooms, so that there was but little communication with each other. She has eight children, but is still a young-looking woman.

But, alas! "the course of true love never did run smooth," and Emeline was doomed to have a rival. When the Prophet "took" Amelia, his last love, poor Emeline was heart-broken. She was taken very sick, and her life was, for a long time, despaired of. From her "sisters" she received no sympathy. The bitter cup which they had been obliged to drink, was now commended to her own lips. From the confiding and happy wife, she has become the rejected and suffering mistress, and must now drag out the remainder of her days a faded, cast-off woman. And Amelia, the present queen, what of her? She too, will soon take her place by the side of Emeline and Mary Ann. Other and younger women will take the place she now occupies, and in their turn be cast off, to suffer with her.

"*Proxy Women.*"

This is a very common term in Utah, and signifies that a woman is married to one man for "time," and sealed to another for eternity. All her children belong to the man to whom she is sealed, no matter which may be their father, or whether the mother ever married the celestial husband "in time." This is a refinement upon the Jewish doctrine, which required a man to "raise up children to his dead brother."

Of this class of women Brigham Young has four, all of whom, while they live with him for "time," are sealed to Joseph Smith for eternity, and to Joseph must they be delivered over, with their children, in the first resurrection.

"Miss" *Eliza Roxy Snow* is of middling stature, dark hair, well silvered with gray; dark eyes, noble intelligent countenance, and quiet and dignified in manner. She is the most intellectual of the women.

Her literary taste and acquirements are good, and she has composed some very creditable hymns for the church of which she is a conscientious and devoted member. A volume of her poems has also been published, some of which evince genius of a high order.

She is quite exclusive in her tastes, and associates but little with the "women." She occupies a small room on the third floor of the Harem, about twelve by fifteen feet in size. A neat carpet covers the floor; a common bedstead occupies one corner. There are some oak chairs grained, with crochet covers, white window-curtains and bed-spread, her "own handiwork." Behind the door is a neat little wardrobe. On a shelf over the window, stands a vase of artificial flowers. A stand, covered with books, usually occupies the centre of the room, and these articles, with a neat little stove, make up the furniture.

This is the *home* of "the sweet singer of Israel." She has cast the charm of her genius over the rude materials, and there is an air of neatness, comfort, and refinement about her little sanctum which is not apparent in any other portion of the house. Here she receives and entertains her company. She occupies her time chiefly in writing, and in needle-work. She is highly respected by the family, who call her "one of the nobles of the earth." When tired of writing and study, she walks out and visits her friends. If any one is sick in the house she looks after the invalid, and shows every kindness and attention. She soothes the afflicted, and cares for the infirm and aged. She and Zina D. Huntington are the most lady-like and accomplished of the wives.

The following verses, written by Miss Eliza R. Snow, will show her style as well as the religious fervor and fanaticism for which she is remarkable.

[For the *Deseret News*.]
"*The Ladies of Utah to the Ladies of the United States Camp, in a Crusade against the Mormons.*

BY MISS E. R. SNOW.

Why are you in these mountains,
    Exposed to frosts and snows?
Far from your sheltering houses,
    From comfort and repose?

Has cruel persecution,
    With unrelenting hand,
Thrust you from home and kindred,
    And from your native land?

Have you been robbed and plundered,
    Till you are penniless,
And then in destitution
    Driven to the wilderness?

No, no; you've joined a crusade
    Against the peace of those
Driven to these distant valleys
    By cruel, murderous foes.

Amid the dreary desert,
    Where hideous red men roam;
Where beasts of prey were howling,
    We've made ourselves a home.

Can woman's heart be callous,
   And made of flint and steel?
Perhaps you'll learn to pity,
   When you are made to *feel*.

Should sickness prey upon you,
   And children cry for bread,
With bitter self-reproaches
   You'll rue the path you tread.

We love with purest feelings,
   Our husbands, children, friends;
We've learned to prize the blessings
   Which God in mercy sends.

We have the ancient order
   To us by prophets given;
And here we have the pattern
   As things exist in Heaven.

We'd fain from human suffering
   Each barbéd arrow draw,
But yet self-preservation
   Is God's and Nature's law.

The Scriptures are fulfilling,
   The spoiler's being spoiled;
All Satan's foul devices
   'Gainst Zion will be foiled.

Great Salt Lake City, Oct. 13, 1857."

This is given not as a fair specimen of her poetry, for she has written much better, but to illustrate how completely she was devoted to the interests of her people at that exciting period of their history.

Zina D. Huntington Jacobs is of large form, well proportioned, high forehead, with light hair and eyes. She is of a melancholy temperament, as is plainly indicated by the expression of her countenance. She has three children, and has charge of the children of Clara Chase.

Zina has some literary ability, and sometimes writes poetry. She has a special office in the family, which is to act as governess for all the young ladies, accompanying them in their attendance to singing-schools and other public places. Zina came to Utah with her husband, Dr. Jacobs. Young became attached to her, sent the Doctor on a mission, and in his absence appropriated to himself the wife and children. Dr. Jacobs is still in California, and is an "apostate." Zina stands in great awe of Brigham, who treats her with marked coldness and neglect.

Amelia Partridge is rather tall, with a fine form, black hair, dark eyes, dark complexion, sweet expression of countenance, and very mild and amiable in disposition. She and her sister Eliza had been servants in the family of Joseph Smith, in Nauvoo.

Amelia has four children, to whom she is devotedly attached. She is a kind and gentle mother, patient and forgiving, — one of the excellent ones of earth. She takes but little interest in family matters, outside of the circle of her own children.

Mrs. Augusta Cobb is a native of Massachusetts, and formerly resided in Boston. She is a large, fine-looking person, — dark hair, gray eyes, and clear complexion. She is very stylish in appearance, and of dignified demeanor. She was converted to Mormonism at Boston, fifteen years ago, left her husband and a very interesting family of children, and with one little girl, Charlotte, came to Utah, and took up her residence at the Harem, as a plural wife of Brigham Young.

She is high-spirited and imperious. She once returned to her family in Boston, and remained two years, but was too deeply involved in the meshes of Mormonism to be satisfied away from Zion, and again returned to Salt Lake. She now lives in a neat little cottage near the Lion House, and is supported by Young. Her son, James Cobb, after finishing his course of study in the East, came to Salt Lake, and after some years, through the influence of his mother, joined the church. Previous to becoming a Mormon, he expressed much anxiety about his mother and sister Charlotte, — now an interesting young lady, — and used many arguments and entreaties to induce them to leave, but finally himself yielded to the seductive influences which surrounded him.

Charlotte at one time enjoyed the proud title of "the belle of Salt Lake." She has steadfastly opposed polygamy, and hence has remained unmarried.

Mrs. Smith is an elderly woman, who admired Brother Brigham very much, and desired to be sealed to him, to insure her salvation. Young did not reciprocate her sentiments toward him, but compromised the matter by sealing her to Joseph Smith for eternity, and to himself for time. After this ceremony had been performed, he committed her to the care of the Bishop of the ward, directing him to support her.

There are many of this class of women in the Territory.

Clara Chase, the Maniac.

This woman was of medium height, dark hair and eyes, rather sullen expression of countenance, low forehead, and her features indicative of deep-seated melancholy. When Young married her, he treated her with marked consideration. He assigned to her an elegant apartment, in which hung the only oil-painting of himself. She from the first distrusted the principle of polygamy, and had many misgivings of conscience in regard to her course in marrying the Prophet.

For a time she lived in this way, in a strait between two opinions. When her husband treated her kindly, she tried to be happy, but when he was cold and unfeeling toward her, she was driven well-nigh to desperation. In the mean time she had four children, two of whom are now living. They are bright and intelligent girls, fourteen and sixteen years of age.

As she approached her fourth confinement, her fits of

remorse became more frequent and more terrible. She reproached herself with having committed the *unpardonable sin.* Her condition was truly pitiable. During her sickness Brigham treated her with such coldness and neglect, that she became actually insane, and raved incessantly. — "Oh, I have committed the unpardonable sin! Oh, warn my poor children not to follow my bad example. I am going to hell. Brigham has caused it. He has cursed me, and I shall soon be there. Oh! do not any of you go into polygamy. It will curse you, and damn your souls eternally." When her husband appeared, she cursed him as the author of her destruction.

The "President" and his two "counsellors" "laid hands" on her, but all of no avail. Dr. Sprague, the family physician, was sent for; but her poor wrecked spirit would no longer abide where it had suffered so much, and she died a raving maniac.

Amelia, or the Last Love.

Amelia Folsom is a native of Portsmouth, N. H. She is tall, and well formed, with light hair and gray eyes, and regular features. She is quite pale, owing to ill health. Has but little refinement of manner. When at the theatre, sitting in the King's box, with her husband, the observed of all observers, she may be seen eating apples, throwing the skins about, chatting with Brigham, and occasionally levelling her glass at some one in the assembly.

She plays and sings, but with indifferent skill and taste. She was, for a long time, unwilling to marry the President, but he continued his suit with a pertinacity worthy a better cause, and by repeated promises of advancement made to herself and her parents, finally succeeded. For several months he had urged his suit, during which time his carriage might be seen, almost any day, standing at her father's door, for hours at a time. He told her she was created expressly for himself, and could marry no one else on pain of everlasting destruction. She plead, protested, and wept, but he persevered, and at length, when all other arguments failed, he told her he had received a special revelation from Heaven on the subject. She had always believed in Mormonism, and had been taught to have faith in revelation. "Amelia," he said, "you must be my wife; God has revealed it to me. You cannot be saved by any one else. If you will marry me, I will save you, and exalt you to be a queen in the celestial world, but if you refuse, you will be destroyed, both soul and body."

The poor girl believed this hellish impostor, and yielding to his wishes, became his wife. For several months after her marriage, Amelia was sad and dejected, but of late she has rallied, and now appears the gayest of the gay. This marriage took place on the 29th day of January, 1863,— more than six months after the passage by Congress of the anti-polygamy law,— and was public and notorious. Here was perpetrated in one act, the double crime of destroying forever the happiness of a young lady and setting before his people the example of an open violation of a law of the land. Yet for both crimes he goes unpunished, and continues to sit in his chair of state, clothed in authority and power, not only the wonder, but the admiration, of thousands outside of the Mormon Church!

Amelia is evidently living under constraint, and acting an assumed character. She is playing the *rôle* of a happy wife, with a breaking heart. At the time of her marriage, her heart had been given to another, to whom she should have been married. That she compromised her character, in marrying Young under the circumstances, is a fact too notorious to be concealed,— and this connection has brought more odium upon polygamy than any the "President" ever formed.

Nevertheless, Amelia stands the recognized Queen of the Harem. She leads the *ton*, and is the model woman for the saints. Thousands bow low as she passes, and think themselves happy to receive her passing recognition. She is now a queen, and is to be a goddess in the celestial world. The new wife sometimes becomes restive and impatient, and treats her liege lord rather shabbily. She is at times notional and imperious, and somewhat coquettish,— to all of which her husband submits with good grace for the present, and pets her as a child.

The Bee-Hive House, formerly occupied by Mrs. Young and her family, has been vacated for Amelia. Servants are at her disposal, and her establishment is extensive and imposing.

Brigham spends much of his time with his new wife, and often dines with her. One evening a friend was taking tea with the newly-married couple. Amelia behaved quite naughtily toward her lord. After tea was finished, they remained at the table, eating nuts and confectioneries. Amelia threw her shells through an open window, on the opposite side of the room. Her husband said, "Amelia, don't do that; put your shells by your plate." "I sha'n't do it," replied the fair one; "I'll throw them where I please." Young was silent for a time, but became so annoyed that he again said: "Amelia, I wish you wouldn't do that any more." "I don't care," replied the spouse, pettishly, "I'll throw the shells where I please, and I'll do as I please, and you may help yourself." And pulling her guest by the dress, she said: "Come, let's go up-stairs, and let him *grunt* it out."

The theatre was dedicated by prayer and a grand ball. This was in the winter of 1862–63. Brigham led off in the dance with Amelia, and all was smiles and sunshine. On another occasion, he honored another one of "the women" with his hand for the first cotillon. This so displeased Amelia, that she refused to dance with him at all. He coaxed, she shrugged her shoulders, and shook her head. It was only after much condescension and solicitation on his part that she granted her forgiveness, and consented to dance with him.

This gay Lothario of sixty-three then led forth his blushing mistress, and "all went merry as a marriage-bell."

Amelia has lovers still, for one of whom she entertains considerable feeling. He was sent to "Dixie," or the Cotton District, in Southern Utah, on a mission. He soon returned, however, to Salt Lake, and by his presence in the city, causes the Prophet considerable anxiety.

Amelia is tyrannical, and rules the women of the Harem with a strong hand. Poor Emeline is quite broken-hearted. Naturally very sensitive, this blow prostrated her upon a bed of sickness, from which it was feared she would never recover. But she lives to drag out a miserable life,— neither wife nor mistress, but a castaway.

In fact all the women are miserable and unhappy. A common remark, in reply to the usual salutation, is, "Oh, I've got the blues to-day."

The Prophet in Love the Thirtieth Time.

Miss Selima Ursenback is a native of Geneva, Switzerland, and with her parents and brother came to Utah in the fall of 1862. She is an accomplished musician, and at once became a favorite with the Mormons. Several concerts were given, at which she figured as *prima donna*, and although she sang in French, the melody of her voice and the artistic character of her music gained for her an established reputation.

Brigham heard, and was delighted. Her voice was music to his ravished ear, and, for the thirtieth time, the little god let slip his arrow, and launched it into the Prophet's heart.

Says a celebrated writer :—

"Now there are various ways of getting in love. A man falls in love just as he falls down-stairs. It is an accident. But when he runs in love, it is as when he runs in debt : it is done knowingly, intentionally, and very often rashly and foolishly, even if not ridiculously, miserably, and ruinously.

"The rarest and happiest marriages are between those who have grown in love. Take the description of such a love in its rise and progress, ye thousands and tens of thousands who have what is called a taste for poetry. Take it in the sweet words of one of the sweetest and tenderest of English poets, and then say whether this is not the way that leads to happiness and bliss.

> "'Ah! I remember well (and how can I
> But evermore remember well) when first
> Our flame began; when scarce we knew what was
> The flame we felt. When as we sat and sighed,
> And looked upon each other, and conceived
> Not what we ailed,—yet something we did ail;
> And yet were well, and yet we were not well;
> And what was our disease, we could not tell.
> Then would we kiss, then sigh, then look; and thus,
> In that first garden of our simpleness,
> We spent our childhood. But when years began
> To reap the fruit of knowledge, ah, how then
> Would she with graver looks, with sweet, stern brow,
> Check my presumption, and my forwardness;
> Yet still would give me flowers, still would me show
> What she would have me, yet not have me know.'

"Falling in love, and running in love, are, as everybody knows, common enough, and yet less so than what I shall call catching love. Where the love itself is imprudent, that is to say, where there is some just, prudential cause or impediment why the two parties should not be joined together in holy matrimony, there is culpable imprudence in catching it, because danger is always to be apprehended, which may have been avoided."

It is plain to be seen, our Prophet did not walk into love, — he did not run into it. He caught it, as a man catches the measles. It broke out, and showed itself all over, in smiles, bows, and sweet honeyed tones. It is also plain that he should not have caught it. Had he not the charming Amelia, dear Emeline, sweet Lucy, pretty Twiss, his darling Lucy No. 2, poetic Eliza, meek Zina, and his dear, dear Jemima, Martha, Ellen, Susan, Hattie, etc., etc. How could any man, much less a prophet, wish for more?

But he said to himself, "I have not a French lady in the family to teach my daughters that charming language. I have no *prima donna* to conduct their musical education. Then my last love — my pretty, naughty, bewitching Amelia — is so cross and fitful, she leads me such a crazy life, she frets and scolds, and I cannot drown her voice, even with my 'sacred fiddle.' [He had frequently boasted that with his violin he could put a stop to the scolding of any of his women.]

"Then my French lady is accomplished. She can receive my foreign guests. She is so clever, that she can assist me in my business projects and plans; and if she should prove unkind, — which God grant she may not, — and if her sweet lips should scold, I should have a great advantage, — *I could not understand her.* Then her name, — Selima! How poetical. None of my wives have such a poetical name. With her in my Harem, I could rival the Sultan himself. Yes, sweet, adored Selima, *you shall be mine.* You shall be the high priestess of my affections, and all my common women shall serve you."

The Prophet plead his suit, but Selima was like stone. He had a young man in his employ who dared to love Selima. The rival lovers met face to face. The Prophet was furious, — "She is not for you, sir, she is not for you. Leave my service, and never dare to aspire to that young lady's hand again."

Alas, that love so devoted, so pure and disinterested as Brigham's, should fail to be rewarded by the object of its choice. But no sooner had the poor singing-master, for such he was, left the Territory for California, than another rival appeared in the field, — a California volunteer, — a dangerous rival; one who would not fear to follow up any advantage he might gain over his spiritual competitor.

To destroy the romance of the whole story, Selima, charming but sensible Selima, becoming disgusted with the whole affair, soon after left for Switzerland again, leaving her lovers to settle the matter among themselves.

For once in his life, Brigham Young was foiled, and that by a woman.

CHAPTER XII.

POLYGAMY.

Condition of Woman among various Heathen Nations. — Influence of Christianity. — Mormonism and Woman. — Brigham offers to set the Women Free. — Arguments in Favor of Polygamy. — The Argument against it. — Abraham and Sarah. — Appeal to Mormon Women. — Their Unhappy Condition. — Evil Effects of the System. — Illustrations.

WOMAN is looked upon and treated by all heathen nations as an inferior being, created for the convenience and comfort of man.

" According to the ancient Rabbis, the rib which had been taken from Adam, was laid down for a moment, and in that moment a monkey came and stole it, and ran off with it, full speed. An angel pursued, and though not in league with the monkey, he could have been no good angel; for, overtaking him, he caught him by the tail, brought it maliciously back instead of the rib, and out of that tail was woman made. What became of the rib with which the monkey got clear off ' was never to mortal known.'

" The Hungarians think it infamous to be governed by a woman, — and when the crown fell to a female, they called her King Mary instead of Queen.

" Aristotle calls woman a monster, and Plato makes it a question whether she ought not to be ranked among irrational creatures.

" Mahomet, too, was not the only person who has supposed that women have no souls. Among the Afghans, twelve young women were given as compensation for the slaughter of one man. Six for cutting off a hand, an ear, or a nose; three for breaking a tooth, and one for a wound of the scalp. By the laws of the Venetians, and of certain other Oriental people, the testimony of two women was made equivalent to that of one man.

"According to the Brahmins, the widow who burns herself with the body of her husband, will, in her next state, be born a male; but the widow who refuses to make the self-sacrifice, will never be anything better than a woman, let her be born again as often as she may."

The Jew begins his public prayer with a thanksgiving to his Maker for not having made him a woman. The Moors do not allow women to enter their mosques or places of worship.

Mussulmen hold that there is a separate paradise for women, considering them unworthy to occupy the same as the men, except such beautiful women as are assigned to the male occupants as a reward for a virtuous and religious life on earth. "Sit not in the midst of women," said the son of Sirach, in his wisdom; "for from garments cometh a moth, and from women wickedness."

"It is a bad thing," said Augustine, "to look upon a woman, a worse to speak to her, and to touch her, worst of all." John Bunyan thanked God that he had made him shy of the women. "The common salutation of women, I abhor," said he, "their company alone, I cannot away with." "Look at the very name woman," says another author, "it evidently means woe to man, because by woman was woe brought into the world."

The Turk does not exclude woman from his heaven, but she is there only to minister to his passions and wants. She bears to his lips the golden goblet, filled with the nectar of the gods.

The Indian hunter believes his squaw, as well as his faithful dog, will bear him company to those shadowy hunting-grounds beyond the dark river.

Among all these heathen and degraded nations, polygamy has prevailed. Among them all, woman has been but the slave of the stronger sex. Her feelings have been outraged, her spirit crushed, and her heart broken; or, which is still worse, her nature has become imbruted and insensible to all the finer feelings and nobler impulses of her sex.

But behold the day-star from on high, the lowly Jesus. He came to bring deliverance to the captive, to let the oppressed go free. No longer is woman to be degraded and despised. The holy covenant of marriage which Moses, by reason of the hardness of their hearts, permitted the Jews to break, was henceforth to be kept inviolate. "It hath been said, whosoever shall put away *his wife*, let him give her a writing of divorcement. But I say unto you, that whosoever shall put away *his wife*, saving for the cause of fornication, causeth her to commit adultery; and whosoever shall marry her that is divorced, committeth adultery." And again, — "For this cause shall a man leave father and mother, and shall cleave to his wife; and *they twain* shall be one flesh."

The position of woman, and her duties in life, are well defined in the New Testament Scriptures. If married, she is to direct her household affairs, raise up children, be subject unto her husband, and use all due benevolence toward him; but his duties are equally well defined. He must love his wife, even as Christ loved his church and gave himself for it; and the fourth verse of the seventh chapter of Corinthians distinctly states that the rights and duties of the marriage relation should be reciprocal, granting no exclusive privilege to either. Is not this reciprocity necessarily and entirely destroyed, when the husband brings other wives into the family?

In the face of the direct and positive teachings of Jesus and his Apostles, the "Latter-Day Saints" of Utah, or rather their leaders, have instituted the heathenish and horrible practice of polygamy. And to add to the blasphemy of the scheme, it is all done in the name of the Lord. In this nineteenth century, they have reduced women to the heathen and Jewish standard.

Foremost in the ranks of their oppressors stands Brigham Young. Following in the footsteps of Mohammed, he declares that women have no souls, — that they are not responsible beings, that they cannot save themselves, nor be saved, except through man's intervention. To be saved, a woman must be "sealed" to a good man, — he can save her; or, if he does not, her sins will be upon his head. Under this system, woman was created expressly for the glory of man; hence the more women and children a man has, the more glory.

This doctrine is openly put forth in the most disgusting form.

Said Brigham, in a public discourse, Sept. 20th, 1856, —

"It is the duty of every righteous man and woman to prepare tabernacles for all the spirits they can; hence if my women leave, I will go and search up others who will abide the celestial law, and let all I now have go where they please."

And in accordance with the same view, he publicly proclaimed that after a certain day which he named, all of his women who were dissatisfied should be free to leave him. The following is his language: —

"Now for my proposition: it is more particularly for my sisters, as it is frequently happening that women say that they are unhappy. Men will say, — 'My wife, though a most excellent woman, has not seen a happy day since I took my second wife.' 'No, not a happy day for a year,' says one; and another has not seen a happy day for five years. It is said that women are tied down and abused; that they are misused, and have not the liberty that they ought to have; that many of them are wading through a perfect flood of tears, because of the conduct of some men, together with their own folly.

"I wish my own women to understand that what I am going to say is for them as well as others, and I want those who are here to tell their sisters, — yes, all the women of this community, — and then write it back to the States, and do as you please with it. I am going to give you from this time to the 6th day of October next (the day the semi-annual Conference was to meet) for reflection, that you may determine whether you wish to stay with your husbands or not, and then I am going to set every woman at liberty, and say to them, 'Now go your way, — my women with the rest, — go your way.' And my wives have got to do one of two things: either round up their shoulders to endure the afflictions of this world, and live their religion, or they may leave, for I will not have them about me. I will go into heaven alone, rather than have scratching and fighting around me. I will set all at liberty. 'What, first wife too?' Yes, I will liberate you all. I know what my women will say. They will say, 'You can have as many women as you please, Brigham.' But I want to go somewhere, and do something to get rid of the whiners." *

It does not appear that these unhappy women availed themselves of this opportunity of getting rid of their misery, by being cast off upon the world, in an Indian country, nearly a thousand miles from civilization.

It may seem very strange, that so many women are led into the snare of polygamy. The most specious arguments are advanced, and inducements held out, by the wicked and designing leaders of the Mormon Church, to blind and deceive unsuspecting and simple-minded women. They are told that "the laws of Christendom differ widely from those of the other three fourths of the whole family of man;" that they are the laws and practices of "a wicked and perverse generation," and differ also from the doctrines taught in the Bible. It is a noticeable fact that the Bible is only quoted on the subject of polygamy. On all other topics, the books of Mormonism are used. These being, as already shown, adverse to their favorite institution, resort is had to the Old Testament Scriptures.

Abraham is constantly cited as the great exemplar and pattern. It is urged that the family order observed by him is the order established among celestial beings, in the celestial world. That God sanctioned the practice, and is himself a polygamist.

That many virtuous and high-minded women should infinitely prefer to unite their fortunes to *one* good man, rather than to have each a wicked husband who could bring her no exaltation in another world. "Shall such virtuous and innocent females, though they may be poor, and low in the scale

* *Deseret News*, October 1, 1856.

of fortune's partial smiles, — shall they be denied the right to choose the objects of their love? Must they, through the operation of hideously contracted laws, be virtually doomed to resort to infamous prostitution, entailing disease, infamy, and death upon themselves and their offspring, or to marry an inferior grade of corrupt, vicious men, — debauchees, gluttons, drunkards, and idlers, — or remain in perpetual celibacy, and frustrate the designs of their creation, and violate the first and foremost command of God, — to multiply and replenish the earth?"

They are pointed to Jacob, also, who had several wives, and who was the father of the twelve patriarchs, after whom all the tribes of Israel were named. From one of these wives, Christ himself lineally descended. Various other instances are cited from the Jewish Scriptures, — especially the fact that the Lord gave unto David some of the wives of Saul. "Hereby we learn that God himself gives many wives to those who are faithful, *and takes them away from transgressors.*" The faith of Abraham was indorsed by Christ and his Apostles, and those who have the same faith are called heirs of the promise. Hence an effort is made to bring the New Testament also to the support of polygamy, notwithstanding it is so plainly condemned in that volume. Indeed, it is unblushingly asserted that not only the Apostles but Christ himself practised polygamy! "The grand reason," said J. M. Grant, one of the First Presidency, in a discourse delivered in the Tabernacle in Great Salt Lake City, " why the gentiles and philosophers of that school persecuted Jesus Christ, was because he had so many wives. There were Elizabeth and Mary, and a host of others, who followed him."

To Abraham and Sarah was the promise made — " In thee and in thy seed, shall all the nations of the earth be blessed " The sisters are called upon to follow the example of Sarah, and to give plural wives to their husbands, even as Sarah gave Hagar unto Abraham. " If you suffer with her (Sarah) you shall reign with her. You shall be heirs of the same promise, and crowned with glory in the celestial world."

By these specious arguments and falsehoods, are thousands lured on to their destruction. Oh! could this volume reach the eye of all such,—as it surely will of many,—to them I appeal to examine carefully the foundation of the system to which they are committing themselves. To them I respectfully and earnestly submit some considerations and facts worthy of their serious attention, before they enter irretrievably upon their own ruin.

Polygamy, or plurality, so called, is not only contrary to the laws of our country, which we are all in duty bound to uphold and obey, but it is adverse to the genius of our free institutions, and is, moreover, contrary to the laws and instincts of our nature, and to the suggestions of a sound reason.

In the first place, is polygamy reasonable or natural?

In pursuing this inquiry, the first fact that stares us in the face is the equality in the numbers of the male and female sexes, in all countries, and in all ages of the world. If polygamy were the natural relation between the sexes, the number of females born into the world would far exceed the number of males. So far from that being the case, there is a larger number of males, and the excess about equal to the greater loss of life, among males, by wars and accidents; thus leaving a substantial equality in the numbers of those living.

The following figures will show the number of males and females in the United States, at the close of each of the last five decades:—

Year.	Males.	Females.	Excess of Males.	Per cent. of Excess.
1820	4,898,127	4,740,004	158,123	3.2
1830	6,529,696	6,336,324	193,372	3
1840	8,688,532	8,380,921	307,611	3.5
1850	11,837,661	11,354,215	483,446	4.1
1860	16,086,059	15,359,021	727,038	4.5

Thus it will be seen, that nature has made no provision for the practice of polygamy in this country. On the contrary, there has continually been an excess of the male population. This fact is owing, in part, to the large excess of males in the immigration from foreign countries.

Let us pursue this subject a little farther. In 1851, the population of **Great Britain** and Ireland was, — males, 13,-537,052; females, 14,082,814. Excess of females, 3 per cent. But emigration, and the heavy wars in which that country had been engaged, had been draining off the male population for many years previous.

In Prussia, in 1849, there were then living, — males, 8,162,805; females, 8,162,382.

The mortality of males is greater than that of females. To compensate for this, more males are born.

In England, the **excess of male births is 5** per cent.; in France and Russia, 6 per cent.; in the United States, from 5 to 12 per cent., according to the locality.

If, now, we turn our attention to the Territory of Utah, we shall find a similar state of facts. By reference to the United States Census of 1850, it will appear that there was, at that time, an excess of males in every county in the Territory, amounting, in the aggregate, to 712; the total number of males being 6,046, and of females, 5,334. The national census of 1860 shows the following result: males, 20,255, — females, 20,018.

There has always been in this Territory, as there is in every new country, a scarcity of females. No person, therefore, could take more than one wife, without, as a necessary consequence, **compelling some other person** to live without any.

This subject is placed in a still stronger light, by reference to the report of the Territorial Superintendent of Common Schools, dated January 14, 1863, and published in the " Deseret News," Vol. XII. No. 31.

By that report it appears that the number of boys between

the ages of six and eighteen, is greater than the number of girls between four and sixteen, in every county in the Territory but one. The total, so far as the Superintendent had been able to obtain reports, is as follows: —

Number of boys between six and eighteen............3950
Number of girls between four and sixteen............3662

Showing an excess of boys, to the number of...... 288

The thanks of the public are due to Mr. Campbell, for bringing to light facts having so important a bearing on this subject.

Thus it will be seen that in this Territory, as well as in all other parts of the country, has nature failed to make any provision for the practice of polygamy. On the contrary, ever true to herself, even now, after polygamy has been practised over ten years, during which time it has been openly encouraged, nature is reëstablishing her own laws, and maintaining the substantial equality in the numbers of the sexes; thus placing the seal of condemnation on this practice, and saying, in the plainest language, "Let every man have his own wife, and let every woman have her own husband."

In considering whether polygamy is reasonable or natural, other arguments present themselves.

This practice tends necessarily to the degradation of woman. Instead of being a companion of man, socially his equal, sympathizing with his moral and intellectual nature, and sharing in all his pursuits and enjoyments, she becomes, under this system, merely the minister to his passions and physical comfort, or the servant to assist in the increase of his worldly store.

It is impossible that several women should live on terms of such intimacy with the same man, all at the same time on a social equality with him and with each other. The idea of plurality necessitates that of subordination and inferiority. Rules must be established and observed, to insure even the appearance of harmony. But this necessary assumption of superiority and power, on the part of the man, at once mars, if it does not destroy, all the finer and holier of the marriage relations. The husband loses respect for her who sits at his feet, rather than by his side. A full and perfect communion of thought and feeling ceases to exist. A sense of inferiority on the part of the wife blunts her pride and ambition, and renders her careless of intellectual and moral progress, and insensible to many of the highest and noblest duties of her sex. She gradually conforms herself to her position, however hard it may be at first to do so, and thus her place in the social scale is lowered.

It need scarcely be asked whether this is an evil. Both reason and history answer the question plainly in the affirmative. In all ages of the world, the most enlightened and prosperous nations have been those who sought to refine and elevate woman by the practice of monogamy, or the one-wife system. Witness Egypt, Greece, and Rome, among the ancient nations; and among the moderns, the United States, Great Britain, France, and other European countries.

A reference to those nations will also illustrate and prove the remark already made, that the practice of polygamy is adverse to free institutions. In all countries where the most freedom has prevailed, has monogamy existed,—a coincidence so remarkable as to authorize the deduction that the relation of cause and effect exists between these facts. The love of home is intimately associated with the love of country and of liberty, and whatever tends to refine and purify the former will inevitably exalt and strengthen the latter.

Again: polygamy tends to destroy the unity and sanctity of home, by permitting a man to have families in different places at the same time. "The supposition," says an eminent jurist, "that a man can have two domicils, would lead to the absurdest consequences." Hence such an idea has always been rejected in courts of justice. And yet this very thing is attempted in Utah, where it is not uncommon to have different families of wives and children located sometimes many miles apart. Indeed, one of the Twelve Apostles has families scattered all along between Salt Lake City and the southern boundary of the Territory, — a distance of over three hundred miles.

Polygamy requires a law of descent peculiar to itself, and this law, differing, as it necessarily must, from that in force in all the surrounding States and Territories, leads to endless difficulty and confusion in the titles to property.

The evils of polygamy are aggravated by the fact that the consent of the first wife is not made necessary to the union of the husband with subsequent ones. The prevailing doctrine on this subject is authoritatively stated in the following words: —

"When a man who has a wife, teaches her the law of God, as revealed to the ancient patriarchs, and as manifested by new revelation, and she refuses to give her consent for him to marry another according to that law, then it becomes necessary for her to state before the President the reasons why she withholds her consent; if her reasons are sufficient and justifiable, and the husband is found in the fault, or in transgression, then he is not permitted to take any step in regard to obtaining another. But if the wife can show no good reason why she refuses to comply with the law which was given unto Sarah of old, then it is lawful for her husband, if permitted by revelation through the Prophet, to be married to others without her consent, and he will be justified, and she will be condemned, because she did not give them unto him, as Sarah gave Hagar to Abraham, and as Rachel and Leah gave Bilhah and Zilpah to their husband Jacob." *

In the case last supposed, in the foregoing extract, if the marriage ceremony is performed in the usual manner, the first wife is obliged to stand between her husband and the hated bride, and falsely admit that she gives her consent, when asked if she "is willing to give this woman to her husband to be his lawful and wedded wife, for time and for all eternity."

The result of such a state of things is what might be ex-

* *The Seer*, Vol. I. p. 41.

pected. Jealousies, strifes, and heart-burnings arise, resulting in most cases in the breaking-up of the family, or the casting-off of the less congenial elements.

It is useless to deny these results. The facts are too patent to admit of any dispute. The alarming frequency, and I may say recklessness, with which divorces are applied for and granted, is a fact familiar to all, and can only be traced to the causes just stated, unless, indeed, we should — as I am unwilling to do — impute it to the promptings of caprice and passion. Having resided in the Territory nearly two years, it would be impossible for me, unless I had, in the mean time, shut my eyes to what was going on around me, to be ignorant of the state of things to which I have briefly alluded.

It has been urged as an argument in favor of polygamy, that it tends to lessen the evils of prostitution. Even if this were true, the argument would have no validity, if at the same time that this evil is abated or suppressed, others are introduced, more serious, lasting, and wide-spread in their influence upon society, our country, and the world. But it never has been clearly shown that polygamy has such an effect. The argument is made by comparing the most favorable localities where polygamy prevails with the most unfavorable monogamic districts; for instance, with the large cities of the United States. But it remains to be seen what condition any one of those cities would be in, with polygamy in full blast; and until it be shown that its condition would be improved, the argument remains of but little force.

Another argument in favor of polygamy, perhaps worthy of notice, is, that it tends to a more rapid increase of population. Admitting the object is a desirable one, it has not been shown that it can be attained in that way. As has been remarked by an able writer, the question is, not whether ten men would not have more children by forty women than by ten; but whether the forty women would not have more children, each woman having " her own husband."

Some other reasons have been given in justification of polygamy, which I consider too absurd to require even a passing notice.

In a former chapter, the so-called Revelation on Celestial Marriage has been given, and it was there shown that polygamy was an innovation upon the Mormon religion.

I desire now to call the attention of the women of Utah to a few observations on the nature of this pretended revelation, and the circumstances under which it was given to the world.

1. It was, even if given as assumed, kept secret for nine years. Polygamy was privately practised by the leaders of the church for several years, during which time, according to Brigham's admission, it was not "preached by the Elders," and was therefore studiously concealed from new converts. Indeed, not only was it "not preached," but it was strongly denounced during the same period.

On the first of February, 1844, the following notice appeared in the "Times and Seasons," the church organ, published at Nauvoo.

"NOTICE.

"As we have lately been credibly informed, that an Elder of the Church of Jesus Christ of Latter-Day Saints, by the name of Hiram Brown, has been preaching Polygamy, and other false and corrupt doctrines, in the County of Lapeer, and State of Michigan:

"This is to notify him and the church in general, that he has been cut off from the church for his iniquity; and he is further notified to appear at the Special Conference, on the 6th of April next, to make answer to these charges.

"JOSEPH SMITH,
"HYRUM SMITH,
"*Presidents of the Church.*"*

This was seven months after the time when, according to Brigham Young and his associates, the Revelation concerning Celestial Marriage had been given to Smith. But here both

* *Times and Seasons*, Vol. V. p. 423.

Joseph and Hyrum Smith call polygamy a "false and corrupt doctrine." Can any true follower of Smith, or believer in his divine mission, believe for a moment, in the face of this declaration, that Smith had received any revelation on the 12th of July, 1843, sanctioning polygamy?

Again, six weeks later, Hyrum Smith wrote as follows:—

"NAUVOO, March 15, 1844.

"To the Brethren of the Church of Jesus Christ of Latter-Day Saints, living on China Creek, in Hancock County, Greeting:

"Whereas, Brother Richard Hewett has called on me to-day, to know my views concerning some doctrines that are preached in your place, and states to me that some of your Elders say, that a man *having a certain priesthood*, may have as many wives as he pleases, and that doctrine is taught here; I say unto you, that that man teaches *false doctrine*, for there is no such doctrine taught here, neither is there any such thing practised here; and any man that is found teaching privately or publicly any such doctrine, is culpable, and will stand a chance to be brought before the High Council, and lose his license and membership also; therefore he had better beware what he is about." *

Polygamy was condemned at the General Conferences of the European churches, in England, during the year 1846, and subsequently.

In July, 1845, Parley P. Pratt, in the "Millennial Star," published at Liverpool, had denounced the "Spiritual-Wife doctrine of J. C. Bennett," — which was one of the earliest manifestations of polygamy in the church, — as a "doctrine of devils" and of "seducing spirits," using this language: "It is but another name for whoredom, wicked and unlawful connection, and every kind of confusion, corruption, and abomination." †

In May, 1848, Orson Spencer, then editor of the "Star,' used the following language: —

"In all ages of the church truth has been turned into a lie, and

---

* *Times and Seasons*, Vol. V. p. 474.
† *Millennial Star*, Vol. VI. p. 22.

the grace of God converted into lasciviousness, by men who have sought to make 'a gain' of godliness, and feed their lusts on the credulity of the righteous and unsuspicious. . . . Next to the long-hackneyed and bugaboo whisperings of polygism, is another abomination that sometimes shows its serpentine crests, which we shall call sexual resurrectionism. . . . The doctrines of corrupt spirits are always in close affinity with each other, whether they consist in spiritual wife-ism, sexual resurrection, gross lasciviousness, or the unavoidable separation of husbands and wives, or the communism of property." *

In July, 1850, at a discussion held at Boulogne, France, John Taylor, a well-known Mormon Apostle, when charged with the belief and practice of this doctrine, said:—"We are accused here of polygamy, and actions the most indelicate, obscene, and disgusting, such that none but a corrupt and depraved heart could have contrived. These things are too outrageous to admit of belief. Therefore, leaving the sisters of the 'White Veil,' the 'Black Veil,' and all the other veils, with those gentlemen to dispose of, together with their authors, as they think best, I shall content myself by reading our views of chastity and marriage, from a work published by us, containing some of the articles of our faith." †
He then read from the Book of Doctrine and Covenants, the article on marriage, already quoted from.

Here we have the following facts:—

In 1830 the Mormon Church organized, and the Book of Mormon was published, in which polygamy is strongly condemned.

In 1831, the same doctrine condemned, in a revelation to Joseph Smith, which was afterward published in the Book of Doctrine and Covenants.

In July, 1843, the revelation in favor of polygamy, *said to have been given* to Joseph Smith.

In February, 1844, polygamy publicly denounced by Joseph and Hyrum Smith.

---

* *Millennial Star*, Vol. X. p. 137.
† *Taylor's Discussion at Boulogne*, p. 8.

In March, 1844, the same practice again denounced by Hyrum Smith.

In June, 1844, the death of Smith.

In 1845, the publication of the article on Marriage, in the Appendix to the Book of Doctrine and Covenants, in which polygamy is called a "crime," and is again strongly condemned and repudiated. The same year the Spiritual-Wife doctrine of J. C. Bennett, denounced by P. P. Pratt, in England.

In 1846, polygamy condemned at the Conferences of the European Mormon churches in England.

In 1848, "polygism" and "sexual resurrectionism" severely denounced in the "Millennial Star," published in Liverpool.

In 1850, polygamy denounced and repudiated by Apostle John Taylor, in France.

And yet, in the face of all these facts, in 1852, we have the same doctrine publicly given to the church, accompanied by the announcement, that it had been believed and practised by the church for many years.

Now, it will not be pretended by any one, that polygamy was any part of the Mormon religion previous to 1843.

Take, then, the period from 1843 to 1852. How was it during those nine years? Which shall be taken as evidence of what was the teaching of the Mormon religion, on that subject, during that time? The Book of Doctrine and Covenants, the Notices published by Joseph and Hyrum Smith, the declarations of Pratt and Spencer, the action of the churches in England, and the assertions of Taylor in France, or the announcement made in Great Salt Lake City in 1852? Are we not, at least, as much authorized to take the former as the latter?

If the Book of Doctrine and Covenants, the writings of Joseph and Hyrum, the continued and persistent declarations of the Mormon leaders, and the action of the Mormon churches be taken, then polygamy was no part of Mormonism up to 1852. And if not previous to that time, it was not afterward, for Young did not pretend to give it at that time as a new revelation, but rested the doctrine entirely on the revelation said to have been given to Joseph in 1843.

2. A singular feature of this revelation is, that in it God is made expressly to contradict what he is represented as having said in the Book of Mormon.

According to the Book of Mormon, as already quoted, God said the polygamy and concubinage of David and Solomon were abominable before him. The following is the language: "Behold David and Solomon truly had many wives and concubines, which thing was abominable before me, saith the Lord."

This was the testimony of the Almighty, as to the manner in which he viewed the conduct of David and Solomon, up to July, 1843, when he is represented in this revelation as indorsing those very acts which, in the Book of Mormon, he had so strongly condemned.

3. Again: This revelation classes Isaac and Moses with Abraham, Jacob, David, and Solomon, as polygamists; when in fact neither Isaac nor Moses ever practised polygamy. How could the All-wise Being make such a mistake?

4. The most remarkable circumstance connected with this revelation remains to be considered, — It was in direct contradiction to the laws of the land.

At that time, July 12, 1843, Smith resided at Nauvoo, Illinois, and was, of course, together with all the other inhabitants of that city, amenable to the laws of Illinois.

The following statute was then in force in that State, the same having been passed February 12, 1833:—

"SEC. 121. Bigamy consists in the having of two wives or two husbands at one and the same time, knowing that the former husband or wife is still alive. If any person or persons within this State, being married, or who shall hereafter marry, do at any time marry any person or persons, the former husband or wife being alive, the person so offending shall, on conviction thereof, be punished by a fine not exceeding one thousand dollars, and imprisonment in the penitentiary not exceeding two years." [The remainder of this section relates to evidence, and prescribes certain exemptions.]

"Sec. 122. If any man or woman, being unmarried, shall knowingly marry the husband or wife of another, such man or woman shall, on conviction, be fined not more than five hundred dollars, or imprisoned not more than one year." *

In the face of this law, which was then in full force, the revelation to Smith declares: " If any man espouse a virgin, and desire to espouse another, and the first give her consent; and if he espouse the second, and they are virgins, and have vowed to no other man, then is he justified." † Thus justifying the violation of both sections of the law. People may well hesitate, before believing in the authenticity of such a revelation.

Here, again, God is made to contradict himself; for not only in the Christian but in the Mormon Bible, He is represented as enjoining upon His disciples to obey the laws and civil authorities. The Book of Mormon abounds in such teachings. The Book of Doctrine and Covenants is to the same effect: —

" We believe that every man should be honored in his station; rulers and magistrates as such being placed for the protection of the innocent and the punishment of the guilty; and that to the laws all men owe respect and deference, as without them peace and harmony would be supplanted by anarchy and terror." ‡

Here, again, I may quote from Mr. Orson Pratt, whose writings have been freely used, as of high authority in " the church."

" Would it be right for the Latter Day Saints to marry a plu-

---

* *Illinois Laws of* 1833, p. 198. See also Gales' *Revised Statutes of* 1839, p. 220, and *Revised Statutes of* 1845, p. 173, the same law having been reenacted in 1845.

† *Revelation*, Sec. 24.

‡ *Book of Doctrine and Covenants*, p. 332.

rality of wives in any of the States or Territories, or nations, where such practices are prohibited by the laws of man? We answer, No; it would not be right; for we are commanded to be subject to the powers that be." *

Since, then, it was not right to violate the laws of the land, then in force in Illinois on this subject, how came God to give a revelation sanctioning such a violation of the State law? And that too, without making, in the revelation, the least allusion to the law which was to be so grossly violated?

Again: Who was authorized to keep this revelation secret, no secrecy being enjoined in the revelation itself?

But enough concerning this extraordinary document. It seems strange, indeed, that any reasonable man or woman can look upon this so-called revelation, announced under such suspicious circumstances, and involved in so many contradictions, as a sufficient authority or excuse for the establishment of a custom which would overturn our most cherished social institutions, and throw us at once back thousands of years in civilization.

The conclusion would not be changed if it were admitted that the doctrine of celestial marriage is a part of the Mormon religion; for that has nothing to do with polygamy. On the contrary, this doctrine is expressly founded upon the relation between Adam and Eve before the fall. The following is the language: —

"The first marriage we have on record is that of our first parents. . . . Here was a marriage in which the Lord in person officiated, — a marriage between two immortal beings. . . . He joined them in one, as one flesh, to be indissolubly united, while eternal ages should roll on, or God himself endure. . . . Did death tear asunder husband and wife, divorce that which God had joined together as 'one flesh,' immortal and eternal in its nature? The atonement of Christ will repair the breach, will restore the immortal Eve to the immortal Adam, will join them again as one flesh, never more to be separated, and will again let the lawful husband enjoy the society of his lawful wife. . . .

* *The Seer*, Vol. I. p. 111.

"Therefore, if the children have been married for eternity, as well as for time, by the authority of God, the same as their first parents were, they will, with them, raise up, after the resurrection, an endless posterity of immortal beings. . . . But those who do not, in this life, enter into the eternal covenant of marriage, after the pattern set by the first immortal pair, can never obey the first great command." *

The foregoing extracts convey a very intelligible idea of this doctrine; and from them it will be seen it is founded entirely upon the relation between Adam and Eve. Those who would enjoy the blessings of celestial marriage, must, "in this life, enter into the eternal covenant of marriage, after the pattern set by the first immortal pair." What was that pattern? Adam and Eve were monogamists. Adam lived with the wife of his youth, and had no other, for nine hundred and thirty years, and according to Pratt, he is to live with the same woman, in the same capacity, throughout all the ages of eternity. Surely he must be very astute who can discover in this "pattern" any sanction for polygamy.

I might enlarge, indefinitely, upon the arguments against polygamy. I might go into the Jewish and Christian Scriptures, and show that it had been, in many ways, condemned by the Almighty. That not only had Adam been limited to one wife at the creation, but when the world was destroyed by a flood, one wife only to each man was taken into the ark;— that God blessed Abraham's posterity through the issue of his first and lawful wife, and in order to do that, worked a miracle upon Sarah; thus sanctioning monogamy in the strongest manner possible. I might refer to the warning of Malachi: "Take heed to your spirit, and let none deal treacherously with the wife of his youth." I might refer to the fact that Lamech, the first polygamist, was a murderer; and that the most prominent polygamists of old were men guilty of the most heinous crimes. And turning from the Old Testament to the New, I might quote the

* *The Seer*, Vol. I. pp. 43–47.

words of Paul, — "To avoid fornication, let every man have his own wife, and let every woman have her own husband;" and the words of Christ, — "From the beginning of creation, God made them male and female. For this cause shall a man leave his father and mother, and cleave to his wife; and they twain shall be one flesh."

But I choose to pass over all these things, and for my present purpose rest the moral character of this practice upon the assertion, already quoted from the Book of Mormon, that the polygamy and concubinage of David and Solomon were abominable before God. No Mormon can gainsay this testimony.

In conclusion, to review what has been said. I have endeavored to show that polygamy is unreasonable, and contrary to the plain provisions and teachings of Nature; that it tends to degrade woman, and to confuse and break up the family relation, thus weakening the attachment to home and country. Other evils consequent upon this system have been pointed out. The arguments by which it is supported have been examined, and have been shown to be weak or invalid.

A word further as to the case of Abraham and Sarah. Did God sanction the polygamy of Abraham?

"Now Sarai, Abram's wife, bare him no children; and she had a handmaid, an Egyptian, whose name was Hagar. And Sarai said unto Abram, 'Behold now the Lord hath restrained me from bearing; I pray thee go in unto my maid; it may be that I may obtain children by her.'" From this it appears that Sarah, and not God, was the author of Abraham's polygamy. She had lost all hope of having children herself, and was willing to adopt those of her handmaid. Hagar being her slave, she intended to own her children. She soon, however, perceived her fatal error. Hagar wished to assume the rights and privileges of a wife. This Sarah would not listen to for a moment.

Hagar despised her mistress, and Sarah appealed to Abraham. Abraham said, "Behold thy maid is in thy hand, do unto her as it pleaseth thee." "And Sarah dealt hardly with her, and she fled from her face." Isaac was born. The son of Hagar was seen mocking, and Sarah desired Abraham to cast him out. "And the thing was grievous in Abraham's sight, because of his son. And God said unto Abraham, '**Let it not be grievous in** thy sight, because **of the lad,** and because of thy bond-woman; in all that Sarah hath said unto thee, hearken unto her voice; *for in Isaac shall thy seed be called.*'"

Again: "God tempted Abraham, saying, 'Take now thy son, thine *only son*, Isaac,'" &c. And again: "Thou hast not withheld thy son, *thine **only son**.*" For this reason God blessed Abraham, and said, "In blessing I will bless thee, and in multiplying I will multiply thy seed as the stars of the heaven, or the sands on the sea-shore;" but, "in Isaac shall thy seed be called."

God thus plainly and unequivocally condemned Abrahamic polygamy, refused to recognize Ishmael as a legitimate son, and disinherited him. He thence went forth, as a cast-out bastard, whose "hand was against every man, and every man's hand against him."

Sisters in Israel! You are told that Sarah is the mother and pattern for all women. She is held up as a bright example of conjugal loyalty and faith for females — wives and mothers — of all ages. Follow, then, her example. **If** through a mistaken faith and false doctrines, you have been induced to give mistresses to your husbands, turn them from you; purify your homes, as Sarah did, and the same God who blessed her will bless you, and multiply your children.

Sisters in Israel! If you have been led astray by wicked and designing men, and have been caught in their snares, arise, and by the help of the Lord your God, break the bonds of wickedness, and go forth and purify yourselves by fasting and prayer; and the God who blessed Hagar in the wilderness will bless you, and show you a fountain, even the **blood of** Christ, which will cleanse you from all sin.

May God guide and direct the afflicted women of Utah, and speedily deliver them from their thraldom.

The practical working of polygamy is what might be expected from a system the fundamental principles of which are in direct opposition to the laws of God and man.

A few instances and illustrations will be given, from among a thousand which might be adduced to show the unhappiness and misery it entails upon all parties concerned, and especially upon those females who are so unfortunate as to be drawn into it.

A Mr. Cushion was engaged to be married to Miss Susan McBride, when he was taken sick and died. He had been a great favorite of Heber C. Kimball, Second President of the Church, who desired he should be saved and glorified in another world. But to that end, he must have a family. Accordingly Heber visited Miss McBride, and urged her to marry the man whom she had loved, *by proxy;* explaining to her that it was a religious duty which she owed to her affianced husband. The poor girl, puzzled and troubled, and desirous of being in the society of the loved one, and contributing to his happiness in the next world, consented.

Heber then applied to Robert T. Burton, and induced him to marry the girl. Burton is the Sheriff of Salt Lake County, and Collector of Internal Revenue for the United States Government! He is a fit instrument to carry out any scheme of the heads of the church, and required but little inducement to undertake this one. The poor girl was thus disposed of, by being sealed to Cushion for eternity, and to Burton, as his third wife, for time. She was taken home, and domiciled with the other two.

These worthy matrons were not pleased with the appearance of a new wife, and claiming their rights as the only real wives, who had been sealed to their husband both for time and eternity, resolved at once to make it exceedingly uncomfortable for the new-comer. This they did effectually, and Susan's life was a very unhappy one. But time passed on, and she became the mother of several children.

Susan was not allowed equal privileges with the other two. She had but one small room, in which she cooked, ate, slept, and spun, while the other two had splendid chambers and parlors,—for Burton is wealthy. When she complained to Burton, he said,—" Susan, you know I have only married you for time, and you must not expect the same privileges which I grant to my other wives, who are married for eternity, and who will exalt and glorify me in the celestial kingdom. You ought to be thankful for what you do receive, and not fret about my other wives."

The first wife takes control of Susan's children, in contradiction to the entire theory of this complex and unnatural relationship, and the mother is frequently obliged to see them severely punished, and suffer in silence. One day the first wife's boys and one of Susan's were in the barn, doing some mischief. The first wife went out and commanded the boys to come away. Her own boys ran past unharmed, but when Susan's boy, the youngest of the three, came out, she caught him, beat him, threw him on the ground, and kicked him.

This is but one of many instances, where women are living in this way, being married to one man for time, and sealed to another for eternity. This narrative was given me by one who had lived in the family for several months, and saw and heard what is herein stated.

A coarseness of feeling and sentiment, scarcely credible, is another result of this state of society. Kimball one day met a Mr. Taussig, a Prussian brother. "Brother Taussig," he said, "are you doing well?" "Yes, sir," was the reply. "Then you do well for the church too," said the Second President; "**how many women have you?**" "Two, sir." "**That** is not enough; you must take a couple more. I'll send them to you. Do you hear?" "Yes, sir." On the following evening, when the brother returned home, he found two women sitting there. His first wife said: "Brother Taussig," (all the women call their husbands "brother,") "these are the sisters Pratt." **They** were two widows of Parley P. Pratt.

One of the *ladies*, Sarah, then said: " Brother Taussig, Brother Kimball told us to call on you, and you know what for." " Yes, ladies," replied Brother Taussig, " but it is a very hard task for me to marry two." The other remarked, " Brother Kimball told us that you were doing a very good business, and could support more women." Sarah then took up the conversation : " Well, Brother Taussig, I want to get married, anyhow." The good brother replied, " Well, ladies, I will see what I can do, and let you know."

The next day, Brother Taussig visited the Bishop, and effected a compromise. By marrying Sarah he was released from the other. After he had lived awhile with the three wives, Sarah became dissatisfied, and applied to Brother Brigham for a divorce. Brother Taussig was summoned before the President, and made but feeble resistance to the application, admitting that he could not properly maintain more than two wives. The divorce was granted, and Brother Taussig was called upon by the clerk for $10. For not having the money, he received a cursing from the clerk, and Sarah was retained in the royal presence, with the assurance that it was " no divorce," until the money was brought in. Brother Taussig went on to the street, borrowed it, and brought it into the office,—and thus ended this disgusting serio-comic conjugal farce.*

Other incidents are more serious in their nature. One of them, which came to my knowledge, would be too horrible to relate, were not the facts well authenticated.

An old man, a brewer by occupation, married a young girl, as a second wife. The husband and the first wife abused her shamefully. Finally, after a long course of ill-treatment, the husband descended to the level of the brute. On one occasion, which was but a few days after her confine-

---

* To explain the part which Brother Kimball acted in this affair, it afterward appeared that he was anxious to have Sarah provided for because he wanted the house that Sarah lived in, for his daughter, who was about to marry a son of Parley P. Pratt.

ment, exasperated by her refusal to yield to his wishes, he dragged her out of bed by the hair, took her down cellar, and kept her there several days and nights, upon bread and water, until her cries and entreaties were overheard by persons in the Overland Stage-Office, which was near by. The matter was investigated, and the poor and almost dying woman released from the clutches of the fiend. She was taken violently ill, and soon after lost her reason entirely.

No notice was taken of this transaction by the church authorities, and the inhuman husband went unpunished.

Wife-whipping is by no means uncommon in Utah. Many names might be mentioned of men of high standing in the church, who make no scruple of using personal violence to keep their wives in due subordination. It is a common saying, that a man who is good at managing cattle, will be able to manage his women.

One would suppose that it would be very difficult to induce women to go into "plurality" under such circumstances. On the contrary, so infatuated are they with the religious view of the subject, that many of them look upon it as a duty to be performed, and a cross to be borne, no matter at what sacrifice.

One of the sisters, in conversation with me, expressed her views upon polygamy as follows: "Oh, it is hard," she said, "very hard; but no matter, we must bear it. It is a correct principle, and there is no salvation without it. We had one, (meaning a plural wife,) but it was so hard, both for my husband and myself, that we could not endure it, and she left us at the end of seven months. She had been with us as a servant, several months, and was a good girl; but as soon as she was made a wife, she became insolent, and told me she had as good a right to the house and things as I had, and you know," she said, "that did n't suit very well. But," continued she, "I wish we had kept her, and I had borne everything, *for we have got to have one*, and don't you think it would be pleasanter to have one you had known, than a stranger?" I told her I thought it would, if it had to be done, but I hoped my husband would not take one. She said, "He'll have to do it, if you and he want to be saved."

That the system of polygamy is really distasteful to the women of Utah, — that they are unhappy and dissatisfied, especially the first wives, is sufficiently shown by the public admissions of the church authorities. The admission of Young to that effect, made in the strongest language, has already been given. Jedediah Grant, one of the "three," also conceded the same fact in a sermon preached at the Bowery, in September, 1856, in the following language: —

"We have women here, who like anything but the Celestial Law of God; and if they could break asunder the cable of the Church of Christ, *there is scarcely a mother in Israel but would do it this day.* And they talk it to their husbands, to their daughters, and to their neighbors, and say *they have not seen a week's happiness since they became acquainted with that law, or since their husbands took a second wife.*"

Nothing but the strong appeals constantly made to their religious faith and moral sentiments, could hold them where they are for a single day. Many instances might be given, illustrating the workings of the system.

The writer has no disposition to bring private individuals into public notice, especially those who deserve only to sink into obscurity. But as this is a subject which affects the whole country, and must eventually be disposed of, upon the basis of *facts*, we shall give two or three other instances, citing cases of persons so well known, that the facts will not be questioned for a moment.

Mr. Townsend, a hotel-keeper at Salt Lake, married a young wife. The other wife became disgusted, and refused to remain in the house. So, in another house back of the hotel, lived the first wife, leading a miserable, unhappy life, looking upon the second wife as an interloper, having an unutterable contempt for her, and refusing to speak to her.

Mrs. Captain Hooper, an intelligent and lady-like woman, says she does not like to think of the subject,— would rather not talk about it; admits that if her husband were to take a second wife, it would make her very unhappy, but says it is a part of her religion, and she believes it would be her duty to submit. It is known that Brigham urges Captain H. to take a second wife, and it is thought the Captain will be forced into it by the absolute power, whose behests he must obey, no matter how contrary to his own inclinations it may be. He was once seen to come out of the President's office with tears in his eyes, after having had a conversation upon the subject.

T. B. H. Stenhouse, an active, intelligent man, holding the office of Postmaster at Salt Lake, under the Federal Government, has a beautiful and accomplished wife, and an interesting family of eight children. For a long time after arriving in Utah, he remained true to his wife. She lived in constant apprehension that her husband would "go into polygamy," and so much was she opposed to it, that she once said to me in his presence, that if he did, she could not and would not live with him longer.

Mr. Cook, the Superintendent and Assistant Treasurer of the Overland Stage Company, who was accidentally killed in California, was, during his lifetime, on intimate terms with Stenhouse, and is supposed to have exercised considerable influence to prevent him from embracing the pernicious system. It is known that on one occasion, Cook, hearing that Stenhouse contemplated something of the kind, threatened him with a prosecution under the Anti-Polygamy Law of Congress.

Cook was killed, as stated, and soon after, Stenhouse, freed from any restraint except the church and his own pliable conscience, married Celia, daughter of Parley P. Pratt, a pert little miss, fourteen years of age, and took her into his family, with his eight children and the wife with whom he had lived so many years. And this too, in open violation of a law of the United States, under the government of which he holds a lucrative commission!

CHAPTER XIII.

THE ENDOWMENT.

Dramatis Personæ.

ELOHEIM, or *Head God*, Brigham Young.
JEHOVAH, Heber C. Kimball.
JESUS, Daniel H. Wells.
MICHAEL, or *Adam*, W. C. Staines.
SATAN, W. W. Phelps.
APOSTLE PETER, Orson Pratt.
APOSTLE JAMES, John Taylor.
APOSTLE JOHN, Erastus Snow.
WASHER, Dr. Sprague.
CLERK, David O. Calder.
EVE, Miss Eliza R. Snow.
TIMOTHY BROADBRIM, *a Quaker*, Wilford Woodruff.
DEACON SMITH, *a Methodist*, Orson Hyde.
PARSON PEABODY, *a Presbyterian*, Franklin D. Richards.
ELDER LONG-FACE, *a Baptist*, Phineas H. Young.
FATHER BONIFACE, *a Catholic*, George A. Smith.
BROTHER and SISTER JONES,
BROTHER and SISTER WHITE,
SISTER MARY BROWN, *to be sealed* } *Endowees.*
  to BROTHER WHITE,
Several other Candidates,

ACT I. SCENE I.

[Enter Candidates.

Clerk. Good-morning, brethren and sisters. Be seated. Brother White, please state the time and place of your birth, date of your marriage, and the time when you were baptized into the church.

Bro. W. I was born November 3d, 1801, in the town of Portsmouth, in New Hampshire. I was married January 1st, 1824, and was baptized into the church April 1st, 1860.

Clerk. Have you paid your tithing punctually? If so, produce your receipts. [These are read, and handed back.] That is sufficient. You are entitled to receive your endowments.

Sister White, will you state when and where you were born, and when you became a member of the church?

Sister W. I was born September 18th, 1815, in the State of New York, and became a member of the church in 1852.

Clerk. Sister Mary Brown, please state when and where you were born, and when you became a member of the church.

Sister Mary. I was born June 20th, 1849, in Great Salt Lake City, and was baptized into the church in 1860.

[The Clerk propounds the same questions to all the candidates, and enters their answers in the record.]

Clerk. You will now proceed to the washing-room, the brethren on the right, and the sisters on the left.

Apostle Peter. You will remove your shoes, that the dust of earth may not pollute the holy ground on which you are about to tread.

[The candidates are then washed in tepid water, and each member blessed with a blessing peculiar to each. They are then pronounced clean from the blood of this generation, and a new name is given to each by the Apostle Peter. They then return to the waiting-room, where the brethren are anointed with oil, the sisters receiving their anointing in their own washing-room.

This ceremony consists in pouring olive-oil upon the head of each, well rubbed into the hair, nose, eyes, and mouth, and allowed to run down over the person. It is accompanied by a blessing, similar to that received at the washing. Brain to be strong, ears to be quick to hear the words of God's servants, eyes to be sharp to perceive, and feet to be swift to run in the ways of righteousness. This is the anointing administered preparatory to being ordained a " King and Priest unto God and the Lamb."

Thus greased and blessed, the "garments" are put on. A dress of muslin or linen is worn next to the skin, reaching from the neck to the ankles and wrists, and in shape like a little child's **sleeping garment.** Over this a shirt, then a robe, made of fine linen, crossing and gathered up in plaits **on** one shoulder, **reaching to the** ground before and behind, and tied around the waist. Over this is fastened a small, square apron, similar in size and shape to a masonic apron, made of white linen **or** silk, with imitation of fig-leaves painted or worked upon it. A cap made from a square yard of linen, and gathered into a band to fit the head, and white linen **or** cotton shoes, complete the dress of the candidates.]

SCENE II. CREATION.

Eloheim, seated upon his Throne.

[*Enter* JEHOVAH, JESUS, *and* MICHAEL.

Eloheim. "Ye powers of Heaven!" This day hath Satan, our rebellious foe, been vanquished. Lest he again presumptuous rise, let us create new worlds, and people them with beings who by slow degrees shall rise and fill the place of those by him deceived. Go forth, ye heavenly messengers; examine well the boundless realms of space, and bring report from thence back to the Eternal Throne.

Jehovah, Jesus, and Michael, [all]. Eternal father! Great Eloheim, Maker and King of the celestial worlds. Joyful we go, thy mandates to fulfil.

[*Exeunt* JEHOVAH, JESUS, *and* MICHAEL.

Eloheim. Far into chaos proudly ride my messengers. Winds bear them onward, o'er the deep profound.

[*Reënter* JEHOVAH, JESUS, *and* MICHAEL.

Jehovah, Jesus, and Michael, [all]. Almighty Ruler. The way is clear. Send forth thy Word alone, and worlds will rise, and circle into space, obedient to thy call.

Elo. "Silence, ye troubled waves! your discord end. Thus far extend, thus far thy bounds. This be thy circumference, O world!"

Jeh. Behold the Earth. "Matter unformed and void; darkness profound covers the abyss."

Mich. But see, "the Spirit of God outspread, and vital virtue infused, and vital warmth throughout the fluid mass. Like things to like! The rest to several place disparted." And in the air, "the Earth, self-balanced, on her centre hangs."

Elo. "Let there be light."

Jesus. "Hail! Holy light. Offspring of Heaven, first born."

Elo. The light is good. Let darkness flee into the shades of night, and light make up the day.

Mich. Hark! "the celestial choirs, when orient light, exhaling first from darkness, they behold, — birthday of Heaven and Earth; with joy and shout, the hollow, universal orb they fill."

Elo. "Let there be a firmament amid the waters, and let it divide the waters from the waters."

Jeh. "Behold the firmament, — expanse of liquid, pure, transparent, elemental air, diffused in circuit to the uttermost convex; partition firm and sure, the waters underneath from those above dividing."

Jesus. The water still doth compass all the Earth, moulding the plastic mass, and doth implant, within her genial breast, the seeds of various life.

Elo. "Be gathered, now, ye waters under Heaven, into one place, and let dry land appear." Land, freed from your prison-house, arise, and be called Earth. Ye waters, — seas. Now "let the Earth put forth the verdant grass, herb yielding seed, and fruit-tree yielding fruit after her kind, whose seed is in herself, upon the Earth."

Mich. Oh, sight sublime! The Earth, till now, barren and fruitless was; "her universal face" now clothed in "pleasant green." Listen, ye Gods! The morning stars, which in the vast expanse of Heaven, circle their rounds, together sing. The sons of God, swift-winged angels, shout for joy.

Elo. "Let there be lights, high in the expanse of Heaven, to divide the day from the night; and let them be for signs, for seasons and for days, and circling years; and let them be for lights, as I ordain their office, in the firmament of Heaven, to give light on the Earth." "Two great lights,— great for their use to man,— the greater to have rule by day, the less by night; the stars I also set in the high firmament, to illuminate the Earth, and rule the day in their vicissitude, and rule the night, and light from darkness to divide."

Jeh. Behold, "the thousand, thousand stars, that now appear, spangling the hemisphere," the luminaries bright, that rise and set, and crown the glory of the fourth new day.

Elo. "Let the waters generate reptile, with spawn abundant; living soul; and let fowl fly above the Earth, with wings displayed, on the open firmament of Heaven, and the great whales, and each soul living, each that creeps, and in the waters generate, and each bird of its kind,— let each be blessed;" "be fruitful, multiply, and in the seas and lakes, and running streams, the waters fill: and let the fowl be multiplied."

Jesus. Let Heaven rejoice, let Earth be glad, and hail the dawning of the fifth new day.

Elo. This is the sixth and last morn of creation. Let every creature forth, from his genial mother, cattle and creeping thing, and beast of earth, each of his kind. All, all is good, and pleasing in my sight.

Jesus. "Now Heaven in all her glory shines. Earth, in her rich attire, consummate, lovely, smiles; air, water, earth, fowl, fish, and beast are here, and yet there wants the master work of all yet done; a creature endued with reason, which erect may stand, and self-acknowledged, govern all the rest."

Elo. "Let us make man, in our own image, man in our similitude, and let them rule over the fish and fowl of sea and air, beast of the field, and over all the earth, and every creeping thing, that creeps the ground." Thou art created male and female, in the form and likeness of the Gods. Go forth, be blessed; "be fruitful, multiply, and fill the earth, subdue it, and throughout dominion hold" over all, all else that breathes upon its bosom. Now all is finished, all complete and perfect. Immortal Gods, let us to our high seat ascend, that from our lofty throne our perfect works we may behold.

[To represent the creation of man, Jehovah, Jesus, and Michael stroke each candidate separately, pretending to form; and by blowing into their faces, pretend to vivify them. They are then supposed to be as Adam, newly made, and perfectly ductile in the hands of their makers. A deep sleep then falls upon the new Adam, and ribs are extracted, out of which, in another apartment, their wives are formed. They are then commanded to awake, and their wives are introduced to them; after which they file by twos into the garden.]

SCENE III. GARDEN OF EDEN.

[*Enter* ADAM and EVE, and Endowees.

Eve. "Well may we labor, still to dress this garden,— still to tend plant, herb and flower, our pleasant task enjoined." "Let us divide our labors," each where seemeth good; and thus, as night draws on, our task will be accomplished.

Adam. "Sole Eve, associate sole, to me beyond compare, above all living creatures dear! A doubt possesses me, lest harm befall thee, severed from me; for thou knowest what hath been warned us, what malicious foe envies our happiness."

Eve. "Offspring of Heaven, and all Earth's Lord! That such an enemy we have, who seeks our ruin, both by thee informed, and from the parting angel overhead; but that thou shouldst my firmness therefore doubt, to God or thee, because we have a foe may tempt it, I expected not to hear."

Adam. "Daughter of God and man, immortal Eve,—

for such thou art; from sin and blame entire; I, from the influence of thy looks, receive access in every virtue. Why shouldst not thou like sense within thee feel when I am present, and thy trial choose with me, — best witness of thy virtue tried."

Eve. "If this be our condition, thus to dwell in narrow circuit, straitened **by a foe, how** are we happy still, in **fear of** harm?"

Adam. "O woman, best are all things as the will of God ordains them; therefore go; for thy stay, not free, absents thee more."

Eve. "With thy permission then, and thus forewarned," I go.

[Enter Satan, **in the** form of a serpent, half man, half snake. He discovers Eve in a bower of roses, and watches her at a distance.]

Satan. "Thoughts, whither have ye led me? — what hither brought **us?** Hate, not love, but all pleasure to destroy." [He approaches Eve.] "Wonder not, sovran **mistress**, fairest resemblance of thy Maker fair, at my appearance, half man, half beast, but approach and view this goodly **tree**, the fruit of which such wonders work."

Eve. "Serpent, we might have spared our coming hither," for "**of** this tree we may not taste or touch; thus hath our God commanded."

Satan. "Indeed! Hath God then said, that of the fruit of all these garden trees ye shall not eat, yet lords declared of all in earth or air?"

Eve. "Of the fruit of each tree in the garden we may eat, but of the fruit of this fair tree, amidst the garden, God hath said, 'Ye shall not eat thereof, nor shall ye touch **it,** lest ye die.'"

Satan. "O sacred, wise, and wisdom-giving plant; mother of science! Now I feel thy power within me clear, not only **to** discern things in their causes, but to trace the ways **of highest** agents, deemed however wise. Queen of this Universe! Do not believe these rigid threats of death;—*ye shall not die.*" Your tyrant ruler knows full well, that in the day ye eat thereof, ye shall be as Gods, and good from evil know. "Goddess humane, reach then, and freely taste."

[Satan plucks the fruit and presents it. Eve receives it, and after considerable hesitation, tastes, and finally eats it. Adam soon after enters.]

Eve. "Hast thou not wondered at my stay? Thee have I missed;" for I have tasted of the tree to us forbidden, and such delight till now have never felt. Taste thou, [offers him the fruit,] and be a God.

[Adam stands amazed and sorrowful, dropping a garland from his hand.]

Adam. "O fairest of creation! Some cursed fraud of enemy hath beguiled thee, and me with thee hath ruined; for with thee certain my resolution is to die." [He eats.] Oh, fruit delicious, fit indeed for Gods. From us withheld, lest being Gods, we cease to obey our tyrant Lord.

[They soon begin to see their true condition. They reproach each other. They discover their nakedness, make aprons of fig-leaves, and wear them. The voice of Eloheim is heard in another part of the garden.]

Elo. "Adam, where art thou? Why hast thou fled and hid thyself? What hast thou done?"

Adam. O Lord, my Maker and Preserver! Thy voice I heard, when thou didst walk amid the trees, but being naked, I did fear to see thy face. Confusion dire and shame filled all my soul.

Elo. "Who told thee thou wast naked? Hast thou then eaten of that tree, to thee forbidden?"

Adam. The woman whom thou gavest me did give this fruit unto my lips; and I did eat.

Elo. O woman, fair but frail. Why hast thou done this deed of sin?

Eve. "The serpent me beguiled, and I did eat."

Elo "Because thou hast done this, thou art **accursed**

above all cattle, each beast of the field. Upon thy belly grovelling thou shalt go, and dust shalt eat, all the days of thy life. Between thee and the woman I will put enmity, and between thine and her seed: her seed shall bruise thy head, thou bruise his heel." And thou, O Eve, "thy sorrow I will greatly multiply by thy conception: children thou shalt bring in sorrow forth, and to thy husband's will thine shall submit; he over thee shall rule." And thou, O Adam, "because thou hast hearkened to the voice of thy wife, and eaten of the tree concerning which I charged thee, saying, 'Thou shalt not eat thereof;' cursed is the ground for thy sake; thou in sorrow shalt eat thereof all the days of thy life; thorns also and thistles it shall bring thee forth unbid; and thou shalt eat the herb of the field; in the sweat of thy face shalt thou eat bread, till thou return unto the ground; for thou out of the ground wast taken; know thy birth; for dust thou art, and shalt to dust return."

Elo. [To Jehovah, Jesus, and Michael.] "Behold the man is become as one of us, knowing good from evil; and now, lest he in some unguarded hour put forth his hand, take of the tree of life, and live forever, we must forth from hence expel him." We will place from Eden eastward cherubims, and flaming sword, turning which way soever he may attempt an entrance.

Adam. "O miserable of happy! Is this the end of this new, glorious world? — and me, so late the glory of that glory? Accursed of blessed, hide me from the face of God, whom to behold was once my height of happiness."

Eve. "O unexpected stroke, worse than of death! Must I thus leave thee, Paradise? — thus leave thee, native soil, — these happy **walks and shades,** fit haunt of Gods, where I had hoped to spend, quiet though sad, the respite of that day that must be mortal to us both? O flowers! that never will in other climate grow, my earliest visitation and my last at even, which I bred up with tender hand, from the first opening bud, and gave ye names! Who now shall rear ye to the sun, or rank your tribes, and water from the ambrosial fount? Thee, lastly, nuptial bower! by me adorned with what to sight or smell was sweet! From thee, how shall I part, and whither wander, down into a world, to this obscure and wild? How shall we breathe in other air, less pure, accustomed to immortal fruits?"

Elo. O man, thy cries of penitence and woe have reached my ears. I will a plan unfold, obedience to which, rendered with deep humility, shall by degrees redeem and bring you back to Heaven.

My holy priesthood I henceforth establish upon Earth. To those endowed with that high calling, as unto me, shalt thou with reverence bow. Their power supreme, commands indisputable, in my stead, I appoint them unto you. They are to act henceforth as I myself.

[Here oaths of inviolable secrecy, with the penalty of throat-cutting, are administered to the awe-stricken and intimidated neophytes. They are sworn to render implicit obedience to the priesthood, and to depend upon them for everything; especially not to touch any woman, unless given through the priesthood.

A sign, a grip, and a key-word are given to the endowees, and the *First Degree of the Aaronic Priesthood* is conferred.]

Elo. You are now endowed with one law of purity, one key of truth, and one power of priesthood. Go forth into the world, ye fallen ones, and seek for truth. Obey the voice of God and his holy priesthood, and I will send to Earth a Saviour, that through faith and obedience you shall again inherit your lost estate, again enjoy the ambrosial fruits in the celestial kingdom of the Gods.

[*Exeunt all.*

SCENE IV. THE WORLD.

[*Enter* ADAM, EVE, Endowees, and Sectarians.

Timothy Broadbrim. I feel the movement of the Spirit to speak unto thee. Thou knowest that the world is lost in sin and wickedness. But ye should "resist not evil," but "overcome evil with good." "If a man take away thy cloak, give him thy coat also." Raise not thy hand to harm a fellow-creature. "Charity suffereth long and is kind!" See that no brother be in want; look ye after the widow and the fatherless.

Deacon Smith. Brethren and Sisters,—I rise to address you a few words, founded upon the following passage of Scripture:—"And there shall be weeping and wailing, and gnashing of teeth." Oh, this is a fearful doom. Oh, ye sinners, hear. There is a lake which burns with fire and brimstone; you are on the very brink; do you not see thousands of the damned weltering in its burning waves? You are, as it were, on a greased plank, sliding, and sliding, as swift as the wheels of Time can roll, down to this awful gulf. [Sisters begin to shriek and faint.] Flee from the wrath to come; fly to Jesus; come to the mourners' bench; cry mightily to God for help. He alone can save you. Come, come, come to Jesus. Brethren and sisters, sing,—

"Where shall the guilty soul find rest?" etc.

Parson Peabody [speaking through his nose]. My dear hearers, this is a fallen world. We are all in the gall of bitterness, and in the bond of iniquity. Satan, the great enemy of mankind, is ever seeking our destruction. Let us close our hearts against his wiles, and come to Jesus, and if we are of the elect, foreordained from before the creation of the world, we shall be saved; and if not, we shall be lost. We can do nothing of ourselves. We are in the hands of a just and wise God, who doeth all things well.

In the language of the divine poet,—

"If you can, if you can't;
If you will, if you won't;
You'll be damned if you do,
You'll be damned if you don't."

Let the brethren remember their covenants, and let them bring their offspring to the altar, and there consecrate them to God, through the ordinance of sprinkling; and if they are to be saved, they will be saved. Otherwise, though not a span long, they will go down to the bottomless pit.

Elder Longface. Brethren, — The subject of my discourse will be found in the following text: "Whom he did predestinate," &c.

We learn from this, — 1st, That we are sinners. 2d, We need a Saviour. 3d, That we must be baptized by immersion. 4th, That we should exclude from the communion-table all such as are not immersed. 5th, That many are called, but few chosen. 6th, That those who are chosen will be saved, without their own action in the matter. 7th, That those who are not chosen will be damned, no matter what they do, in and of their own strength; and lastly, in order to have the least opportunity to be saved, you must join the Baptist Church.

The Lord grant that many may embrace the truth as it is in Christ Jesus, and unite with "our church," and be saved. The brethren will sing, —

"O, when shall we see Jesus," &c.,

Father Boniface [with pages, robes, candles, &c.]. *Te Deum laudamus.* [They sing.] O Divine Queen of the skies, Holy Mother of God, to thee we lift up our voices. Grant us thy divine intercession with thy dear Son, that we, through his precious blood, may be made clean. Bless thy believing children, make them faithful to their Holy Father the Pope, diligent in counting their beads, and saying their matins and vespers. O Holy Mother, keep them from all sin; especially grant them grace to eat no meat on Friday, and we will ever adore and bless thee, Father, Son, and Holy Spirit. Amen.

Let the choir sing *Ave Maria. Benedicite.*

[*Enter* SATAN.

Satan. Good-morning, brethren. I love you all; you are my friends. I am gratified to find you so faithful in assisting me to build up my kingdom. Rest assured, you shall be rewarded. You shall be kings and princes when I succeed in setting up my throne upon the Earth.

[*Enter Apostles* PETER, JAMES, *and* JOHN.

Peter. Why dost thou tempt the children of men, and lie in wait to deceive them?

Satan. "Let me alone. What have I to do with thee," thou follower of Jesus? I know thou hast the holy priesthood of God, —

Peter, James, and John, [all.] And in the name of the Lord Jesus Christ, and of the holy priesthood, we command you to depart from hence.

[The Devil foams, hisses, and rushes out, chased by the Apostle Peter.]

James. My children, hearken now unto my voice. When in these last days God saw the lost condition of mankind, his heart was moved with pity, and He sent with me Peter and John, and commanded us, saying, " Go ye to Earth, and seek me a good man, of the lineage of Joseph, who was carried away into Egypt, and of the lineage of the prophets, even Joseph Smith." Restore to him the lost priesthood. Bestow upon him the keys of power; make him Prophet, Seer, and Revelator, and let him reëstablish my church upon the Earth." Behold, this was done, and the same power and authority has now descended from Joseph to Brigham. Hear ye him, the representative of God on Earth. Him reverence and obey, and ye shall advance toward the kingdom of Heaven.

[An oath, penalty, the heart to be plucked out, with agonizing details, is administered. The utmost secrecy is impressed, and the *Second Degree of the Aaronic Priesthood* is conferred, with signs, grips, &c.]

ACT II. SCENE I.
Room with an altar in the centre.

[*Enter Apostles* PETER, JAMES, *and* JOHN, with the candidates for endowment.

Peter. Dearly beloved, you are now in the way of salvation. Be faithful to each other, and all your brethren. Betray not the secret things of Zion to the ungodly gentiles. Think not with your own thoughts, but come to the priesthood. They are the mediators between God and man. Obey, without murmuring, whatever they command, though it may seem to you unjust or unreasonable. Your hearts are not so fully sanctified as to enable you to judge as to the merit of their acts. Be ever ready and willing to forsake father or mother, husband or wife, houses or lands, for the glory of Zion, and the upbuilding of God's kingdom on the Earth. And more especially, brethren, as you value your eternal salvation and temporal welfare, speak no evil of the Lord's anointed.

[An oath is now administered, with particulars the most disgusting and revolting. Another sign, key-word, and grip, are communicated, and the *First Degree of the Melchisedec Priesthood* is conferred.]

SCENE II.

Another room with an altar in the centre; on it the Bible, Book of Mormon, and Book of Doctrine and Covenants. Jehovah in the room, and Eloheim in the next, looking on. The candidates are ranged round the altar. The Apostles are also present.

Peter. You are now in a saved condition, and acceptable in the sight of God. You are to enter on the work of the Lord, in truth and sincerity.

"Behold now," saith the Lord, "the wicked and ungodly gentiles; they have slain the Prophet Joseph, persecuted the saints, and mocked at my priesthood. Therefore, O Israel, arise in thy strength, go forth and revenge the wrongs of my people on this perverse generation. They have spilled the blood of the saints, and wasted their substance. Therefore let their blood be spilled, and let their substance be wasted

Let the curse of God rest on this nation and Government. Let wars and famine, and cruel pestilence overtake them, and let the Church of God, in its glory and power, rule over all the nations, and fill the whole earth.

Therefore, brethren, be ye vigilant; and let no opportunity pass to vindicate the name of **your** God; and if you cannot do it, teach it to your children. Let them take it from their mother's breast. Teach it to them from your bed of death, and leave it for an inheritance, that all people may know that the God of Israel has set his hand to gather his people, and to destroy the wicked **from off** the face of the earth.

[Here another oath is administered, binding the endowee to revenge the death of Joseph Smith on this generation; to cherish constant enmity toward the United States Government, doing all in his power for its overthrow; to baffle its designs, to refuse submission and renounce all allegiance, and to obey the church authorities, and no other.

Curses the most frightful, penalties the most barbarous, accompany the obligation, to add to its binding efficacy, **and to** insure secrecy. A new sign, grip, &c., complete **the** *Second Degree of the Melchisedec Priesthood.*]

John. You are the children of the Most High, endued **with powers** and blessings. Your robes of righteousness, which you must henceforth wear, in token of your covenants, are on the wrong shoulder, and none but God's priesthood can set them right. [The robes are changed to the other shoulder, and the candidates are stationed in a circle, around the altar.]

Peter. Little children, you are now chosen of God to carry on his mighty work, and He, through his servant, will teach you how to pray, that your supplications may reach the eternal throne, and call down an immediate answer.

[Peter kneels on his right knee, takes hold of the hand of one of the standing brethren, all of whom are united by a fantastic intertwining of hands, and prays slowly, all repeating his words after him:]

"O, God, ruler of the celestial world, we have this day taken upon ourselves covenants and powers from thy hand. Make us faithful to those covenants; and if we obey not thy commands, let thy curses descend upon our heads. Make us quick to hear and obey God's servants in the holy priesthood, and if we ever divulge anything that we have received, let the curses this day pronounced, fall upon our heads. Make us faithful in Zion and in the upbuilding of her cause, and at last receive us into thy celestial kingdom, with all the gifts, powers, and blessings this day pronounced upon the faithful in Israel. Amen.

Peter. Brethren, you are now members of the holy orders of God's priesthood. Henceforth you are entitled to all the blessings and privileges of the same.

[The endowees, fitted for Heaven and celestial glory, pass "behind the vail," a new name is whispered very softly and quickly to each; certain marks, resembling the Masonic square and compass, are cut in the under garment, on the left breast; also a similar one on the knee. The candidates are then ushered into the full light and glory of the celestial kingdom. The brethren turn back to the vail, and admit their wives, whose garments are marked in a similar manner.]

SCENE III. THE CELESTIAL KINGDOM.

In the centre of this apartment is an altar, nicely cushioned, with a cushioned ledge to kneel upon. The men kneel upon one side and the women upon the other, each brother holding the hand of his wife, also of the woman to whom he is to be sealed, with the patriarchal grip. The ceremony of sealing for eternity then commences.

Eloheim. Children of Earth, you have been redeemed by the blood of the Lamb, and the power of my holy priesthood. You have been faithful unto the end, and shall now receive a crown of glory. In like manner as I gave Eve unto your father Adam, while he was yet pure and holy, I give unto you wives and children, that you may be Gods in your season, and that worlds may be peopled by your posterity. [Each candidate is asked the usual questions, and after the answers have been received, Eloheim **proceeds :**]

Because of your faithfulness in all these things, I seal upon you the blessings of the Holy Resurrection, with **power to come** forth in the morning of the first resurrection, clothed with glory, immortality, and eternal lives; and I seal upon you the blessings of thrones and dominions, and principalities, and powers, and exaltations; together with the blessings of Abraham, Isaac, and Jacob; and say unto you, be fruitful and multiply, and replenish the earth, that you may have joy and rejoicing in your posterity, in the day of the Lord Jesus. All these blessings, together with all other blessings pertain**ing to the** new and everlasting covenant, I seal upon your **heads,** and enjoin your faithfulness unto the end.

[The candidates dress, get a lunch, and return **to the** "celestial kingdom" to hear a lecture by Kimball, explanatory of the whole scheme. The signs, tokens, marks, and idea*r* **are many of** them taken from the Masonic Order. " **The in tention** of the mystery **is to** teach unlimited obedience **to** Brigham, and treason against the country."]

CHAPTER XIV.

BRIGHAM AS GRAND ARCHEE OF THE ORDER OF THE GODS.

Organization of the Order of the Archees. — The Grand Archees. — The Archees. — The Danites. — Organization of Brigham's Celestial Kingdom. — Doctrine of Adoption. — Case of Dr. Sprague. — Description of Leading Danites: Bill Hickman, Porter Rockwell, Robert T. Burton. — Affidavits. — Recent Attacks on Emigrant Trains.

> " There on that throne, to which the blind belief
> Of millions raised him, sat the Prophet Chief.
> . . . .
> On either side, with ready hearts and hands,
> His chosen guard of bold believers, stands;
> Young fire-eyed disputants, who deem their swords
> On points of faith more eloquent than words;
> And such their zeal, there's not a youth with brand
> Uplifted there, but, at the Chief's command,
> Would make his own devoted heart its sheath,
> And bless the lips that doom'd so dear a death."

THE Order of the Danites has been, for many years, an established institution in the Mormon Church.

Brigham and his two Counsellors form the First Presidency of this Order, under the style of Gods, or Grand Archees. These are, at present, Young, Kimball, and Wells. A few, also, of the Apostles, hold the rank of Grand Archees. These have the power of life and death.

Next in importance, is a body of men called Archees. They are entitled to sit in Council with the Gods or Grand Archees, in matters relating to the taking of life. This "Quorum," as it is called, also includes some of the Bishops and Presidents of other quorums in the church. Their office is to examine cases of offenders thought to require a summary disposal, and submit the result of such examination to the Grand Archees. In some cases, where the utmost discretion is required, they act as agents and swift-winged messengers, to carry into effect the decrees of the Gods.

The Archees have discretionary and independent power over the lives of all gentiles and "apostates."

Next in rank are the Danites, whose office is to assist the Archees in the execution of their bloody deeds. These are formed into bands of fifty men each. One band, at least, belongs to each Archee, they serving under him as minutemen. These "Danite Bands" are generally composed of inferior officers and teachers, constables, and policemen, and those who, having committed heinous crimes, as murder, theft, adultery, &c., would sooner be sworn to serve in this bloody office, than have their deeds exposed and receive their justly merited punishment.

The officers in all these grades are solemnly sworn to secrecy, and to the duties of their respective offices, on pain of instant death.

Where the danger of discovery is imminent, and the matter in hand too important to be trusted to the Danites, the Archees meet and perform the dirty work themselves; as in the case of Secretary Babbett, Brewer, and the unlucky attempt on Dr. Hurt. In other cases, the Danites are called upon; instance the Parishes, Potter, Bowman, Mountain Meadows, &c.

The Danites are also expected to act as spies upon the federal officers and other gentiles; to watch the feelings and spirits of the saints, and to report the first indications of disaffection. Such cases are at once attended to, and if they are deemed of a dangerous character, are summarily disposed of.

The spoil is divided, one half going to the Grand Archees, and the other half to the Archees and Danites who are employed in the commission of the crime.

When Judge Cradlebaugh attempted to bring to justice the perpetrators of the Mountain-Meadow Massacre, and various other crimes, several bishops and many other leading Mormons fled to the mountains, where they remained several weeks. Their place of refuge they named "Mount Kolob," which means "the residence of the Gods."

The remark is frequently made in Utah, — "Brigham is the only God I care a d— about." The deep meaning of this is only to be explained by reference to this organized system of crime, taken in connection with the organization of the "celestial kingdom."

The theory is, that Brigham Young is a God in embryo. That he is laying the foundation here for a celestial kingdom. That there will be created for him a world, which his posterity will inhabit, and of which he will be the King and God.

His kingdom will be constituted as follows: —

1st. Himself as God.

2d. His wives as Goddesses and Queens, each ruling her own posterity, with Brigham as husband and God.

3d. His sons and their families.

4th. The daughters, by the celestial law, would, when married, pass out of their father's kingdom, and be added to the husbands'. To obviate this difficulty, every man who marries one of the President's daughters, is obliged to be adopted by and sealed to his father-in-law. The daughter is thus retained to augment her father's kingdom, by the addition of her family. This is one reason why female children are so lightly esteemed in Utah. They cannot add to the father's glory, but must go to glorify others.

5th. Many young men who have no families, and therefore no kingdoms, are sealed to Brigham, to add to his celestial glory, — in some instances, also, men of families, who have not ambition enough to aspire to kingdoms of their own. This relationship pertains to this world as well as to the next. Brigham becomes a father to them here, supports them if necessary, and demands their respect and obedience.

A case recently occurred in Salt Lake, which fully illustrates the power which Young exercises over this class of his subjects.

Dr. Sprague, an Eastern man, has been at Salt Lake about twelve years. During most of that time he has officiated in the Endowment House, in the washings and anointings. He has also had charge of the Tabernacle, and acted as family physician to the inmates of the Harem.

He has a wife and two children. His son is on a mission, and the daughter, a little girl of thirteen, is an invalid. Mrs. Sprague is a model New-England housewife. She has toiled early and late to procure the comforts, and some of the luxuries of life. By the most persevering effort, they at length succeeded in building a beautiful house, and Doctor Sprague's garden is the prettiest in Salt Lake.

The family removed to their new residence in the fall of 1862, and had but just furnished it. By the Mormon law of adoption, the property of the adopted child belongs to the father, or is under his control. Dr. Sprague is the adopted son of Brigham Young. His whole property is worth not less than $10,000.

Mrs. Emeline Free Young has been very melancholy since Brigham married Amelia. Her health continued to decline until it was thought advisable to remove her from the Lion House, the scene of her joys and sorrow, and situate her more pleasantly. Accordingly one day Brigham called on Dr. Sprague and wife, and coolly told them that he wanted their place for three or four years, for Emeline, until he could build her one. At the end of that time they could have it again, and in the mean time they could live in the house formerly occupied by J. M. Grant, which he would have repaired for their use.

The husband and wife were astonished and confounded at this request, and Mrs. Sprague, under the first impulse of her indignation, said "she did not relish the idea of giving up her house to people who read novels every day." "Very well," replied the Prophet, "if you prefer to incur my displeasure rather than to let me have your home, you can do so." With this he left them.

The Doctor and his wife began thinking the matter over. It would never do to incur the displeasure of Brother Brigham. He was their father in this world, and their God in the celestial kingdom. Then the Doctor was advancing in years, and should he lose his situation in the Endowment House and Tabernacle, where would be the support for himself and family in his declining years? He had served his adopted father so long and faithfully, should he break with him now? It would never do; so, after many sleepless nights and much anguish of spirit, he made up his mind to make the sacrifice. As to Mrs. Sprague, she cared not for herself, but her poor sick child! She had lived for years almost entirely in the beautiful garden, and how could she leave it now? With frail and faltering step she had wandered amid the flowers and fruit, culling this bright geranium and that lovely rose, plucking this beautiful strawberry, and that luscious bunch of grapes, and by this sweet communion with Nature, the child seemed to receive afresh the life-giving principle. She was now to be torn from her little paradise, by whom, and for what? No wonder if the heart of the mother grew somewhat stony at the reflection.

When the poor girl heard that she must leave these "delightful shades," she wept until oblivion wrapt her senses, and in a fit of convulsions, she forgot, for the time being, at least, her cruel fate.

The sisters came to condole with Sister Sprague; said it was too bad. "Sister Sprague, it is too bad, but you had better do it than to have Brother Brigham's curse resting upon you."

Emeline, who is really a kind-hearted creature, came and wept with Sister S., saying she did not want her home, "but Brigham," said she, "has set his mind upon it, and we don't any of us *dare* to speak to him about it."

Young remained inexorable,—the change was made; and to-day the whilome favored wife and now cast-off mistress of Brigham Young, occupies the beautiful residence of Dr. Sprague, the fruit of his many years of toil and economy.

Bill Hickman is one of the most notorious of the Danite leaders. He is now about fifty years of age. He is a man of medium size, heavy set, of florid complexion, troubled of late years with weak eyes, causing him to wear goggles. He is of Southern birth, and a strong secessionist, but professes much friendship for the United States Government, and the federal officers. He is wily and cunning, with much of the *suaviter in modo*, and is something of a lawyer. He glories in a household of seven "women" and about twenty children, but does not maintain them in the highest style.

Porter Rockwell, another noted character, is somewhat of the same style of Hickman. Shorter of stature, with the Utah floridity of complexion, and very voluble in conversation. Anything that is all right with Rockwell, is "on the square." It is "wheat"; and nearly every act and expression of a stranger, is of that character.

Robert T. Burton, Sheriff of Salt Lake County, and Collector of Internal Revenue, who bids fair to rival or outdo all the others in his lawless deeds, is a tall, wiry man, one it would be hard to hit with a bullet. He is cool and imperturbable; in fact, never thrown off his balance, never wanting in case of an emergency. No fitter person to carry out the plans of Young could be found within or without the Territory, and upon him Brigham relies implicitly. With or without a "writ," he is always ready.

It is not my purpose to enter into a history of the many crimes to be traced with more or less certainty to the doors of these and other Mormon leaders. Some of them will be found collated in the appendix to the speech of Judge Cradlebaugh, already mentioned. Others are touched upon in the pages of this volume.

One or two affidavits, from a large number in the writer's

possession, will here be given, to illustrate the workings of the Mormon system, and to show how little the perpetration of crime stands in the way of the prosecution of the plans and purposes of the church leaders.

"UNITED STATES OF AMERICA,} ss.
TERRITORY OF UTAH.

"——— of said Territory, being duly sworn, says:—

"About ——— years ago, I was living on the ——— River, in the ——— Ward, and was Bishop of that Ward. Was in good standing in the Mormon Church.

"During that summer, a man who had had a difficulty with a Bishop living near me, was killed. When the man was missed, the Bishop refused to help look for him. Myself and several others turned out, and after considerable search, found the body. It was perforated by two balls. One had entered the back, the other, the back of the head. The difficulty related to a girl, whom the Bishop wanted to marry, for a plural wife.

"A relative of the murdered man went to Salt Lake City, and related all the facts to Elias Smith, Probate Judge of Great Salt Lake County, (Mormon,) asking his advice. This relative told me afterward, that Judge Smith said, 'Keep still for a while.' Nothing was ever done. No examination, coroner's jury, or investigation of any kind.

(Signed) ——— ———

"Subscribed and sworn to before me, at Salt Lake City, this 18th day of April, A. D. 1863.

"CHARLES B. WAITE,
"*Associate Justice for Utah Territory.*"

[Taken in presence of two witnesses.]

"UNITED STATES OF AMERICA,} ss.
TERRITORY OF UTAH.

"———, of said Territory, being duly sworn, says:—

"I have resided in the Territory of Utah about eight years. Some time in the fall of 1855, two men, one of them named Frank Keene, rented a house on East Weber, in Weber County, in this Territory. They rented of a Mr. Cox, and paid the rent up to the last day of March ensuing. Some time in February Cox endeavored to take possession of the house. The tenants remonstrated, and the matter was referred to the Teacher of the district. Cox was a Mormon; the tenants were not. The Teacher decided they should remain until the lease expired. Cox appealed to the Bishop of the Ward, Abiah Wadsworth. Wadsworth heard the case. The Bishop at first confirmed the decision of the Teacher; but immediately afterward, he said, as the tenants were gentiles, they must leave; and turning round to his clerk, directed him to write a notice to them to leave within a week. There were two or three feet of snow on the ground. Frank Keene was destitute of means. They both left as ordered. Nearly a month remained of the time for which rent was paid, and there was no pretence that the lease had been broken. It was a very severe winter, and a famine was prevailing.

"The next winter, a man by the name of Jones was denounced, and his life threatened, in a church meeting. The cause was this: He had loaned Lorenzo Snow, in England, one hundred pounds sterling, to print the 'Book of Mormon' in the Italian language. Upon arriving in the Territory, Jones tried to get payment of the money, but could not. It was because he insisted upon having his money, that he was denounced.

"The meeting was held at Centreville; and so much excitement was raised against Jones, and so many threats made against him, that he fled for his life. At the same time, the order was given, that no one should feed or entertain him, but he should be left to perish. Stoddard, one of the High-Priests, told me that the Bishop was so angry that he came down from the stand to kill Jones, in the meeting, but he fled. I saw Jones some weeks afterward. He corroborated these statements, and said the Bishop tried to kill him.

"I have often heard the doctrine of cutting the throats of apostates preached from the pulpit, particularly during the year 1856, when, for several months, I scarcely attended meeting without hearing such preaching. They would say, 'If you find a man with his throat cut, pay no attention to it.'

"At one time, my life was threatened by a Danite, and his intention to take my life was sanctioned at a meeting, by the Bishop and authorities. No cause was alleged, except a trivial remark made by my wife, reflecting slightly on one of the First Presidents. The remark had been exaggerated and attributed to me, and although it was fully explained, I was followed and threatened for over a year. At that time my wife and myself were members of the Mormon Church, in good standing.

"In December, 1857, Bishop Abiah Wadsworth, of East Weber Ward, gave permission to his friends to steal cattle for beef, from gentile merchants, and aided them in so doing. In carrying on these operations, they took cattle belonging to Mormons who had purchased them of gentile merchants. Having the brand of those merchants upon them, it was supposed they belonged to gentiles. The taking of the Mormon cattle gave rise to a church meeting to investigate the affair. I was present at that meeting. The result was, that those who had taken cattle which were proved to belong to Mormons, should pay for them. It was also determined at the same meeting, that those who had taken cattle belonging to gentiles, should pay their value to Brigham Young, as Trustee of the Emigrating Fund. The gentile owners of these cattle had been driven out of the Territory.

(Signed) ————————

"Subscribed and sworn to before me, this 2d day of May, A. D. 1863, at Great Salt Lake City.

"CHARLES B. WAITE,
"*Associate Justice for Utah Territory.*"

The names of these affiants, and some of the circumstances tending to identify them, are omitted, as the writer does not feel at liberty to place their lives in danger. We do not hesitate to say, however, that the evidence furnished by them is entirely reliable. Both of these witnesses saw Burton shoot Morris, and corroborate Dow's affidavit on that point.

Many of the murders committed on the Plains, and attacks on emigrant trains, usually attributed to Indians, may be traced to the Mormons. Some light is thrown upon these transactions by the following statements furnished by men who were crossing the Plains in the summer of 1863.

Statement of James P. Veatch.

"I am going to Oregon. Am from Newbern, Marion County, Iowa.

"We travelled on the road from Salt Lake City to within eight miles of the City of Rocks, when we turned north, and went about three miles. There we struck the old California Road, which passes by the City of Rocks. Just before reaching the road, we came to a large camping-ground, or corral, covering about an acre.

"Here we saw rifle-pits and entrenchments, and some half a dozen ox-yokes, — also bones of cattle. We then proceeded east, on the same road, some three or four miles, where we found a wagon-bed, — also a letter written by a man named Bradley, and directed to Indianola, Warren County, Iowa. About half a mile farther, we found a small provision-box. [This statement was made at a camp on Snake River, a few days after Veatch and his party had passed the scene of the massacre.] We also found a Bible, a copy of Wesley's Sermons, and a large Testament. These books were pretty well decayed. Some of them we still have. Also a volume entitled 'The Wide, Wide World.'

"About seventy-five yards farther, we found two graves of grown persons; no names on them. They had the appearance of being last year's graves. We then drove four or five miles, and camped near a creek emptying into Raft River.

"Next morning, after going about two miles, we came to where five or six wagons had been corralled. Here feather-beds had been opened, and feathers scattered; many were still matted on the ground. There was an old chair or two partly burned; also a chest, with the hinges torn off, and the lock broken open. Also several books: a spelling-book, Bible, melodeon note-books, etc. Also 'The Journeyings of the Children of Israel.' The name of James H. Smith was in the Bible and another book; that of Caroline Smith in another. [Some of these books are now in the writer's possession.]

"There were also the bones of twelve or fifteen head of cattle, which must have been killed last summer. There were signs of men having been there within a few days. There is no emigration on the road this season; but there were the fresh tracks of three wagons, — mule and horse teams.

"About three fourths of a mile beyond this place, we crossed the creek. There I saw three or four skull-bones. Others of the company saw more of them. At this place a skeleton was found, nearly complete. A little farther on, we found a cast-iron cooking stove, broken in pieces. Men had lately been at this place. A handful of buckshot was found.

"Near the junction of this with the Oregon road, we saw two graves,—one of a man from Keokuk, Iowa, buried in August, 1862; the other, of a lady 23 years of age, named L. J. Adams, and marked, 'Shot by Indians on the 9th, and died on the 12th of August, 1862.'

"Fourteen wagon-tires *and a twelve-pound cannon-ball* were found at this place. We carried the ball to our camping-ground, and there left it.

"Two young men, Francis Kelsey and Harrison Edwards, told us, that when they went down, about five weeks ago, they saw two wagons nearly complete, at the place where we noticed the wagon-bed, but when we passed, they were gone.

"I know that a train went from Newbern, Iowa, starting about the 11th of May, 1862, bound for Oregon. George Leeper, from that train, was killed by Indians. A train from Indianola, Iowa, was attacked by Indians last summer, their property taken, and several of their number killed and wounded. The survivors were assisted back to Salt Lake City, *by the Mormons*. John Gamble, of Knoxville, Iowa, can give further information concerning this matter; also Rev. Joseph Howard, Newbern, Marion County, Iowa."

Statement of W. F. Lawrence.

"I am from Appanoose County, Iowa. At our first camp, after striking the Oregon Road, I saw three wagons approaching; they were going eastward. A man from the wagons came to our camp. He was a short, thick-set person, with light complexion, light hair, and full, round face, considerably freckled; downcast look. He said he was from the outside settlements of Salt Lake, near Lovelands, and was out here gathering up old irons. Said they came to a place on Snake River, where they could walk across on the rocks, but did not dare to go farther, for fear the Indians would steal their horses. Said his party consisted of three white men and one Ute Indian, whom they had brought along to recover their horses, should the Indians steal them.

"He asked if they could camp with us; and being told they could, said he would go up and drive the wagons down; but instead of doing so, the party went off in a direction which would be twenty miles to water,—and this was near sundown.

"The night before, a man had been among our cattle, and when our guide cried 'Halt!' he ran off toward the road." This man was supposed to be young Bernard, the '*Mormon from the outside settlements.*'

CHAPTER XV.

RECENT EVENTS. — CONCLUSION.

Personal Appearance and Character of Brigham Young. — His Aims and Purposes. — Solution of the Mormon Question. — New Complications. — Military Reviews of Mormons. — Governor Durkee. — Counteracting Influences. — The Mines and Miners. — Rev. Norman McLeod. — The "Salt Lake Vedette." — Administration of General Connor. — Murder of Brassfield. — Order of Young for the Expulsion of the Gentiles. — Order for the Murder of Eighty Men. — Difficulties concerning the Public Lands. — Murder of Dr. Robinson. — The Gentiles flee in Terror. — The Government fails to protect its Officers and Citizens. — The Hero of Three Wars of the Republic hunted through the Territory. — Rev. Mr. McLeod warned not to return to Utah. — The Reign of Terror commenced. — The Gentiles call for Help.

BRIGHAM YOUNG is a man of medium height, compact frame, with a manner deliberate and impressive. There is less of ostentation, however, in his bearing toward strangers than might be expected in a religious pretender. His hair is sandy, and inclined to curl; features regular, and expressive of great determination.

In conversation he is pleasant and affable, but is restive under the slightest contradiction or opposition. Strangers are favorably impressed with the first visit to his office. They go to see and hear, and Brigham looks well and is a good talker. He has talent, and is not destitute of genius; when, therefore, he is master of the field, and has the choice of topics, he never fails to make himself interesting, if so disposed. Indeed, is it not in itself interesting to see and hear the Mohammed of America?

His early education was very limited, and his sermons are illiterate. But in that most important of all fields of education, a knowledge of mankind and of human nature, he is proficient. It is true, that even here he sometimes grossly errs in his estimate of men. This is because his experience is mostly confined to certain phases of human nature. In those phases he is an adept. Outside of them, he brings to bear a strong judgment, upon a limited range of facts, and if he misses the conclusion, he has the tact to retrieve his error as speedily as possible. He has no pride of consistency, which conflicts in the slightest degree with the accomplishment of his purposes. If necessary to attain his ends, he is one thing to-day, and another to-morrow, and all in the name of the Lord!

Much has been said as to his sincerity in his religious professions and belief. In his younger days he may have been sincere; doubtless was. The character of his religion, and the degree of his sincerity, at the present time, may be inferred from the following incident.

A physician at Salt Lake was urged by Brigham to join the church. He had lived in the city several years, and was doing a good business, and it was pressed upon him as a reciprocal duty. The Doctor, like too many of his profession, was tainted with infidelity. "I wouldn't mind joining your church," said he, "but I don't believe in your religion. In fact," he added, with emphasis, "I don't believe in *any* religion." "Oh," replied Brigham, "that don't make any difference. Come and be baptized, and it will all be right!"

The Doctor *was* baptized, and became a good enough Mormon. He received as his reward, from the hand of Brigham, a beautiful young lady as a "second wife."

Young's talent is all of a practical character, — his shrewdness is ever ready to extricate him from any difficulty or emergency. As a financial and political leader, he is far superior to Joseph Smith. As a religious leader, he is much his inferior. Smith was brave; Young is cowardly. Smith was enthusiastic and impetuous, while Young is cool and calculating.

Brigham is a good speaker. Oratory, however, he uses as a means to accomplish certain ends; and he seldom, even when most excited, says anything that has not its object.

His manner in the pulpit is impressive and authoritative; and he sometimes rises to a high degree of eloquence. His illustrations are apt, his sentences frequently pungent and sarcastic.

He is lamentably deficient in moral sense. No falsehood staggers him, no blasphemy shocks him. Why, then, should he hesitate at the perpetration of any crime which will conduce to the accomplishment of his life-purpose. Even the traveller Burton, his admirer and panegyrist, thus frankly expresses his doubts as to this phase of his character: "I cannot pronounce about his scrupulousness; all the world over, the sincerest religious belief, and the practice of devotion, are sometimes compatible not only with the most disorderly life, but with the most terrible crimes; for mankind mostly believes that '*Il est avec le ceil des accomodements.*' He has been called hypocrite, swindler, forger, murderer. No one looks it less." This is, perhaps, true; but therein lies his hypocrisy.

We have already shown that polygamy originated in the passions and lusts of himself and followers, and was afterward reduced to a system and promulgated as part of the Mormon religion. So with other phases of the system. The Celestial Kingdom, the Grand Archee, the Prophet, the Seer, the Revelator, — all tend to self and self-aggrandizement. Everything must yield and become subservient to the purposes of his unholy ambition. Principles, conscience, the moral sense, Christianity, the divine brotherhood of man, human liberty and republican institutions, the sacred associations of the home-fireside and of the family altar, all the thrilling sentiment and ennobling effect of love, the purity and fidelity of the marriage relation, all the rights of property and life, all the relations of man to God, — yea, God himself, with all the machinery of Heaven and the spiritual world, including angels, spirits, and demons,— are brought under contribution to this one man, and made to revolve about him, — a confused constellation of chaotic elements from the mental and moral world. Neither social nor political restraint does he recognize. Setting himself above all law, human and divine, he becomes a law to himself and his deluded followers.

How long this state of things is to last, how big this God-defying creature is yet to swell ere he is checked in his tyrannical and blasphemous career, how long this theocratic monarchy is to stand in the centre of the Republic, remains to be seen.

But the question will be asked, "Is there any remedy other than by the strong hand? And would not that increase rather than diminish the number of his followers? Whether there can be any peaceful solution of the question is doubtful. Inflamed by power, blinded by ambition, he will not tamely submit to the laws and the constituted authorities, so long as he has thousands of obedient followers around him, ready to move as a single man at his word of command.

The only hope of a peaceful result lies in the gradual assimilation of the "gentile" with the Mormon element. A wonderful change is already in progress in this respect, caused by the presence of United States volunteers, the influx of miners, and the preaching of true religion. This is seen by Young, who already trembles, as he turns his thoughts into the future.

Fearful that the migration of miners into the Territory would tend to lessen his power, and desirous of removing the government troops from Camp Douglas, he spent several months in the spring of 1864, in inducing the farmers to unite in raising the price of their produce, and enlisting the people generally in favor of a combination against the gentiles. To the same end he has been laboring for years.

On Monday, the 8th of August, 1864, a Convention of Delegates from the several Wards in the Territory assembled, in accordance with this scheme and by direction of the " President," at the Tabernacle, in Great Salt Lake City, to adopt measures for the establishment of the prices of produce *upon a gold basis.*

The scheme signally failed. Temporarily, supplies for the

troops were brought across the Plains, and were purchased as they could be had. But General Connor more than hinted that if this plan should be persisted in, what supplies he could not purchase at a fair price with the currency of the country, he would *take*. This had the desired effect, and after some further spasmodic efforts, this attempt to lay an embargo upon the traffic of the people with the Government, was abandoned.

This meeting, like every other in Utah, merely gave expression to the preconceived views and preconcerted measures of the leaders. No steps were taken to raise the wages of the mechanic or laborer. Brigham denounced the mechanics bitterly, because they were opposed to raising the price of produce, calling them a parcel of thieves and rascals. He indulged in a tirade of abuse and vulgar language, unfit for publication.

This may be cited as one of the instances in which he misjudged human nature. By espousing the interests of one class against those of the other, instead of attempting to reconcile them, he introduced a new element of discord into his already inharmonious kingdom. Two of the delegates at the meeting had sufficient manly dignity and moral courage to plead the cause of the mechanic and laborer; also of the poorer class generally; showing the amount of misery and suffering that would be entailed upon them by the adoption of the proposed measures. To which Young replied, in a tone of sarcasm and contempt, that even if he were to build houses for the poor, and provide them with all the necessaries and comforts of life, they would not be satisfied unless they had free admission to his house and the privilege of listening to his daughters playing on the piano.

The fact that leading Mormons were found to vindicate the people, notwithstanding the degraded condition which such language implies, and openly to oppose Young's measures in a public meeting, is a hopeful one, and of deep significance.

In pursuance of the same policy of segregation of the

faithful, and preparatory to the accomplishment of his ambitious schemes, Young has established a system of militia training and reviews, confined exclusively to Mormons. This system he sedulously fosters and maintains, commanding the Mormon militia as *Governor of the State of Deseret.*

On the 2d of November, 1865, such a review was held on the plains of Salt Lake Valley, near the Jordan River. On that occasion Governor Durkee, who had lately arrived in the Territory as the successor of the lamented Doty, visited the Mormon troops and marched in a procession headed by Brigham Young. The Organic Act of Utah makes the Governor the Commander-in-Chief of the Militia, and it would seem to have been more consonant with the spirit of that provision, and more conservative of the dignity of his position, to have headed the procession, or if not permitted to do so, to have dispersed it as an illegal assemblage.

General Connor, who has lately returned to Salt Lake from a brilliant Indian campaign, is the military commander of the Department of Utah. He does not look with favor upon the marshalling of military forces composed exclusively of Mormons, and considers such gatherings but little better than displays of rebels in arms. The progress of events will soon determine whether the military organization of the Mormon militia is conducive to loyalty and good order, or to anarchy and rebellion.

Notwithstanding these attempts to organize and nationalize his followers, there are, within the dominions of Brigham Young, and among the masses of his adherents, various conflicting elements, furnishing hopeful indications to the statesman and the lover of his country. It may reasonably be expected that Young will soon appear to the deluded people in his true character; not as a branch of the Divinity, but as a selfish, corrupt, ambitious, and very dangerous man.

To this end, every attempt to enlighten and disabuse them, should be encouraged, and such changes in the Organic Act should be made as may be necessary to protect the rights of gentiles resident in the Territory. The extraordinary jurisdiction now exercised by the Probate Courts should be taken away and limited to the District Courts. The Governor should not only be authorized, but *required* to take the leadership and control of the militia of the Territory. The laws of Congress against polygamy should be rigidly enforced. Mormon postmasters and other Mormon federal officers should be removed. These and kindred measures should be adopted and enforced, until the authority of the Federal Government shall be fully vindicated and acknowledged.

Among the agencies already at work to accomplish this desirable end, and to redeem Utah from her enthralment, may be mentioned the discovery of mines of precious metals, and the large influx of miners, — the preaching not only of a purer Mormon faith, under the auspices of Joseph Smith Jr., but the promulgation of the Gospel itself, and of the principles of Christianity in their purity, by Rev. Norman McLeod, a Congregational minister of great boldness and talent, who is now firmly established in the Territory, — the extended and controlling influence of the " Union Vedette," a daily and weekly paper published at Salt Lake City, and edited with an ability which is but a synonym for immense moral, intellectual, and political power, — and above all, the military administration of General Connor, who, by the discreet but firm hand with which he has held a check upon the movements of unprincipled church leaders, by the establishment and support of the journal just mentioned, and by the encouragement given to gentiles and disaffected Mormons, has done more to undermine and overthrow the whole system of Mormonism than all other influences combined!

Much is to be expected from the discovery of valuable mines of gold, silver, and copper, in various localities in Utah. Already mining camps have been established, mining companies formed, and villages and settlements of miners are springing up in different directions. In Rush Valley, west of the Oquirrh, or West Mountain, about forty miles southwest from Salt Lake City, is a flourishing mining town called Stockton, which has been built entirely since the winter of 1863-4. The mines in this valley are good, and are attracting much attention abroad. Over fifty ledges have been discovered, which prospect well in gold and silver. In Cottonwood Canyon copper mines have been discovered yielding 75 per cent. of pure ore. Extensive arrangements have been made for bringing on machinery, building mills, &c.

It has steadily been the policy of Brigham to discourage prospecting, and to prevent, if possible, the opening of these mines to the gentile public. It has long been known that such mines existed, not only from the whisperings and traditions of dissatisfied saints, but by the boastings of Young himself, whose vanity would not permit him to be entirely silent upon a subject so well calculated to magnify his own importance. On one occasion he said to Bishop Simpson, "I can stand in my door and see plenty of gold and silver."

These hidden riches, thank God, have been brought to light. Miners are flocking in by thousands, and their rights will be protected, if necessary, by the strong arm of a strong government.

Mormonism must soon give way before the advancing tide of American civilization.

Brigham Young, with his band of desperadoes, may not much longer despise and trample upon our laws, and outrage the rights of our people. If he is to be permitted to continue his system of heathen polygamy, he will be obliged to leave the Republic he has discarded and would have overthrown, and fleeing from the scenes of his impieties and his crimes, set up his kingdom in some new refuge,—perchance in the Sandwich Islands, which have long been one of the stakes of Zion.

The events of the last two years have not been of a character to inspire confidence either in Young and his associates, or in the policy, or rather want of policy, of the government, in connection with the affairs of that Territory. The same spirit of lawlessness and violence which has marked the entire history of the Territory still prevails. Partially repressed for a few years, and kept in check by the determination and known bravery of General Connor and his officers, it has now, since their retirement from the service and the withdrawal of nearly all the military stationed at Camp Douglas, broken out more fiercely than ever.

The disbanding of the volunteers was immediately followed by denunciations of the gentiles, and threats and warnings of every description. A letter containing the representation of a bloody hand was sent to the "Vedette" office.

Anonymous communications were frequently received by leading gentile citizens. Fiery and vehement declamation was indulged in from the rostrum; and the prophecy was frequently made that in a few months not a gentile would be left in the Territory. Yet that class of proscribed citizens kept on in the even tenor of their way; the "Vedette" appeared as usual, always bold and determined in its opposition to the wrong and injustice prevailing around it. There was danger that the prophets would be brought into disrepute and contempt.

At this juncture, it having been determined "in council" that a blow should be struck, the community was startled by the announcement of one of the most atrocious murders recorded in history.

On the evening of the second of April, 1865, Squire Newton Brassfield, a resident of Austin, Nevada, temporarily residing in Salt Lake, was shot down in the streets while in the company of the United States Marshal, and under his protection. The particulars, as well as the pretext for this bloody murder, are fully given in the following editorials taken from the "Salt Lake Vedette," of April 4th, 1865: —

"We are called upon this morning to chronicle one of the most cold-blooded and inhuman murders that has ever fallen under our notice — unparalleled even in the bloody record of Utah's foulest crimes. The victim of this last exhibition of the hellish doctrine of 'blood atonement,' promulgated by these fiends of hell from the rostrum of their Tabernacle, is Squire Newton Brassfield, late a resident of Austin, Nevada, by business a freighter, and aged about thirty years. The circumstances which led to his murder are briefly as follows:—

"On the evening of the 27th ult. Mr. Brassfield was married by Judge McCurdy, of the Supreme Court, to Mary, *second* wife of A. N. Hill, a Mormon missionary now in Europe. A short time after the marriage, Brassfild went with his wife to her late residence to get her clothes and household goods which had been packed up ready for removal. While there he was arrested by the city police, charged *with resisting an officer*, and lodged all night in the county jail. The next morning he was taken before the Probate Court to answer the charge, and bound over in the sum of five hundred dollars to await the action of the Grand Jury. The next day two indictments were brought against him, one on the charge above named, and the other for larceny,— for being present and assisting in taking away his wife's goods and clothing. He gave bail in the sum of one thousand dollars. On Monday last his counsel, Major C. H. Hempstead, quashed the indictment for resisting an officer, and proceeded to trial on the charge of larceny. The trial was not concluded when the court adjourned on **Monday**, and was to have been continued on the following day.

"The wife had two children, one nine and the other five years of age. About these children a contest was evident — Mrs. Brassfield claiming them, and the friends of Hill being determined to keep them from her. The mother obtained a writ of *habeas corpus* from Judge McCurdy, and the Hill party from the Probate Court, each claiming the right to the custody of the children. The writ of Judge McCurdy was first executed, and a hearing held by him last Saturday night. Major Hempstead argued the case for the petitioner, and claimed that as Hill had a wife living at the time of his alleged marriage with Mrs. Brassfield, it was illegal and void, and that, as there was no legal father, the mother was entitled to the custody of the minor children. Thus the legality of polygamous marriages was made a direct issue in the case. Judge Snow appeared against the petitioner and in the capacity of Deputy Attorney-General of the Territory, and desired further time to prepare the case of the defendant, and the hearing was continued until Monday evening at seven o'clock.

"At that hour the house was crowded, the friends of both parties being present in large numbers. After a few preliminary remarks and the filing of some papers by Judge Snow, the hearing was again adjourned until Wednesday morning at ten o'clock. The children in the mean time had been committed to the custody of the United States Marshal, Hosmer, until further orders of the court, and on Monday the writ from the Probate Court was served on him, when he appeared before Judge Smith and stated that he held the children by order of Judge McCurdy, and declined to produce them in that court, when he was threatened with an attachment for contempt, and warned that unless he produced the children *he would be imprisoned in the county jail!* The Probate Court of Salt Lake, imprisoning a United States Marshal, for obeying an order of the Supreme Court! Our readers can make their own comments.

"Thus stood the several phases of the case at the adjournment of Judge McCurdy's court on Monday evening. The court adjourned at about half-past eight o'clock, and on his way home, and while in company with the United States Marshal, Hosmer, Mr. Brassfield was shot and killed; adding another to the long list of victims of Mormon 'law' and Mormon 'justice.'"

"STATEMENT OF MARSHAL HOSMER.

"About half-past eight o'clock on Monday evening, the second instant, I was accompanying Mr. Brassfield home to the National Hotel from Independence Hall. As we turned the corner by the small building west of the hotel, a man who stood between the bay-window and door of that building advanced one step from the corner and fired at Mr. Brassfield, the shot taking effect in his arm and side; four buck-shot entered the arm, one striking the elbow joint and breaking the arm. The fifth shot, which was much larger than the others, entered his right side. When the gun was fired Mr. Brassfield fell, and said, 'O my God! I am shot!' He was carried into the International Hotel, where he lingered in agony about forty-five minutes and then expired. The assassin, after firing, ran across the street, and turning the corner by the theatre, continued in a northerly direction. As he passed the St. Charles Restaurant, he was fired at twice by a policeman. I lost sight of him as he turned the corner of the theatre."

"THE FEELING AMONG THE PEOPLE.

"It would be useless to deny the fact that in the opinion of the gentile community of this city, the killing of Mr. Brassfield was a deliberately planned scheme, concocted and advised by men high in authority in the Mormon Church. It is a reminder of the days that were, and a foretaste of what will be again 'when the troops are removed.' The community is struck dumb at the appalling audacity of the affair. Men say but little, but the lowering brows and compressed lips everywhere visible, bespeak a rising storm, which, when it bursts, will be very hard to control."

"THE SPIRIT OF ASSASSINATION.

"From time to time during the past nineteen years, the people have been almost palsied with the announcement of dark and fearful crimes committed within the limits of this Territory — crimes of the greatest magnitude and of the blackest character have been perpetrated, and in no known instance have the guilty parties been brought to the tribunal of justice.

"The Mountain Meadow massacre, the Parish, Potter, and Forbes murders, the assassination of Sergeant Pike on the main street of Salt Lake City, in broad daylight, were all committed with an impunity and immunity from punishment having no parallel elsewhere in the country.

"Last Monday evening the community was astounded with the intelligence of another foul assassination committed on Theatre Street, only a few steps east of Main Street.

"The man who was assassinated was known throughout Nevada, and more particularly at Austin and Reese River, as one of the best and most reliable citizens of that State, and was engaged in the freighting business between this place and Reese River. His conduct, while here, was that of a good, quiet, peaceable citizen, violating no law of the land, interfering in no way with the legitimate business of any person, and honored and respected by all who knew him."

This high-handed outrage was immediately followed by a fulmination from Brigham Young, warning the gentiles to leave the Territory, and throwing out various dark hints of the consequences in case the warning should be disregarded.

The serious character of this order was well understood in that community, and had the effect to cause many citizens to quietly take themselves out of harm's way.

For the information of those who may doubt whether anything criminal was intended by this edict, or whether Young would scruple in the use of means in carrying out his plan of getting rid of the gentiles, we refer them to the Order of Brigham issued in 1858, for the murder of eighty men by his Danite followers. The following is a copy of the Order :—

"SALT LAKE CITY, *April* 9, 1858.
"SPECIAL ORDER.

" The officer in command of escort is hereby ordered to see that every man is well prepared with ammunition and have it ready at the time you see those teamsters a hundred miles from the settlements. President Young advises that they should be all killed to prevent them from returning to Bridger to join our enemies. Every precaution should be taken and see that not one escapes. Secrecy is required.

" By order of Genl. DANL. H. WELLS.
JAMES FERGUSON, *Asst. Adjt. Genl.*"

The teamsters alluded to were eighty in number, discharged from Johnson's command when at Fort Bridger, and were *en route* to California. Maloney, who commanded the escort, is and has been for four years employed at Camp Douglas. He was too humane to execute the order. He however preserved it, and it is now in the possession of Hon. John Titus, Chief Justice of the Territory. The signature of Ferguson is authenticated under oath, by two prominent Mormons of Salt Lake. The Mormons have on several occasions attempted to take the life of Maloney, and only a short time since destroyed a house of his near Camp Douglas.

About this time a new source of difficulty arose in the settlement of the public lands. The entire body of land in the Territory belongs to the United States Government, subject to the claims of Indian tribes roving through the country. The land has never been open to market. But very little of it, indeed, has ever been surveyed.

The Mormons claim to own the valley of the Salt Lake, and all the adjacent country; not only that which they have reduced to possession, but the square miles of adjoining land untouched by human being.

But the gentiles were not disposed to concede the rightfulness of these claims. In the summers of 1865–66, various settlements were made upon the public lands in Utah, under the National Homestead Act, by anti-Mormon or gentile citizens.

The Mormons affected to consider this an infringement of their rights, and from denunciations and threats proceeded to open violence to prevent these intrusions.

Some account of these outrages is given in the following extracts from a letter written by Captain S. E. Jocelyn, and published in the " Chicago Republican," of January 4, 1867.

As the writer is fully posted in relation to the recent history of the Territory, I have given other quotations also, from the same letter: —

"CHICAGO, *Dec.* 28, 1866.

" It has been my fortune to reside in Utah Territory during the last four years, whence I have recently arrived in your city. While *en route*, and since my arrival in 'America'—for so the gentiles are accustomed to call the Eastern States—I have observed a great and universal interest existing on all hands concerning affairs among the Mormons.

" As early as last spring threats were made by the Mormon authorities toward certain parties, not Mormons, then doing business of one kind or another in Salt Lake City, looking to the forcible entry of their premises and the destruction of property without due process of law. These threats were of a general character, and it was believed that, under cover of breaking up certain places where disreputable business was carried on, it was the intention to destroy other establishments of a different character, but interfering with certain monopolies of the city and church patriarchs. To prevent this, the local military commander, under constructive orders from Gen. Sherman, called upon Brigham Young to exact a promise that no violence should be done to private property without due process of law, which, after some hesitation, was obtained. Matters progressed smoothly until the adjournment of Congress, for, fearing the effect on that body of any violent measures inaugurated against gentiles, Brigham kept his promise strictly. But no sooner did the telegraph flash across the continent the announcement of the adjournment of Congress, than his pent-up wrath broke forth, and he openly urged the policy of violence toward the gentiles. With regard to the public lands, he said repeatedly that he owned land, and plenty of it, and any man who attempted to 'jump' the same should have 'a preemption title which would last till the resurrection.' This was called forth by the fact that a number of locations had already been made by discharged soldiers and others upon unoccupied land lying along the west bank of the Jordan River, contiguous to Salt Lake City, and there was considerable talk of many others following in the same course, induced by the prospective coming of the Pacific Railroad, and a desire to obtain as eligible situations for homes convenient thereto as possible. But the idea of allowing gentiles to settle in any considerable numbers in the vicinity of Mormon communities is totally at variance with the well-understood policy of the leaders, and must, therefore, be prevented by every possible means — else, what would become of polygamy? Hence the hostility of Brigham Young to any such scheme as they contemplated, for in it he scented danger to his favorite institution, and hence, too, his threat of death to 'land jumpers.'

"Now the fact is that there has never been, to my knowledge, one foot of land '*jumped*' in Utah; in other words, no locations whatever have been made or attempted by gentiles except upon totally unoccupied lands. But, in violation of the Territorial organic act, the Legislative Assembly of Utah has, from time to time, granted away to Brigham Young, and others, certain valuable timber and tracts of arable lands for a nominal consideration, and it is to protect these from gentile intrusion, as well as for reasons already stated, that a reign of terror has been inaugurated.

"As early as last August, the writer of this article called attention, in the columns of the 'Salt Lake Vedette,' to the threats being made by the Mormon Head Centre to inflame the passions of his followers, predicting the result which has already been reached, and putting his language on record, that it might be known who should be held responsible when the event transpired.

"On the night of September 24th occurred the Jordan outrage, in which a number of land preëmptors were attacked about midnight by a gang of some forty or fifty ruffians, disguised and armed, and flagrantly abused, their houses destroyed, themselves thrown into the river, and their lives only saved by a promise to leave the Territory within forty-eight hours. One in attempting to get away, was fired upon and wounded, but effected his escape — very fortunately for the entire party beyond a doubt, for there can be little question that the original purpose was to put them all out of the way, which would certainly have been accomplished had any of the forty or fifty shots fired at the fugitive taken fatal effect. The better nature of some of the party prevailed over the malignant influence of the master whom they served, and they probably hoped to reach the result he desired — terror to gentiles — by less sanguinary means than those he contemplated. The result proved them wrong, for the parties warned did not leave the Territory, though any further attempts to secure homesteads were abandoned. Then followed the demolition of a portion of Dr. Robinson's premises, three of the city police, including the chief, being identified as accomplices, and held to answer therefor. Then the abduction of Mr. Weston, of the 'Vedette,' to a remote part of the city, where he escaped with his life only by the approach of a rescue party."

These outrages were closely followed by another atrocious murder, only equalled in ferocity and cold-blooded cruelty by that of Brassfield.

On the 22d day of October, 1866, Dr. J. K. Robinson, a prominent and influential citizen of Salt Lake City, who had recently had some difficulty with the city authorities, was shot in the streets, but a few steps from his own door. He had retired for the evening, when he was called up and requested to go a short distance to attend upon a neighbor, who, it was alleged, had broken his leg.

He quickly obeyed the call, followed his summoners a few rods from the house, when he was brutally assassinated by those who had him in charge. The following allusion to this murder is from the letter of Captain Jocelyn already quoted from : —

"I do not hesitate to state my most earnest conviction that Brigham Young is the author of Dr. Robinson's assassination, and in this I do not go one iota beyond the public opinion of all gentiles in Salt Lake City, and, I have no doubt, of the Mormons as well, could their secret thoughts be known. He signified his consent, which was the victim's death warrant; some of his satellites — probably Daniel H. Wells — made the detail for the execution; and not the least hideous feature of the whole affair is, that, in all probability, the perpetrators of that most atrocious crime feel no guilt for this deed, have no visitations of remorse or compunctions of conscience in consequence, but consider that they have only done their duty and proved their faith in thus obeying the behests of their Prophet. I will trace the chain of evidence leading to the foregoing conclusion; Brigham Young is the Mormon Church, since therein his word is law. It is the deliberate policy of the church to isolate Mormonism from the intrusion of persons averse to the peculiar faith it teaches. That such is the burden of the discourses of its leaders throughout the Territory, and has been for years, will not be seriously disputed by any sensible Mormon. Hence their strenuous efforts to settle up the valleys, or the more desirable portions, by gathering the saints together from all parts of the world, and concentrating their force in Utah. In Missouri they controlled one county by this means; they now control, and will, if possible, perpetuate their authority over an entire Territory which they hope may become a State, under the absolute dominion of Brigham Young. To effect this, gentiles cannot be permitted to mingle with Mormons unopposed, nor to settle in their vicinity, on account of the dangerous influence they would thus exert. The control of the church authorities over personal actions extends to every possible circumstance. When the headquarters of the District of Utah were established in Salt Lake City by order one year ago, his authority was exercised to prevent the lease of any buildings for that or any other public purpose, and the person from whom they were finally obtained was afterward 'cut off' from the church for disregard of 'counsel' in that particular, and has since been subjected to all manner of petty persecution in consequence. Dr. Robinson had leased certain city property, which he managed without regard to the wishes of the Mormon magnates. Formerly the property of an elder in the church, it was now the place where the 'Vedette' newspaper found refuge, when driven from every other covert. Moreover, **Dr. Robinson was** foremost in encouraging the idea that gentiles, **as well as Mormons**, had rights in Utah, and among them a right to a portion of the public domain, whereon to build themselves homes. Acting upon this unorthodox theory, he, with others, had procured the survey of certain lands **near the city**, including the famous Warm Sulphur Springs, **and** had taken all the necessary steps to perfect a title, according to act of Congress regulating **the** location of cities on the public domain.

"The buildings in **process of erection thereon were demolished**, and there the **matter rested for more than** a year, when it was formally revived by **Dr. Robinson, who** brought the case before **the United States Third District Court**, praying to be put in possession of his property, from which he was unlawfully restrained.

"About the **same time** other parties began locating on vacant **land near the city, as** already stated. No objection was made by any person, however, until Brigham Young began his inflammatory **harangues**, giving the key-note of assassination. Early **in** October the semi-annual **conference convened** in Salt Lake City, and it was attended beyond all precedent. To the thousands there assembled he repeated all his violent language, — and no man knows better how to inspire his hearers with his **own purposes**, — concluding by taking a vote, in effect, whether the policy thus strenuously urged should be adopted and **at once inaugurated**.

"What more **was necessary** for him to do? Not to strike the blow, surely, for there were hundreds ready to do that; all they **wanted was to be** told *who*, *where*, and *when*. The event was predicted by the writer in a communication to the 'New York Tribune,' dated ten days previous to Dr. Robinson's assassination. None knew, indeed, on whom the blow would descend, but all felt sure **it was impending. To my personal** knowledge many of those who believed **or knew themselves under** ban took extraordinary precautions to meet the **threatened danger**.

"On Saturday, October 20th, Dr. Robinson, acting under legal advice, called **on Daniel H. Wells**, Mayor of the city, 'Lieutenant-General' of the **Utah** militia, and only second to Brigham Young in the church, to demand payment of the city for damages done to his premises by police acting under Wells's orders without due process **of law**. Wells no sooner learned that he was the person contesting the Warm Springs case, than he ordered him from his house, with every circumstance of gross insult. On the night of Monday following Dr. Robinson was murdered. The full moon made the night almost as light as day. There were at least seven of the assassins. They did the deed, knowing that within twenty steps a witness was observing them. They did not rifle the pockets of their victim. The deduction is irresistible. No mere murderers would commit so heinous a crime under such circumstances, unless certain of adequate backing and sure protection. He had no personal enemies. Who desired his death? Who could protect his murderers? I leave the answer to public opinion, which, I trust, may soon compel our timid lawgivers to do their duty. For myself, I have no doubt on the point. I know as well as I ever hope to know who caused the murder of Dr. Robinson. I feel and write warmly on the subject, for the victim was my intimate friend. Not three days before his foul murder, he expressed to me a sense of the danger he felt himself exposed to in attempting, single-handed, to fight the Mormon authorities of Salt Lake City. The event very soon proved how prophetic were those fears. I was by his side only a few minutes after he was stricken down — held his hand and felt the last faint pulse that flitted from his heart when he died. Who could look upon such a sight — a strong man basely stricken down in his early prime by assassin hands, his family crushed with the awful weight of such a sorrow — and not feel it a duty to use every means which honor allows to bring the perpetrators to punishment. During my residence in Utah I have carefully studied the Mormon system, and confidently assert it to be dangerous to the commonweal. I have traced the connection between public utterances of the leaders and crimes wherewith they have been charged, and entertain no doubt of their guilt from evidences found in their own record.

"Well, Dr. Robinson sleeps in the cemetery at Camp Douglas, the second victim of Mormon hatred to gentiles, within the year, whose ashes repose therein. They sleep as do the Parishes, the innocents slaughtered at the Mountain Meadows, and the hundreds of other victims who have perished to appease the insatiate demon of blood-atonement — the tutelary deity by whose fell assistance Brigham Young maintains his power, and hopes to accomplish his evil purposes."

The following comments upon the same affair, together with the closing portion of the eloquent speech of Governor Weller before the Coroner's Jury, are taken from the "San Francisco Bulletin" of November 16th, 1866:—

"SAN FRANCISCO, *Nov.* 16th.

"The gentiles of Salt Lake may find very great attractions in a business way in that city, but they do not dwell in very secure habitations. Now and then one of their number is taken off as stealthily as when a wolf pounces down upon the fold. Bassfield made himself obnoxious by a marriage, and his days were numbered. The manner of his taking off was well known, but it availed nothing to trace the crime to its perpetrators. Mormon vengeance selects a shining mark even though it lets its bolts fly in the dark, and there is always a Mormon moral to the tragedy.

"The recent assassination of Dr. J. K. Robinson, in Salt Lake City, does not differ in its diabolical features from others which preceded it. He was a representative man, and as such, the murder may have peculiar significance.

"Robinson in 1864 was Assistant Surgeon of United States Volunteers, and soon after took charge of the hospital at Camp Douglas, near Salt Lake City, and sometime after, being mustered out of the service, he settled down in that city as a regular practitioner of medicine, which pursuit he followed with success, and was a leading man, at least among the gentiles. Indeed, it was said that no man stood higher, socially or morally. It seems that Robinson was at the time contesting a claim known as the Warm Springs, before the United States Territorial Court, and with good prospect of ultimate success. His opponents were, of course, Mormons, and may have chosen a more expeditious way of quieting title by quieting the claimant at the same time. But certainly a Mormon jury could have settled the claim without blood; only there might not have been such an impressive and saintly moral for the benefit of the gentiles.

"But there were other reasons why Robinson's permanent absence was deemed far more desirable than his presence. He had been very active in educational and religious enterprises, not altogether after the pattern prescribed by the saints. Nearly two years ago Rev. Norman McLeod, a Congregational minister, commenced preaching at Camp Douglas, and finding so much encouragement from Gen. Connor and the whole gentile community, he established a preaching station in the city, and finally organized a church. An intelligent congregation was gathered every Sunday to hear a gentile preacher in the city of the saints. Money was liberally subscribed, and a church edifice, we believe, was in process of erection. A Sunday-school was organized, and considerable assistance was sent from this city. Dr. Robinson was the Superintendent of the Sunday-school, and was very effective in all matters connected with the new religious society. Some time in March last, Rev. Mr. McLeod was summoned to Washington by a Congressional Committee to state the results of his observations concerning the attitude of the Mormons toward the Federal Government, and such other knowledge concerning the workings of Mormonism as he possessed. There being no alternative, he obeyed the summons. But previous to his departure Dr. Robinson, his intimate friend and room-mate, was united by him in marriage with the daughter of the late Dr. Kay, a lady identified also with the new religious enterprise. Six months or more afterwards, and before McLeod's return, Robinson was called up in the night on pretense that he was wanted professionally, waylaid and murdered.

"A fact of some significance comes out at this juncture. Gen. Connor, who had taken a warm interest in the religious society, and was the fast friend of Robinson and McLeod, telegraphed to the latter, who is still at the East, advising him not to return as his life was in danger. Thus, the leading layman in the society was assassinated, and the pastor warned by his best friend that it is not safe to return. It may be said that the gentile society had, from the beginning, exerted a quiet but powerful influence against polygamy, and already much of doubt and skepticism on this point had begun to pervade the Mormon community. In New Zealand and some other places, the natives sometimes roasted and ate a missionary. In Salt Lake they assassinate him and throw him to the dogs. At the coroner's inquest, ex-Governor John B. Weller being present as counsel on behalf of the friends of the murdered man, addressed the jury and submitted the following suggestive propositions:—

"'And upon this evidence I have a few plain questions to propound, which I will leave you and others to answer. I do not propose to discuss them, simply because I could not do so without increasing the excitement which already exists, and producing an exasperated state of feeling, which could not at the present time result in any public good.

"1. If my associate, Judge Stout, the City Attorney, had been murdered under the circumstances Dr. Robinson was, would the police have exhibited a greater degree of vigilance and energy?

"2. Would the attention of the 4000 people who assembled at the 'Tabernacle' (where secular affairs are often discussed) on the succeeding Sabbath have been called to the crime and exhorted to use every effort to ferret out the assassins?

"3. Could any prominent Mormon be murdered under the same circumstances and no clew whatever found to the murderer?

"4. Would any portion of the five hundred special police have been called into requisition or ordered on duty?

"5. Would any of the numerous witnesses who saw the assassins fleeing from their bloody work, have been able to recognize and name them?

"6. Have we not utterly failed to prove, after full investigation, that Dr. Robinson had a personal enemy in the world, and have we not proved that he had had difficulties with none except the city authorities?

"7. Is there any evidence that he had done anything to make personal enemies, unless it was having the Chief of Police and two others bound over to answer a charge of riot?

"8. Would he have been murdered if he had not by his land claim raised a question as to the validity of the city charter?

"9. Would the ten-pin alley have been destroyed if it had not been his property, and that he had a suit pending against the city?

"10. Would the Mayor of the city have ordered him out of his house two days before he was murdered, if he had not understood that he claimed damages from the city for the wanton destruction of his property?

"11. Is it not remarkable that a gang of men could go to a bowling alley, nearly surrounded by houses, within sixty steps of the most public street in the city, between the hours of eleven and twelve o'clock at night, demolish the windows and break up with axes and sledges the alley, and no witnesses found to identify the men or who knew anything whatever about the perpetrators of the act?

"12. Are not the jury satisfied that some witnesses have withheld evidence calculated to fasten guilt upon certain parties, because they feared personal violence?

"13. Is there not an organized influence here which prevents the detection and punishment of men who commit acts of violence upon the persons or property of gentiles?

"14. If a Mormon of good standing had been murdered, would the Mayor, to whom the Chief of Police reports, have been informed of the act before ten o'clock the next day?

"15. Would the Chief of Police have gone to bed as soon as he heard of the crime, and waited three days before he visited the scene of the murder?

"16. Was the murder committed for the purpose of striking terror into the gentiles and preventing them from settling in this Territory?

"17. Is it the settled policy of the authorities here to prevent citizens of the United States, not Mormons, from asserting their claims to a portion of the public domain in the regularly organized judicial tribunals of the country?

"18. Are all legal questions which may arise in this city between Mormons and gentiles to be settled by brute force?

"19. Do the public teachings of the Tabernacle lead the people to respect and obey the laws of the country, or do they lead to violence and bloodshed?'

"He then referred to the practices and teachings of the Mormons and the natural results that flowed from them:—

"'Whilst following the practices of some of the patriarchs of old they have also adopted the creed, "An eye for an eye, and a tooth for a tooth." What has been the result of these teachings upon society here? There are a number of respectable men in this city, some of whom have families, who dare not go upon your streets at night! Nor are they men who are afraid of shadows. They have shown their courage upon the field of battle in defence of the honor of the country, and would not shrink from meeting any of them single-handed in the light of day. But they do not choose to meet an organized band of assassins at midnight. They dare not go to your theatre or other public places of amusement. Is it not hard that here, in an American Territory, supposed to be under the protection of our national flag, citizens who have perilled their lives to sustain the supremacy of our laws and the integrity of the government, are compelled to remain in their houses at night to escape the hands of murderers? men who have violated no law, trespassed upon the right of no one, but have simply incurred the displeasure of the dominant party? Can this state of things be tolerated on American soil? A government which habitually fails to give protection to its people must soon cease to command their confidence or respect. But I do not choose to pursue this subject further.

"In this connection, however, I feel called upon to notice the extraordinary efforts which have been made and are still being made at the Tabernacle, as well as by the press, to destroy the confidence of the people in the courts established by the Federal Government in this Territory. Judges selected by the government, because of their legal attainments and sterling integrity, have been sent out here to administer the laws and preserve the peace and order of society. If, in the faithful discharge of their duties under the oath they have taken, they make a decision in conflict with the interests or the opinions of the dominant party, they are bitterly denounced and every effort made to impair their power and lessen their influence. To effect this, slander and ridicule are generally employed. If a Federal Judge will decide every question which arises between a Mormon and gentile in favor of the former, he can have an easy and quiet time. He can have as much fulsome praise as he deserves. But if he decides in favor of the latter, " uneasy lies the head that wears a crown.'"

The murder of Dr. Robinson, following so closely upon that of Brassfield, and the outrages upon Williamson and his companions, quite unsettled the nerves of those gentiles who had had the hardihood to remain, and they now fled in terror from before the face of the infuriated fanatics, to whose tender mercies they had been turned over by that government which should have afforded them the fullest protection.

The garrison stationed at Camp Douglas, instead of being strengthened as it should have been, had been disbanded and withdrawn, till scarcely a corporal's guard remained; not enough to inspire the least respect for the government or its representatives. General Connor, whose name had been a terror to the offender for three years, now found himself an outcast and a refugee, in the land which had so lately been under his control. Finding his life constantly in danger in Salt Lake City, he removed with his family, a few months after the assassination of Robinson, to Stockton, in Rush Valley, forty miles west of Salt Lake, where he now resides. He is engaged in mining operations, and having considerable capital invested in developing the silver mines in that locality, cannot well leave without much financial sacrifice. His life is in constant danger, as well as that of every anti-Mormon resident of the Territory.

The following extract from a letter of General Connor, dated Salt Lake, December 26, 1866, written just before his removal to Stockton, will give some idea of the condition of the Territory at that time: —

"Matters are getting worse here. You will see by the 'Vedette,' that the merchants have addressed a card to Brigham Young, in reference to his action in not permitting the people to trade with gentile merchants. Several gentiles established themselves in business in the outer settlements. Some of them have been ordered to close their stores, and are doing so, and are glad to get away with their lives.

"Of the hundreds who came here to spend the winter, all or nearly all have left, and many of the old gentile inhabitants are leaving, or preparing to do so in the spring, if nothing is done for us by Congress or the Administration."

The Rev. Mr. McLeod who, previous to the murder of Robinson, had made a visit to the States, was cautioned by his friends, by telegraph, not to return, as his life was in danger.[1]

Many fled the Territory. But a small number remained.

[1] Rev. William Roberts, also one of the ablest ministers on the Pacific coast, was deputed, at the last annual Methodist Conference of Oregon, to act as a missionary at Salt Lake. He proceeded to execute the mission, but after a short stay, returned to his former charge in Idaho, there to remain till such time as American citizens in Utah should be protected in their lives and property.

And from that Spartan band the cry now comes up for aid and protection.

Will that cry be heeded by the government of their country? Or will that same masterly inactivity which has hitherto characterized the course of the Federal Government on this subject, still prevail?

This is a question which now demands the serious attention of Congress and of the country.

If the Mormons are to remain in the country, it would seem to be time that some system were adopted to enforce the execution of the laws among them. I am aware that the subject is one of some difficulty, but one would suppose that among all those who have been grappling with the great questions of Southern reconstruction, enough statesmanship might be found to devise some efficient mode of protecting life and property in Utah.

Let us at least hope the attempt will be made.

THE END.

www.ingramcontent.com/pod-product-compliance
Lightning Source LLC
Chambersburg PA
CBHW030808230426
43667CB00008B/1120